Computers as Mindtools for Schools

Computers as Mindtools
for Schools

Engaging Critical Thinking

SECOND EDITION

David H. Jonassen

Pennsylvania State University

Merrill
an imprint of Prentice Hall
Upper Saddle River, New Jersey   *Columbus, Ohio*

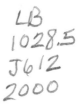

CATALOGUED

Library of Congress Cataloging-in-Publication Data

Jonassen, David H.
    Computers as mindtools for schools : engaging critical thinking / David H. Jonassen.—2nd ed.
      p. cm.
    Rev. ed. of: Computers in the classroom. ©1996.
    Includes bibliographical references and index.
    ISBN 0-13-080709-5
    1. Computer-assisted instruction. 2. Critical thinking—Study and teaching. I. Jonassen, David
H. Computers in the classroom. II. Title. III. Title: Computers as mind-tools for schools.
    LB1028.5.J612   2000
    371.33'4—dc21
                                                    99-32758
                                                      CIP

Editor: Debra A. Stollenwerk
Editorial Assistant: Penny S. Burleson
Production Editor: Mary Harlan
Copy Editor: Lorretta Palagi
Design Coordinator: Diane C. Lorenzo
Photo Coordinator: Anthony Magnacca
Text Designer: Mia Saunders
Cover Designer: Thomas Mack
Cover Photo: ©Unicorn Stock Photography
Production Manager: Pamela D. Bennett
Electronic Text Management: Marilyn Wilson Phelps, Karen L. Bretz, Melanie N. King
Illustrations: Christine Marrone
Director of Marketing: Kevin Flanagan
Marketing Manager: Meghan Shepherd
Marketing Coordinator: Krista Groshong

This book was set in Garamond by Prentice Hall and was printed and bound by R. R. Donnelley & Sons
Company. The cover was printed by Phoenix Color Corp.

©2000, 1996 by Prentice-Hall, Inc.
Pearson Education
Upper Saddle River, New Jersey 07458

Previous edition entitled *Computers in the Classroom: Mindtools for Critical Thinking.*

Photo Credits: Scott Cunningham/Merrill: pp. 58, 207, 245; Anthony Magnacca/Merrill: pp. 3, 21, 35, 83, 108, 136, 155, 175, 194, 233, 271, 280.

Printed in the United States of America

10 9 8 7 6

ISBN: 0-13-080709-5

Prentice-Hall International (UK) Limited, *London*
Prentice-Hall of Australia Pty. Limited, *Sydney*
Prentice-Hall of Canada, Inc., *Toronto*
Prentice-Hall Hispanoamericana, S. A., *Mexico*
Prentice-Hall of India Private Limited, *New Delhi*
Prentice-Hall of Japan, Inc., *Tokyo*
Prentice-Hall (Singapore) Pte. Ltd., *Singapore*
Editora Prentice-Hall do Brasil, Ltda., *Rio de Janeiro*

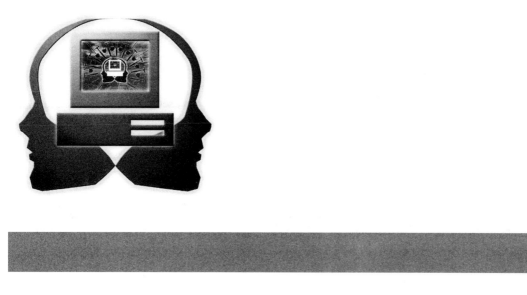

Preface

Computers as Mindtools in Schools: Engaging Critical Thinking is the second edition of "the Mindtools book." The first edition of this book, along with my other writings, provided an alternative model for how to integrate technology with the learning process in order to engage learners more mindfully and meaningfully. Feedback indicates that many educators from around the world have accepted and adopted the idea of using computers as Mindtools. I hope that they are not doing so to the exclusion of many other valuable and productive applications of computers. I also hope that they are using Mindtools an intellectual toolkit for engaging learners in constructive, critical thinking about whatever they are learning. Thinking emerges naturally from purposeful activity. Mindtools provide a set of computer-mediated activities that foster thinking.

New to This Edition

The Mindtools concept is as dynamic as the computer technology and learning psychology fields that underlie it. This book reflects the changes in thinking technologies since the first edition. Based on my own reading and research, feedback from reviewers, and feedback from users of the book, I have substantially reorganized the content of the book. I have added chapters on systems modeling tools, visualization tools, intentional search tools, and synchronous and asynchronous conferencing tools, and have deleted the chapter on computer programming

Not only has the structure of the book changed, but also the internal structure of each chapter. Within each chapter I used consistent chapter structures to facilitate access and comparisons and contrasts between the tools. Each chapter includes descriptions of what the tool is and how it can be used as a Mindtool. The latter sections include more specific descriptions and examples of how to use the tool as a Mindtool. I added a section on Coaching Student Construction of Mindtools. I deleted the sections on Evaluation of Software as Mindtools (too redundant), Software Tools (too dynamic; check various Mindtools websites), and Fostering Collaboration (also too redundant). However, in the Evaluation section of each chapter, I retained the analysis of critical thinking skills engaged by each Mindtool and added assessment rubrics that you can use for evaluating student Mindtools projects.

Organization

Part 1 of this second edition begins with describing the Mindtools concept and critical thinking, which is the goal of using Mindtools. Part 2 describes Semantic Organization Tools, including databases and semantic networking tools (concept mapping). Part 3 includes Dynamic Modeling Tools, such as spreadsheets (with new sections on analysis and reasoning, mathematical comprehension, and simulation modeling), expert systems, systems modeling tools (these are the most powerful Mindtools yet), and microworlds. Part 4 (Interpretation Tools) is all new, including chapters on intentional information searching and visualization tools. For those who must have a chapter on the Internet, chapter 9 on intentional information searching is it. The Internet is not a Mindtool. It is a repository of fact and opinion that modern students desperately need to know how to search and evaluate. This chapter provides some clues. Part 5 (Knowledge Building Tools) includes only hypermedia construction tools (including website construction). Part 6 (Conversation Tools) includes two new chapters, synchronous and asynchronous conferencing tools. Finally, Part 7 reflects on the processes of implementing Mindtools with chapters on entailments and assessment. The latter chapter provides a set of rubrics for assessing learning with Mindtools.

The book is still designed as a handbook to be accessed, used, and experimented with, so the chapters in Parts 2 through 6 share a similar structure and features that clarify the ways in which various tools can be used as Mindtools. The focus of this book is still practical, with an emphasis on experimentation.

The current edition of "the Mindtools book" reflects the state of the art in early 1999. The concept will continue to change as rapidly as the technologies and learning theories that underlie it. While those changes are challenging, the excitement generated by the potential of these tools to effect meaningful reform in learning justifies our anxiety while trying to accommodate those changes. The point of this book is that technologies can make a difference in education if they are used to engage learners in meaningful and mindful thinking. Although that sounds like a simple solution,

I am sensitive to the complexities and difficulties imposed by individual differences, social values, cultural beliefs, competing interests, and personal intentions and motivations. I continue to believe that Mindtools cannot and will not reform education. However, educators, parents, and students who want to refocus the emphasis of education on thinking will need a set of tools to use. Ergo, Mindtools.

ACKNOWLEDGMENTS

I would like to acknowledge the help of many people, including the designers and developers of the many tools that I describe in this book. They have advanced computing and thinking more than they know. I also want to express my thanks to the many students who have tested out many of the ideas, methods, and beliefs described in this book. Authoring is a difficult process, which was aided in Chapter 9 by Susan Colaric and in Chapter 12 by Chad Carr.

In addition, I would like to thank the reviewers of this book: Temba C. Bassoppo-Moyo, University of Memphis; Edward Caffarella, University of Northern Colorado; Dennis Danielson, National University; Edwin J. George, Florida Gulf Coast University; and Joan Hanor, California State University, San Marcos.

Discover the Companion Website
Accompanying This Book

THE PRENTICE HALL COMPANION WEBSITE:
A VIRTUAL LEARNING ENVIRONMENT

Technology is a constantly growing and changing aspect of our field that is creating a need for content and resources. To address this emerging need, Prentice Hall has developed an online learning environment for students and professors alike—Companion Websites—to support our textbooks.

In creating a Companion Website, our goal is to build on and enhance what the textbook already offers. For this reason, the content for each user-friendly website is organized by topic and provides the professor and student with a variety of meaningful resources. Common features of a Companion Website include:

For the Professor—

Every Companion Website integrates **Syllabus Manager**™, an online syllabus creation and management utility.

- **Syllabus Manager**™ provides you, the instructor, with an easy, step-by-step process to create and revise syllabi, with direct links into Companion Website and other online content without having to learn HTML.
- Students may logon to your syllabus during any study session. All they need to know is the web address for the Companion Website and the password you've assigned to your syllabus.
- After you have created a syllabus using **Syllabus Manager**™, students may enter the syllabus for their course section from any point in the Companion Website.
- Class dates are highlighted in white and assignment due dates appear in blue. Clicking on a date, the student is shown the list of activities for the assignment. The activities for each assignment are linked directly to actual content, saving time for students.
- Adding assignments consists of clicking on the desired due date, then filling in the details of the assignment—name of the assignment, instructions, and whether or not it is a one-time or repeating assignment.
- In addition, links to other activities can be created easily. If the activity is online, a URL can be entered in the space provided, and it will be linked automatically in the final syllabus.
- Your completed syllabus is hosted on our servers, allowing convenient updates from any computer on the Internet. Changes you make to your syllabus are immediately available to your students at their next logon.

For the Student—

- **Topic Overviews**—outline key concepts in topic areas
- **Electronic Blue Book**—send homework or essays directly to your instructor's email with this paperless form
- **Message Board**—serves as a virtual bulletin board to post—or respond to—questions or comments to/from a national audience
- **Web Destinations**—links to www sites that relate to each topic area
- **Professional Organizations**—links to organizations that relate to topic areas
- **Additional Resources**—access to topic specific content that enhances material found in the text

To take advantage of these and other resources, please visit the Companion Website for *Computers as Mindtools for Schools* at

www.prenhall.com/jonassen

Brief Contents

Contents

PART ONE

What Are Mindtools?
What Do They Do?

Using computers as Mindtools implies a change of thinking about how computers can be and should be used in schools. In Part 1 of this book, I lay the conceptual foundation for using computers as Mindtools, providing theoretical, pedagogical, and practical reasons why using computers as Mindtools represents an important new approach to using computers in education. Part 1 consists of two chapters:

Chapter 1   What Are Mindtools?
Chapter 2   Critical Thinking: The Goal of Mindtools

In Chapter 1, I present conceptual arguments for using computers as Mindtools. After describing traditional uses of computers in schools (learning *from* and learning *about* computers), I discuss psychological, educational, and practical reasons why computers are better used as knowledge representation tools, that is, tools for thinking (learning *with* computers). I also provide some criteria for evaluating the usefulness of any computer application as a Mindtool.

In Chapter 2, I describe the primary intellectual reason for using computers as Mindtools: they necessarily engage students in critical thinking. I

1

then provide some background on critical thinking, which for purposes of this book is defined in terms of critical, creative, and complex thinking skills. These skills are used throughout most of the rest of the book to evaluate the mental outcomes of using each of the Mindtools described in Chapters 3 through 13.

In Part 1, I present arguments that Mindtools represent a new and alternative way for using computers in education to engage students in critical thinking while they represent what they know, not what the teacher knows. Mindtools are knowledge representation and reflection tools. I do not argue that computers should only be used as Mindtools. I do argue that if you want students to think critically, then Mindtools will help them do so.

What Are Mindtools?

INTRODUCTION

This book is about using computers to support meaningful learning. In it I recommend a significant departure from traditional approaches to using computers in schools. I promote the idea of using selected computer applications as cognitive tools (which I call Mindtools) for engaging and enhancing multiple forms of thinking in learners. How are Mindtools a departure from traditional applications? Technologies have been used traditionally in schools to "teach" students, much the same as teachers "teach" students (tell students what they know and assess their recall and comprehension of what they were told). I do not believe that students learn *from* computers or teachers—which has been a traditional assumption of most schooling. Rather, students learn from thinking in meaningful ways. Thinking is engaged by activities, which can be fostered by computers or teachers. Thinking is engaged by representing what students know in the forms required by different Mindtools.

Mindtools, therefore, are computer applications that require students to think in meaningful ways in order to use the application to represent what they know. I argue that students cannot use the applications described in this book without thinking critically (engaging the mind). So the most effective uses of computers in classrooms are for accessing information and interpreting, organizing, and representing personal knowledge. Just as carpenters cannot build furniture or houses without a proper set of tools, students cannot construct meaning without access to a set of intellectual tools to help them assemble and construct knowledge.

Traditional computer learning applications assess the effects *of* computer technologies on the learner where the learner has no input into the process (Salomon, Perkins, & Globerson, 1991). Mindtools assess the effects of learning *with* computer technologies when learners enter into an intellectual partnership *with* the computer. Learning with Mindtools depends "on the mindful engagement of learners in the tasks afforded by these tools," which raises the "possibility of qualitatively upgrading the performance of the joint system of learner plus technology" (Salomon et al., 1991, p. 4). In other words, when students work *with* computers, they enhance the capabilities of the computer, and the computer in turn enhances their thinking and learning. The result of this partnership is that the whole of learning becomes greater than the potential of learner and computer alone. Carpenters use their tools to build things; the tools do not control the carpenter. Similarly, computers should be used as tools for helping learners build knowledge rather than controlling the learner.

The purpose of this chapter is to lay the conceptual foundation for using the various Mindtools described in Chapters 3 through 13. In the next section of this chapter, I will briefly review three phases in the short history of computers and learning—learning *from* computers, learning *about* computers, and learning *with* computers. The latter phase includes Mindtools, which I will later justify with several theoretical and practical rationales.

LEARNING *FROM* COMPUTERS: COMPUTER-ASSISTED INSTRUCTION

Throughout the history of educational computing, a primary use of computers has been to deliver computer-assisted instruction (CAI), including drill and practice, tutorials, and, more recently, intelligent tutorials. CAI represents learning *from* computers, where the computer is programmed to teach the student, to direct the activities of the learner toward the acquisition of prespecified knowledge or skills.

Drill and Practice

Throughout the 1970s and much of the 1980s, the most prominent form of CAI was drill-and-practice programs. These electronic ditto sheets presented problems—most commonly mathematical problems—for learners to solve. Learners would enter answers and receive feedback about the accuracy of their responses, often receiving graphic rewards (smiley faces, explosions, or other distractions to learning) in response to correct answers. Drills were based on behaviorist beliefs about the reinforcement of stimulus–response associations. The reward (visual reward) enhanced the likelihood that learners would make a particular response when presented with a specific stimulus. More complicated drill-and-practice strategies, consisting of large item pools, placement algorithms, mastery learning, and review strategies, enhanced drill-and-practice programs. Unfortunately, the behaviorist principles underlying drill and practice are unable to account for, let alone foster, the complex thinking required for meaningful learning required to solve problems, transfer skills to novel situations, construct original ideas, and so on.

The best rationale for the use of drill-and-practice applications was automaticity (Merrill, Tolman, Christensen, Hammons, Vincent, & Reynolds, 1986). To learn complex, higher order skills, the argument goes, it is necessary for learners to first be able to perform the lower level subskills automatically. So, overlearning these subskills on a computer enables learners to gain automaticity. That is true. Computers are certainly patient, tireless, and accurate drillers. However, what drill and practice does not facilitate is the transfer of those skills to meaningful problems.

The thousands of drill programs that were made available to educators were easy for publishers to produce, and they satisfied the demands of administrators that teachers be innovative and use computers. The irony of their existence and use was that they replicated one of the oldest and most meaningless forms of learning, rote learning. While drill programs did help some remedial learners who needed practice, they are not, I argue, the most effective way to use powerful computer technologies.

Tutorials

The cognitive revolution in learning psychology in the 1970s provided the foundations for computer-based tutorials, which sought to respond to individual differences in learning by providing remedial instruction when learners' responses were incorrect. The archetypal tutorial would present some information in text or graphics and then ask the learners a question to assess their comprehension of what had been presented. The student would respond, most often in multiple-choice format, and the tutorial software would compare the student's response with the correct answer stored in the computer's memory. Correct responses were rewarded, while incorrect responses resulted in the presentation of remedial instruction. Sometimes the remediation strategies were fairly sophisticated, with the software providing instruction geared to the nature of the student's error. The program sometimes branched to alternative forms of instruction. Following the remediation, the program typically presented the problem again, providing the student another opportunity to respond correctly. Tutorials consisted of sequences of these presentation–response–feedback cycles. Many tutorials also provided orienting strategies, such as objectives, advance organizers, overviews, summaries, and personalization (e.g., responding to the learner by name). More modern tutorials adapted to learners' entry level of learning, allowed learners to select the amount and form of instruction they preferred, or advised them about how much instruction they needed.

Although tutorials represented an important intellectual advance from drill-and-practice programs, there were problems. For instance, every form of learner response and appropriate instruction has to be anticipated and programmed into the computer. Anyone who has taught students realizes that it is impossible to anticipate how every student or even most students will interpret instruction. The other weakness of tutorials, according to learning theories described later in this chapter, is that they do not allow learners to construct their own meaning but rather seek to map a single interpretation of the world onto what students know. Students are not encouraged or even able to determine what is important, reflect on and assess what they know, or construct any personal meaning for what they study. What they too often acquire from tutorials is *inert* knowledge because they are not applying it.

Intelligent Tutoring Systems

The most sophisticated form of CAI is an intelligent tutoring system (ITS), sometimes referred to as intelligent CAI. ITSs were developed throughout the 1980s and 1990s by artificial intelligence (AI) researchers to teach problem solving and procedural knowledge in a variety of domains. What ITSs add to tutorials is intelligence in the form of student models, expert models, and tutorial models. Expert models describe the thoughts or strategies that an expert would use to solve a problem. How the student performs while trying to solve the problem in the ITS (captured in a student model) is compared with the expert model. When discrepancies occur, the student model is thought to have bugs in it, and the tutorial model diagnoses the problem and provides appropriate remedial instruction. ITSs have more intelligence than traditional tutorials and so can respond more sensitively to learners' misinterpretations.

Although ITSs are more powerful than traditional tutorials, there are many problems with the expert/student modeling procedures used in them. For example, Derry and LaJoie (1993) claim that the student model cannot possibly specify all of the ways in which students may go about trying to solve a problem. And providing "canned" text as feedback cannot possibly offer the same sensitivity as a good human tutor. More important is the issue of whether computers should be used to diagnose learners' understanding, because many educators believe that the most important goal of education is for students to learn how to reflect on and diagnose their own performance. Students should be encouraged to become "reflective practitioners" (Schön, 1983). Derry and LaJoie also note that good ITSs are technically difficult to implement, often costing millions of dollars to develop. There are relatively few intelligent tutors available, and most are used in universities; virtually none have seen widespread use in public schools. Finally, the student modeling methods most commonly used in intelligent tutors are useful only for diagnosing a limited kind of knowledge and so are not generalizable. ITSs resemble powerful instructional devices that benefit most, I argue, the professionals who develop them. Mindtools represent AI in reverse: rather than having the computer simulate human intelligence, get humans to simulate the computer's unique intelligence and come to use it as part of their cognitive apparatus (Salomon, 1988). When learners internalize the tool, they begin to think in terms of it. Why not let the learners assume responsibility for setting their own goals, determining their own strategies, and monitoring their own learning?

LEARNING *ABOUT* COMPUTERS: COMPUTER LITERACY

In the 1980s, microcomputers proliferated, so educators (as they had with most other technologies like radio, film, and television) began grappling with how to use them. The unfortunate result of their deliberations was that most educators felt that it was important for learners to learn *about* computers. So, we taught students about the hardware components of computers. And because useful applications were not available, we taught students how to program the computers, too often using BASIC. Definitions of computer literacy evolved to guide the use of computers in schools, such as "the skills and knowledge needed by all citizens to survive and thrive in a society that is dependent on technology for handling information and solving complex problems" (Hunter, 1983, p. 9). Although computer literacy experts such as Luehrmann (1982) stressed that, beyond verbal awareness of computer components, computer literacy is the ability to do something constructive with the computer, what too many students learned on the way to becoming computer literate was how to memorize the parts of a computer, based on the "strong belief that vocabulary implies knowledge" (Bork, 1985, p. 34). It is a mistake to believe that if students memorize the parts and functions of computers and software, then they will understand and be able to use them. The following questions (from a test given to my fifth-grade daughter when she was learning about computers in school) were used to assess computer literacy:

_____ **1.** bug	A.	programs for computers
_____ **2.** programmer	B.	a mistake in a program
_____ **3.** software	C.	like a typewriter
_____ **4.** CPU	D.	person who writes games
_____ **5.** printer	E.	the brain of a computer
_____ **6.** Storage is where the information is saved. (True or False)		
_____ **7.** A floppy disk is a piece of hardware. (True or False)		

Unfortunately, it is much easier to assess vocabulary than thinking, so computer literacy too often denoted rote memorization.

For a number of reasons, computer literacy is no longer a major issue in schools. First, many more students are able to use computers without instruction. Many students have computers in their homes, and most are exposed to computers at an early age in preschools and elementary schools. Given a useful purpose, most children naturally experiment with computers and learn to use them without a lot of assistance.

Second, the de-emphasis on computer literacy has resulted from discovering that learners do not have to understand the computer in order to use it productively. Computers are intellectual tools and, like most tools, should support the desired functionality in an efficient, comprehensible way. Students generally should not need to study a tool—especially one as powerful as a computer—in order to understand how to use it. Was it necessary to complete a course on "washing machine literacy" in order to use the last new washing machine that you encountered? Yet today's washing machines are complex, computer-controlled (using fuzzy-logic controllers) machines. Newer software better uses the computational power of the computer to make application programs and tools friendly or even transparent. This trend in software transparency will only continue to improve software interfaces, making computer literacy even more irrelevant.

The third reason for the de-emphasis on computer literacy is that most of the applications or skills that students learned about did not support the educational goals of schools. Tools are really useful only if they help you perform a task you need or want to perform. Millions of students in the United States were forced to acquire computer-related skills and knowledge that had no relevance to them and did not support meaningful learning goals.

I am not arguing here that knowledge of computers is irrelevant. Some knowledge of any tool is required in order to use that tool. That is why I begin Chapters 3 through 13 with brief summaries of the software to be used as Mindtools. Clearly, skill in using Mindtools will require practice. However, the practice needs to be embedded in some meaningful activity. When we use a tool to perform some meaningful task, we focus less on the tools themselves and more on their affordances (what they enable us to do). Memorizing the parts of a computer is relatively meaningless if the computers are not used to do something useful. Understanding arises from meaningful activity, not memorizing.

LEARNING *WITH* COMPUTERS: A CONSTRUCTIVIST PERSPECTIVE

The latest phase in the history of educational computing has rejected the assumptions of CAI and computer literacy. The ways in which we use technologies in schools should change from their traditional roles of technology-as-teacher to technology-as-partner in the learning process. Before, I argued that students do not learn from technology, but that technologies can support meaning making by students. That will happen when students learn *with* technology. Students learn *with* technologies when:

- ■ Computers support knowledge construction
  - for representing learners' ideas, understandings, and beliefs
  - for producing organized, multimedia knowledge bases by learners
- ■ Computers support explorations
  - for accessing needed information
  - for comparing perspectives, beliefs, and world views
- ■ Computers support learning by doing
  - for simulating meaningful real-world problems, situations, and contexts
  - for representing beliefs, perspectives, arguments, and stories of others
  - for providing a safe, controllable problem space for student thinking
- ■ Computers support learning by conversing
  - for collaborating with others
  - for discussing, arguing, and building consensus among members of a learning community
  - for supporting discourse among knowledge building communities
- ■ Computers are intellectual partners that support learning by reflecting
  - for helping learners to articulate and represent what they know
  - for reflecting on what they have learned and how they came to know it
  - for supporting learners' internal negotiations and meaning making
  - for constructing personal representations of meaning
  - for supporting mindful thinking (Jonassen, Peck, & Wilson, 1999).

Next I will provide several definitions for Mindtools and later elaborate several rationales for why they represent an effective departure from traditional uses of computers.

MINDTOOLS FOR CONSTRUCTIVE LEARNING

Numerous meanings can be ascribed to Mindtools. The purpose of describing those different definitions is not to confuse you, but rather to lay different conceptual foundations for understanding Mindtools. So, let's begin.

Definitions of Mindtools

Mindtools are computer-based tools and learning environments that have been adapted or developed to function as intellectual partners with the learner in order to engage and facilitate critical thinking and higher order learning. These tools include (but are not necessarily limited to) databases (Chapter 3), semantic networks (computer concept maps) (Chapter 4), spreadsheets (Chapter 5), expert systems (Chapter 6), systems modeling tools (Chapter 7), microworlds (Chapter 8), intentional information search engines (Chapter 9), visualization tools (Chapter 10), multimedia publishing tools (Chapter 11), live conversation environments (Chapter 12), and computer conferences (Chapter 13).

Mindtools are cognitive amplification and reorganization tools. They amplify the learner's thinking by transcending the limitations of the mind. Throughout our history, we have developed mechanical tools to facilitate and amplify physical work. The wheel and the lever provided humans with an enormous mechanical advantage. The industrial revolution added artificial sources of power to extend that advantage and the amount of physical work that could be performed. The information revolution has further extended that advantage by extending the functionality and speed of tools. As Salomon (1993) points out, tools are not just implements; they also serve culturally defined purposes and require a skilled operator in order to function usefully. Computers can amplify cognitive functioning. Pea (1985) argues that the amplification metaphor is inadequate, that cognitive tools reorganize (fundamentally restructure) how learners think.

Mindtools are generalizable computer tools that are intended to engage and facilitate cognitive processing—hence cognitive tools (Kommers, Jonassen, & Mayes, 1992). Cognitive tools are both mental and computational devices that support, guide, and extend the thinking processes of their users (Derry, 1990). Mindtools do not necessarily reduce information processing (that is, make a task easier); rather, their goal is to make more effective use of the mental efforts of the learners. They are not "fingertip" tools (Perkins, 1993) that learners use naturally, effortlessly. In fact, learning *with* Mindtools requires learners to think harder about the subject-matter domain being studied than they would have to think without the Mindtool. Students cannot use Mindtools without thinking deeply about the content they are learning, and, if they choose to use these tools to help them learn, the tools will facilitate the learning and meaning-making processes.

Mindtools (as discussed in Chapter 2) are critical thinking devices. They do this by modeling—in their functions—critical thinking skills. For example, learners cannot construct semantic nets (Chapter 4) or expert systems knowledge bases (Chapter 6) without analyzing and therefore thinking critically about the content they are studying. The tools scaffold meaningful thinking; they engage learners and support them once they are engaged. Mindtools (as shown in Figure 1.1) actively engage learners in creation of knowledge that reflects their comprehension and conception of the information rather than replicating the teacher's presentation of information.

Mindtools are intellectual partners. In most partnerships, responsibility is assigned to the partner who is better able to perform specific functions. In intellectual partnerships, learners should be responsible for recognizing and judging patterns of information and then organizing it (tasks which humans perform better than computers), while the computer should perform calculations and store and retrieve information (tasks which computers perform much better than humans).

Finally, Mindtool is a concept. Although these definitions have focused on computers, computers are not implicitly Mindtools. Search the literature on computers and learning or any software catalog, and you will not find Mindtool research or Mindtools for sale. Mindtools represent a constructivist approach for using computers or any other technology, environment, or activity to engage learners in representing, manipulating, and reflecting on what they know, not reproducing what someone tells them. When using a Mindtool, knowledge is built by the learner, not

Figure 1.1
Learning Processes of Mindtools

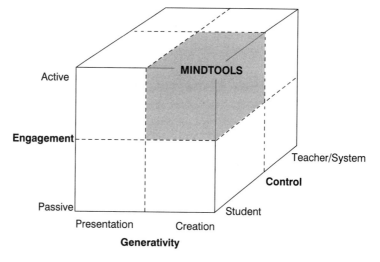

provided by the teacher. Mindtools can assume many forms. As a child, I collected discarded electronic equipment in a basement room which functioned as a Mindtool for testing theories about electricity (most of which failed, by the way). Mindtools are just that, tools for engaging the mind.

WHY USE MINDTOOLS?

Theoretical Reasons for Using Mindtools

Meaningful Learning.   Mindtools foster meaningful learning. Jonassen, Peck, and Wilson (1999) argued that meaningful learning is:

- *Active (manipulative/observant)*—learners interacting with an environment and manipulating the objects in that environment, observing the effects of their interventions and constructing their own interpretations of the phenomena and the results of the manipulation
- *Constructive (articulative/reflective)*—learners integrating new experiences and interpretations with their prior knowledge about the world, constructing their own simple mental models to explain what they observe
- *Intentional (reflective/regulatory)*—learners articulating their learning goals, what they are doing, the decisions they make, the strategies they use, and the answers that they found
- *Authentic (complex/contextual)*—learning tasks that are situated in some meaningful real-world task or simulated in some case-based or problem-based learning environment

■ *Cooperative (collaborative/conversational)*—learners working in groups, socially negotiating a common expectation and understanding of the task and the methods they will use to accomplish it.

Knowledge Construction.   Learning theory applied to technologies is in the midst of a revolution in which researchers and theorists argue about what it means to know and how we come to know. The new theory is *constructivism*. Constructivism is concerned with the process of how learners *construct* knowledge. How learners construct knowledge depends on what they already know, which depends on the kinds of experiences that they have had, how they have organized those experiences into knowledge structures, and the beliefs they use to interpret objects and events that they encounter in the world. Mindtools are tools for helping learners organize and represent what they know.

Constructivists claim that we construct our own reality through interpreting our experiences in the world. Teachers have always assumed that if they tell the student something, the student should understand it as the teacher does. However, learners cannot learn from only listening to teachers since they don't share a set of common experiences and interpretations. Learners must think about what the teacher tells them and interpret it in terms of their own experiences, beliefs, and knowledge.

A common misinterpretation of constructivism suggests that if learners end up constructing their own individual knowledge representations, then intellectual chaos will result. If all learners have their own set of perceptions and beliefs, how can they share meaning? Constructivists believe this naturally occurs through social negotiation. Socially, we collaborate in determining the meaning of certain perceptions. For example, we socially agree on the meaning of a red traffic light, and society negotiates laws to solidify those interpretations. Social negotiation enables us to construct common interpretations of events and objects. Mindtools are media for collaboratively negotiating meaning. That process is required in order to build the kinds of knowledge representations provided by Mindtools.

Constructivist approaches to learning strive to create environments in which learners actively construct their own knowledge, rather than recapitulating the teacher's interpretation of the world. In constructivist environments such as Mindtools, learners are actively engaged in interpreting the external world and reflecting on their interpretations. Active, constructive learning combats the occurrence of inert knowledge, which may be remembered but cannot be used. If learners actively build their own interpretations of the world, they have more ownership of those thoughts, so those thoughts are less likely to degenerate over time. The foundations and implications of the constructivist debate can be investigated further (Duffy & Jonassen, 1992; Jonassen, 1991). The implication of the debate for this book is that Mindtools are constructivist knowledge construction tools.

Reflective Thinking.   Donald Norman (1993) distinguishes between two forms of thinking—experiential and reflective. *Experiential* thinking evolves from one's experiences with the world; it is reflexive and occurs automatically. You experience something in the world and react to it. *Reflective* thinking, on the other hand, requires deliberation. You encounter a situation, act on it, and then think about what you did, make inferences from the experience, determine implications, and retain the experiences and reflections. A common criticism of constructivist approaches to learning is that learners are so active that they do not have time to think about what they are doing. The antidote is reflective thinking that helps us make sense of what we have experienced and what we know. Computers may support reflective thinking, Norman contends, when they enable users to compose new knowledge by adding new representations, modifying old ones, and comparing the two. So, in addition to actively engaging in experiences, knowledge requires that learners reflect on what they have done, what it means, and what else they need to do and know. When learners perceive and declare an intention to learn, what they learn is not inert. Mindtools engage learners in these forms of reflective learning. That is, using Mindtools necessarily engages learners in reflective thinking, which supports knowledge construction.

Cognitive Partnership Tools.   Cognitive technologies are tools that may be provided by any medium and that help learners transcend the limitations of their minds, such as limitations to memory, thinking, or problem solving (Pea, 1985). The most pervasive cognitive technology is language. Imagine trying to learn how to do something complex without the use of language. Language amplifies the thinking of the learner. Computers may also function as cognitive technologies for amplifying and reorganizing how learners think.

Unlike most other tools, computer tools can function as intellectual partners that share the cognitive burden of carrying out tasks (Salomon, 1993). When learners use computers as partners, they off-load some of the unproductive memorizing tasks to the computer, allowing learners to think more productively. Perkins (1993) claims that learning does not result from solitary, unsupported thinking by learners. So our goal should be to allocate to learners the cognitive responsibility for the processing that they do best while we allocate to the technology the processing that it does best.

For example, rather than focusing exclusively on how the computer screen presents information, we should also analyze what the learner is doing with the computer. Rather than using the limited capabilities of the computer to present information and judge learner responses (neither of which computers do well), while asking learners to memorize information and later recall it (which computers do with far greater speed and accuracy than humans), we should assign cognitive responsibility to the part of the learning system that does it best. Their performance is enhanced, leaving some "cognitive residue" in the learners that will likely transfer in situations where they use the tool again (Salomon, 1993).

Scaffold Thinking.   Mindtools scaffold new forms of thinking and reasoning in their zone of proximal development, the zone between learners' existing and potential capabilities. The Vygotskian perspective stresses the functional reorganization of cognition with the use of symbolic technologies (Pea, 1985). Mindtools engage new forms of reasoning that fundamentally reorganize the ways in which learners represent what they know. If these forms of reasoning lie within their zone, then learners will internalize the formalism. Mindtools represent cognitive scaffolds. This book is about developing and adapting computer-based tools as Mindtools to amplify and restructure cognitive functioning during learning, to engage learners in cognitive processes while constructing knowledge that they would not otherwise have been capable of (Pea, 1985).

Practical Reasons for Using Mindtools

A number of practical rationales also exist for using Mindtools that make their use in schools more feasible than other applications of computers.

Lack of Software.   The first practical reason for considering the use of computers as Mindtools is the lack of availability of traditional instructional software. Since the late 1970s, CAI has been available to support learning. Surveys have shown that approximately 85% of that software was either drill-and-practice or tutorial software that was designed to support rote learning. Even assuming that you wanted to use drills or tutorials, it is unlikely that you would be able to find a program to drill the specific skill that students needed to learn. Despite the thousands of instructional programs that have been published, the sum still does not cover a fraction of school curricula. There simply is no software available to teach in any traditional way the bulk of subjects and skills taught in schools. Also, the difficulty of locating, selecting, previewing, and implementing each program, which typically covers only a single objective in the curriculum, is impossible for teachers and librarians. Mindtools require that only a few programs or software packages be learned, most of which are already available in schools. These application programs can be used across the curricula. That is, you can develop Mindtool knowledge bases (using the tools described in Chapters 3 through 13) in every math, science, social studies, literature, and health course taught in schools.

Cost of Computing.   The second practical rationale for using Mindtools is cost. As indicated before, each computer-based instructional program constructed by a separate software producer typically addresses only a single instructional objective or goal, or, at best, a set of related instructional goals. So, addressing a significant portion of the science curriculum would require many individual computer-based instructional programs. Most of these instructional programs—especially the higher quality ones—will cost well over $100 for a single-station license and several hundred dollars for a school-site license, so the cost of providing computer-based simulations or thought-provoking software for each school to cover even the science curriculum, for example, would likely be tens of thousands of dollars. Most of the software for engaging students with Mindtools is either already available in the schools or is available as public domain software.

Efficiency.   The third and related practical rationale for using Mindtools is efficiency. Because Mindtools can be used in many ways in any course to engage meaningful learning, and because the cost per application is relatively low, the cost per student is extremely inexpensive. Mindtools can be used in a great deal more of the curriculum at a lower cost than other currently available computer-based approaches to learning.

Not only do Mindtools provide cost efficiency, they also provide learning efficiencies. Each computer-based instructional program constructed by a separate software producer possesses a different set of outcomes and means for achieving those outcomes. Learning to use individual software applications requires time and effort, which reduces the cognitive effort that can be applied to the ideas being learned. Learning the procedures for using each program requires the teacher to study the software and related instructional materials for each individual lesson. Having to adapt each instructional program to the needs and abilities of each class is not an efficient use of teachers' time. Mindtools require the development of learner skills on a limited number of programs that can be applied to the broad range of subject content. Mindtools simply represent a more efficient use of time and effort.

EVALUATING SOFTWARE AS MINDTOOLS

The software applications described in this book do not represent all of the possible Mindtools. New computer applications are being developed constantly, and many existing applications may be repurposed as Mindtools. To assess the potential of any application as a Mindtool, I will first distinguish Mindtools from productivity tools and knowledge-building tools from information-using tools and then provide a set of criteria for evaluating and using any application as a Mindtool.

Mindtools versus Productivity Tools

Throughout this chapter, I have argued that learning *from* computers and learning *about* computers should be replaced by learning *with* computers. Learning *with* computers means using the computer as a tool to learn with. Computers are frequently used in schools and the workplace as tools to help students or workers produce work, that is, as productivity tools. Using computers in this way involves computers as a medium for helping the user accomplish some task, making the user more productive. Word processing, computer-assisted design (CAD) tools, graphics packages, and outlining programs are essential productivity tools for classrooms and should be used whenever they can facilitate student work. Productivity tools are an appropriate and useful application of computers in classrooms. However, in this book I advocate going beyond productivity to engaging learners in a level of learning that is not possible using productivity tools. So, it is important to distinguish between Mindtools and productivity tools in order to explain why tools such as word-processing programs and paint programs were not included in this book as Mindtools.

Tools such as word-processing (the most commonly used) programs, graphics and paint programs, and CAD programs have significantly enhanced the productivity of users. They are powerful productivity tools and can make us more productive writers, artists, and mechanical drawers. For example, most academics and writers have repressed their memories of the cumbersome nature of the writing process before word processors. Using even primitive (by today's standards) word processors like "Electric Pencil" on 8-kilobyte computers with cassette tape drives in the mid-1970s represented to me a revolution in the process of composition. Most of us believe that word processors have made all of us more efficient, effective, and productive writers. What is questionable is whether, as many advocates claim, word processors have made us *better* writers. In an unscientific study, Halio (1990) claimed that the use of more powerful and friendly Macintosh word processors by college students resulted in sloppier, simplistic, more banal, and grammatically incorrect compositions. The friendliness of the interface causes writers to perceive the computer more as a toy than as a tool, and this may arrest writing at an immature stage of development. Clearly, the ease of editing ideas makes us less careful during initial composition, but does that make us more *creative* writers? While Halio's findings have been widely criticized, I am not convinced that word processors significantly amplify the user's ability to write. They certainly facilitate the process—that is, writing is a conceptual talent that can be facilitated by productivity tools—but they do not necessarily amplify that process. I am not convinced that William Faulkner's novels or the characters in them would have been significantly enhanced had Faulkner used a word processor rather than his manual Royal typewriter.

Word processors, graphics, CAD programs, and other productivity tools are not included in this book because I believe that they do not *significantly* restructure and amplify the thinking of the learner or the capabilities afforded by that thinking. Word processing does not restructure the task of writing. It does not provide an alternative formalism for representing ideas. The formalism of writing is language, which is the richest and most flexible yet complex formalism for representing knowledge. Word processing does not fundamentally change that representation process.

You may ask, then, "Why include productivity tools such as databases and spreadsheets?" They are also used most commonly as productivity tools. However, I believe that databases and spreadsheets, like the other applications described in this book, can also function as cognitive tools for enhancing, extending, amplifying, and restructuring the way learners think about the content they are studying. These applications provide alternative conceptualizations of the content for the learner. They provide new formalisms for thinking. That makes them Mindtools.

Some will argue that the newer generations of idea-processing tools, which integrate note taking, outlining and structuring of compositions, and drafting and proofing of the text, are more powerful tools and can function as Mindtools. Examples of such programs are Writer's Toolkit (from the Scottish Educational Technology Council) and Writer's Assistant (Sharples, Goodlet, & Pemberton, 1992). While these are powerful tools for supporting the composition process, they merely assist learners in using language in appropriate ways to represent their ideas. These programs do not restructure the knowledge representation process; in fact, they supplant much of the thinking that has traditionally been required to represent knowledge through composition.

Mindtools are intellectual partners that enhance the learner's ability to think. Although productivity tools significantly enhance the ability to produce ideas, they do not provide alternative ways of thinking. It may be possible for you to justify word processors, graphics, and CAD programs as Mindtools. In fact, I began writing chapters on word-processing and graphics programs more than once but could not justify their inclusion. In the next section I will present the critical attributes for my conception of Mindtools. I do not believe that word processors and graphics programs meet enough of those criteria to be included. Perhaps you can include word processors and graphics programs in *your* conception of Mindtools. As indicated before, *Mindtool* is a construct or concept as much as it is a real thing, and my construct for Mindtool may be less inclusive than yours. If this is the case, I would encourage you to construct your own word-processing and graphics activities to supplement this text.

Knowledge Building Tools versus Information-Using Tools

Many readers will note the absence of chapters about the Internet and World Wide Web (WWW) as Mindtools. Most contemporary books about computers and learning concentrate on the WWW. It is new, and many educators believe that it will revolutionize education. But will the WWW improve learning?

I do not believe that the WWW is a Mindtool. It is an information source. Searching the WWW may provide learners with different perspectives or information, thereby facilitating their construction of knowledge bases using other Mindtools. However, information searching without an intentional purpose will not necessarily lead to meaningful learning. In fact, it may and often does impede meaningful learning. A generation of learners is learning to use the WWW as an electronic encyclopedia to copy from (a process that is made easier), rather than constructing and representing their own ideas. That form of learning is antithetical to the concept of Mindtools.

Yet the Internet is included in this book. Chapter 9 focuses on search engines to support intentional searches, and Chapters 12 and 13 focus on the use of the Internet for engaging and amplifying learner conversations. Once again, Mindtools depend on how you want learners to think and learn and how you can use computers to support and amplify that learning. Again, my construct for Mindtool may be less inclusive than yours. If so, extend my concept and construct your own WWW activities to supplement this text.

CRITERIA FOR EVALUATING MINDTOOLS

In this final section, I will provide some criteria for assessing whether or not an application you encounter qualifies as a Mindtool. These are not absolute criteria, but rather indicators of "Mindtoolness." Each of the Mindtools described in this book exhibits these characteristics. In the first edition of this book, I evaluated each computer application using these criteria, but the reviewers believed that they were redundant. I agree, so each of the Mindtools chapters will not include that.

1. *Computer-based.* Doubtless there are many noncomputer applications that can function as Mindtools, but this book is about how to use computers more effectively as Mindtools, so they should be computer mediated.

2. *Available applications.* The software applications that are used as Mindtools are readily available, general computer applications. Good Mindtools may also function in ways that support other computing needs (productivity tools, tutors, even baby-sitters). For example, databases have a range of applications other than serving as a Mindtool, such as record keeping, scheduling, information access, and producing the index for this book.

3. *Affordable.* Additionally, Mindtools should be affordable. Most Mindtool applications are available in the public domain or as shareware. Others are integrated into suites of software (like Microsoft Works or Office) that are often bundled with computers. Most are available from vendors at a reasonable cost. A few, like Stella (Chapter 7) are expensive, but their learning effects are so powerful that they are worth it.

4. *Knowledge construction.* The application can be used to construct and represent content or personal knowledge.

5. *Generalizable.* The application can be used to represent knowledge or content in different areas or subjects. Most Mindtools can be used in pure science (chemistry, physics, biology) or applied science (engineering) courses, math courses, literature courses, social science (psychology, sociology, political science) courses, philosophy courses, home economics and health, and even many physical education and recreation courses.

6. *Critical thinking.* Using Mindtools engages learners in critical thinking about their subject (see Chapter 2). That thinking is deeper, higher order, and/or more meaningful than memorizing and paraphrasing what someone else (the teacher or the textbook) said about the content.

7. *Transferable learning.* Using Mindtools results in the construction of generalizable, transferable skills that can facilitate thinking in various fields. This is different than number 5 above, which stated that Mindtools can be used in different subjects. This criterion suggests that critical thinking developed in the context of using Mindtools in science classes will transfer to (be applicable in) English classes. Mindtools are interdisciplinary tools. They facilitate the transfer of knowledge across domains.

8. *Simple, powerful formalism.* The formalism embedded in the Mindtool is a simple but powerful way of thinking. The thinking required to build databases or produce multimedia, for instance, is deep. Expert systems require learners to think causally. Each Mindtool requires learners to organize and represent what they know in a somewhat different way.

9. *Easily learnable.* The mental effort required to learn how to use the software should not exceed the benefits of thinking that result from it. If weeks of effort are required to learn software, the software becomes the object of learning, not

the ideas being studied. The syntax and method for using the software should not be so formal and so difficult that it masks the mental goal of the system. Software programs that are overly complicated to use are not good Mindtools. The basic functionality of the software should be learnable in 1 to 2 hours. You may want students to think causally about information in a knowledge domain, but if the system requires weeks of agonizing effort to learn, the benefits of thinking that way will be outweighed by the effort to learn the system.

SUMMARY

Mindtools are knowledge representation tools that use computer application programs such as databases, semantic networks (computer concept maps), spreadsheets, expert systems, systems modeling tools, microworlds, intentional information search engines, visualization tools, multimedia publishing tools, live conversation environments, and computer conferences to engage learners in critical thinking. The process of using these tools as formalisms for representing the ideas being learned in personal knowledge bases represents an alternative approach to integrating computers in schools. Mindtools represent an effective and efficient way of integrating computers in schools. They can be used across the school curricula to engage learners in thinking deeply about the content they are studying. Mindtools are intellectual partners that facilitate knowledge construction and reflection by learners.

References

Bork, A. M. (1985). *Personal computers for education.* New York: Harper & Row.

Derry, S. J. (1990). *Flexible cognitive tools for problem solving instruction.* Paper presented at the annual meeting of the American Educational Research Association, Boston, April 16–20.

Derry, S. J., & LaJoie, S. P. (1993). A middle camp for (un)intelligent instructional computing: An introduction. In S. P. LaJoie & S. J. Derry (Eds.), *Computers as cognitive tools.* Hillsdale, NJ: Lawrence Erlbaum Associates.

Duffy, T. M., & Jonassen, D. H. (Eds.). (1992). *Constructivism and the technology of instruction: A conversation.* Hillsdale, NJ: Lawrence Erlbaum Associates.

Halio, M. P. (1990). Student writing: Can the machine maim the message? *Academic Computing, 6*(1), 18–19.

Hunter, B. (1983). *My students use computers.* Reston, VA: Reston Publishing.

Jonassen, D. H. (1991). Objectivism vs. constructivism: Do we need a new paradigm? *Educational Technology: Research and Development, 39*(3), 5–14.

Jonassen, D. H., Peck, K. C., & Wilson, B. G. (1999). *Learning with technology: A constructivist perspective.* Upper Saddle River, NJ: Merrill/Prentice Hall.

Kommers, P. A. M., Jonassen, D. H., & Mayes, T. M. (1992). *Cognitive tools for learning.* Heidelberg, Germany: Springer-Verlag.

Luehrmann, A. (1982, May/June). Computer literacy: What it is; why it is important. *Electronic Learning,* pp. 20–22.

Merrill, P. F., Tolman, M. N., Christensen, L., Hammons, K., Vincent, B. R., & Reynolds, P. L. (1986). *Computers in education.* Upper Saddle River, NJ: Prentice Hall.

Norman, D. A. (1993). *Things that make us smart: Defending human attributes in the age of the machine.* Reading, MA: Addison-Wesley.

Pea, R. D. (1985). Beyond amplification: Using the computer to reorganize mental functioning. *Educational Psychologist, 20*(4), 167–182.

Perkins, D. N. (1993). Person-plus: A distributed view of thinking and learning. In G. Salomon (Ed.), *Distributed cognitions: Psychological and educational considerations.* Cambridge: Cambridge University Press.

Salomon, G. (1988). AI in reverse: Computer tools that turn cognitive. *Journal of Educational Computing Research, 4*(2), 123–139.

Salomon, G. (1993). On the nature of pedagogic computer tools. The case of the writing partner. In S. P. LaJoie & S. J. Derry (Eds.), *Computers as cognitive tools.* Hillsdale, NJ: Lawrence Erlbaum Associates.

Salomon, G., Perkins, D. N., & Globerson, T. (1991). Partners in cognition: Extending human intelligence with intelligent technologies. *Educational Researcher, 20*(3), 2–9.

Schön, D. (1983). *Educating the reflective practitioner: Toward a new design for teaching and learning in the professions.* San Francisco: Jossey-Bass.

Sharples, M., Goodlet, J., & Pemberton, L. (1992). Developing a Writer's Assistant. In J. Hartley (Ed.), *Technology and writing: Readings in the psychology of written communication.* London: Jessica Kingsley.

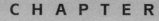
Critical Thinking: The Goal of Mindtools

INTRODUCTION: CONCEPTUALIZATIONS OF THINKING

During the past couple of millennia, philosophers, theologians, and psychologists have developed many theories of thinking. They have developed a range of conceptions, from the simple disposition to behave in certain ways all the way to mysterious acts of sorcery. Contemporary research into the components of intelligence, cognitive learning strategies, and critical thinking have all confirmed that thinking is a complex, multifaceted process. What separates humans from lower orders of mammals is their highly developed cortex, which affords them incredible thinking processes.

A detailed treatment of the evolution of thinking about thinking is beyond the scope of this book, however I will introduce the complexity of human thinking by briefly describing one of the more popular contemporary psychological conceptions of thinking, Gardner's "multiple intelligences." Gardner and his colleagues examined the literature in cognitive capacities in individuals of all types in order to produce a theory of multiple intelligences (Gardner, 1983; Gardner & Hatch, 1989). This theory contends that there are seven different kinds of intelligence, each with its characteristic use:

- *logico-mathematical*—using logical and numerical patterns and deductive reasoning; used by mathematicians, scientists, and logicians
- *linguistic*—sensitivity to sounds and meanings of words and language abilities; used by writers and literature teachers
- *musical*—sense of rhythm, pitch, and melody, and appreciation of musical expressions; used by musicians
- *spatial*—spatial memory and manipulating and transforming perceptions of visual objects; used by artists and architects
- *bodily-kinesthetic*—control of bodily movements and proprioceptive abilities; used by athletes and skilled artists
- *interpersonal*—understanding and dealing with the moods, temperaments, motivations, and behaviors of other people; used by counselors, social workers, and salespersons
- *intrapersonal*—understanding one's own feelings, motivations, needs, strengths, and weaknesses; used in guiding one's own behavior.

Most individuals use most or all of these kinds of thinking, with varying levels of skill. And when we engage in complex learning tasks, we use combinations of these different kinds of thinking.

Because developing meaningful thinking through using computers is the focus of this book, and because my purpose is to contrast the thinking required by various Mindtools, it will be necessary to use a single interpretation of what meaningful thinking should be in schools. Among the contemporary conceptions of thinking in schools, I believe that the concept of critical thinking (generalizable, higher order thinking, such as logic, analyzing, planning, and inferring) is the most common and therefore the most useful way to describe the outcomes of Mindtools. Therefore, I will use critical thinking as the metric for comparing the effects of using Mindtools.

So, the primary hypothesis of this book is that the use of computer-based Mindtools necessarily engages learners in critical thinking about the topics they are studying, which, in turn, results in better comprehension of the topics and the acquisition of useful learning skills. Each Mindtool described in the following chapters will be compared in terms of critical thinking skills, which I will describe in the following sections.

CRITICAL THINKING IN SCHOOLS

Traditional Models of Critical Thinking

Critical thinking as an issue emerged during the 1970s and 1980s as an antidote to reproductive, lower order learning (Paul, 1992). Reproductive learning, resulting from memorizing and regurgitating what the teacher or textbook says, leaves students with fragments of information that are not well connected or integrated: "What they have in their heads exists there like so many BBs in a bag." So Paul equates meaningful thinking with critical, logical thinking—"disciplined, self-directed thinking" (p. 9). Paul's elements of thought include the "ability to formulate, analyze and assess the

- problem or question at issue
- purpose or goal of thinking
- frame of reference or points of view involved
- assumptions made
- central concepts and ideas involved
- principles or theories used
- evidence, data, or reasons advanced (interpretations and claims made)
- inferences, reasoning, and lines of formulated thought
- implications and consequences that follow" (1992, p. 10).

Paul's conception of critical thinking, like most traditional models, regards it as "reflective thinking focused on deciding what to believe or do" (Ennis, 1989, p. 4), consisting of skills such as

- grasping the meaning of a statement
- judging whether there is ambiguity in a line of reasoning
- judging whether certain statements contradict each other
- judging whether a conclusion follows necessarily
- judging whether a statement is specific enough
- judging whether a statement is actually the application of certain principles
- judging whether an observation statement is reliable
- judging whether an inductive conclusion is warranted
- judging whether the problem has been identified
- judging whether something is an assumption
- judging whether a definition is adequate
- judging whether a statement made by an alleged expert is acceptable.

According to Ennis, these skills occur in three dimensions: *logical* (judging the relationships between meanings of words and statements), *critical* (knowing the criteria for judging statements covered by the logical dimension), and *pragmatic* (considering the background or purpose of the judgment and the decision as to whether the statement is good enough for the purpose). So, the skill of judging the reliability of a statement, for example, involves judging whether a statement makes sense in terms of what it says, knowing the criteria that make a statement reliable, and understanding the source of the statement and the context in which it is used. This is because critical skills are critical in different ways in different circumstances. Such a conception of critical thinking, like most of the traditional conceptions of critical thinking, is very logic oriented. Traditional conceptions describe a restricted set of tasks that can be applied to ideas that already exist, but they do not account for generating original thoughts and ideas, which I believe must be the hallmark of any conception of critical thinking.

Current Models of Critical Thinking

Walters (1990) describes the outcomes from traditional conceptions of critical thinking as the *vulcanization* of students. Vulcans, as exemplified by Spock in the television series *Star Trek,* are incapable of thinking or acting illogically. Spock's ability to stick to the evidence and draw logical conclusions made him unparalleled at problem solving and critical analysis. He never succumbed to prejudices, hidden agendas, or emotional confusion. He was the epitome of objectivity. However, he was also devoid of imagination, intuition, insight, and the capacity for metaphorical thinking. The literalness of his thinking made imaginative speculation and practical adaptability to novel situations impossible. His reasoning was reactive and not innovative. He was unable to suspend the rules of logic, even when his predicament required him to. Spock believed that logical thinking—or rationality—is good thinking.

Walters holds that there is a more holistic view of rationality, one that includes, along with the logical processes, intuition, imagination, conceptual creativity, and insight. He argues that much of the bandwagon effect of critical thinking assumes that critical thinking is logical thinking. Although Walters agrees (as do I) that logical inference, critical analysis, and problem solving are fundamental elements of good thinking, they are practically useful only if they are supplemented by imagination, insight, and intuition, which he considers essential components of discovery. Concentrating only on logical thinking will produce Vulcans and not students who appreciate the multiple perspectives necessary for meaningful knowledge construction.

There are numerous other conceptions of critical thinking. Closer to the constructivist position I described in Chapter 1, Litecky (1992) defines critical thinking as "the active, mental effort to make meaning of our world by carefully examining thought in order to better understand content" (p. 83). Resnick and Klopfer (1987) also include aspects of thinking that are not included in traditional models of critical thinking. Rather than proffering a precise definition of higher order thinking, they list its key features:

- Higher order thinking is *nonalgorithmic.* That is, the path of action is not fully specified in advance.
- Higher order thinking tends to be *complex.* The total path is not visible (mentally speaking) from any single vantage point.

■ Higher order thinking often *yields multiple solutions,* each with costs and benefits, rather than a unique solution.

■ Higher order thinking involves *nuanced judgment and interpretation.*

■ Higher order thinking involves the application of *multiple criteria,* which sometimes conflict with one another.

■ Higher order thinking involves *self-regulation of the thinking process.* We do not recognize higher order thinking in an individual who allows someone else to "call the plays" at every step.

■ Higher order thinking involves *imposing meaning,* finding structure in apparent disorder.

■ Higher order thinking is *effortful.* Considerable mental work is involved in the kinds of elaborations and judgments required.

Model of Complex Thinking

All of these conceptions are useful in helping us to understand the kinds of thinking that Mindtools engage. However, to compare and contrast the effects of using Mindtools, it is easier to use a single conception of critical thinking. Therefore, I have selected as a model one of the most comprehensive and useful models of critical thinking, the Integrated Thinking Model (Iowa Department of Education, 1989). It defines complex thinking skills as an interactive system, not a collection of separate skills. It also describes the various processes that are referred to as "thinking," and their relationships to each other. I will use this model to analyze and compare the effects of Mindtools discussed in this book.

This model has three basic components of complex thinking (see Figure 2.1): content/basic thinking, critical thinking, and creative thinking (the three circles surround the complex thinking core). Complex thinking, the synthesis of content, critical, and creative thinking, includes the "goal-directed, multi-step, strategic processes, such as designing, decision making, and problem solving. This is the essential core of higher order thinking, the point at which thinking intersects with or impinges on action" (Iowa Department of Education, 1989, p. 7). It makes use of the other three types of thinking in order to produce some kind of outcome—a design, a decision, or a solution. I will discuss these four types of thinking in turn.

Content/Basic Thinking. Content/basic thinking represents "the skills, attitudes, and dispositions required to learn accepted information—basic academic content, general knowledge, 'common sense,'—and to recall this information after it has been learned" (Iowa Department of Education, 1989, p. 7). Content/basic thinking thus includes the dual processes of learning and of retrieving what has been learned. Content/basic thinking describes traditional learning, except that it is important to note that this content-based knowledge is in constant interaction with critical, creative, and complex thinking because it is the knowledge base from which they operate. Because the hypothesis of this book is that Mindtools engage learners in critical thinking (which, in this model, consists of critical, creative, and complex thinking), I will use only those thought processes in the analysis of the outcomes of each Mindtool.

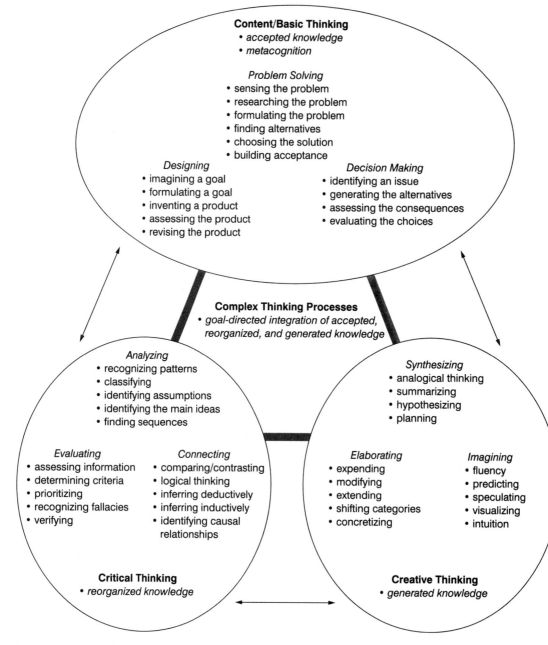

Figure 2.1
Integrated Thinking Model

26

Critical Thinking.   Critical thinking involves the dynamic reorganization of knowledge in meaningful and usable ways. It involves three general skills: evaluating, analyzing, and connecting.

Evaluating involves making judgments about something by measuring it against a standard. Evaluating is not expressing a personal attitude or feeling. It involves recognizing and using criteria in different instances. Recognizing criteria is important when criteria are unstated; otherwise, the learner is required to use a publicly available set of standards. It is also important that students be able to determine which criteria are appropriate. Evaluating information involves skills such as

- assessing information for its reliability and usefulness, and discriminating between relevant and irrelevant information (e.g., evaluating the meaningfulness of criticism of a film based on the ability of the critic; evaluating an historical account in terms of its accuracy)
- determining criteria for judging the merits of ideas or products by identifying relevant criteria and determining how and when they will be applied (e.g., developing an evaluation sheet for critiquing research studies; establishing evaluation guidelines for judging an art show)
- prioritizing a set of options according to their relevance or importance (e.g., ranking a set of interventions for solving a child's behavioral problem; rating a set of bonds for long-term gain)
- recognizing fallacies and errors in reasoning, such as vagueness, non sequiturs, and untruths (e.g., propaganda in political campaigns; sales pitches that promise more than they can deliver)
- verifying arguments and hypotheses through reality testing (e.g., solving proofs in geometry; checking the accuracy of arguments in court actions)

Analyzing involves separating a whole entity into its meaningful parts and understanding the interrelationships among those parts. Manipulating part/whole relationships helps learners understand the underlying organization of ideas. Analyzing knowledge domains involves skills such as

- recognizing patterns of organization (e.g., meter and rhyme schemes in poetry; arithmetic series)
- classifying objects into categories based on common attributes (e.g., sets in math, plant/animal classifications; economic, social, or political groups)
- identifying assumptions, stated or unstated, including suppositions and beliefs, that underlie positions (e.g., postulates in geometry; meaning in advertising campaigns)
- identifying the main or central ideas in text, data, or creations, and differentiating core ideas from supporting information (e.g., discovering the theme of a series of paintings; finding important arguments or themes in a passage or poem)
- finding sequences or consecutive order in sequentially organized information (e.g., determining sequences for preparing dishes in a meal; determining the order of operations in solving math problems).

Connecting involves determining or imposing relationships between the wholes that are being analyzed. Connecting compares and contrasts things or ideas, looks for cause-and-effect relationships, and links the elements. Connecting builds on analyzing because it often compares wholes based on the parts that were analyzed. It involves skills such as

- comparing/contrasting similarities and differences between objects or events (e.g., comparing business plans; contrasting different phyla of animals in terms of locomotion)
- logical thinking, required to analyze or develop an argument, conclusion, or inference or provide support for assertions (e.g., evaluating the logic used in a geometric proof or a position paper in economics; using a method for determining an unknown element in chemistry)
- inferring deductively from generalizations or principles to instances (hypothetico-deductive or syllogistic reasoning) (e.g., proving theorems given a set of axioms; solving logic problems in philosophy)
- inferring a theory or principle inductively from data (e.g., developing a theory of animal behavior from observing animals in the wild; drawing conclusions from collections of data such as tables or charts)
- identifying causal relationships between events or objects and predicting possible effects (e.g., predicting the effects of a physics experiment; inferring the causes of social strife in a country)

Creative Thinking.   Creative thinking requires going beyond accepted knowledge to generate new knowledge. Many creative thinking skills are closely tied to critical thinking skills. Critical thinking makes sense out of information using more objective skills, such as analyzing and evaluating information using established, external criteria. Creative thinking, on the other hand, uses more personal and subjective skills in the creation of new knowledge, not the analysis of existing knowledge. That new knowledge may also be analyzed using critical thinking skills, so the relationship between critical and creative thinking is dynamic. The major components of creative thinking are synthesizing, imagining, and elaborating.

Synthesizing involves skills such as

- thinking analogically, which involves creating and using metaphors and analogies to make information more understandable (e.g., creating characters to describe different chemicals or chemical groups; finding everyday occurrences to relate to fictional events in literature)
- summarizing main ideas in one's own words (e.g., summarizing the meaning of a story in English or a foreign language; stating a personal method for solving math problems)
- hypothesizing about relationships between events and predicting outcomes (e.g., sampling classmates' attitudes about new laws and projecting their parents' beliefs; predicting the reaction of chemicals in a laboratory simulation)

■ planning a process, including a step-by-step procedure for accomplishing activities (e.g., developing a new study sequence for improving course grades; developing a plan for completing a term paper)

Creative thinking also involves *imagining* processes, outcomes, and possibilities. It involves intuition and fluency of thinking, and often calls on students to visualize actions or objects. Visualization is a skill that some students will find difficult to develop because of individual differences in thinking abilities. Although imagining skills are not as concrete or easily taught as other skills, they are nonetheless important for generating new ideas. Imagining includes skills such as

■ expressing ideas fluently or generating as many ideas as one can (e.g., thinking of things that are red and round; generating an adjective checklist to describe individuals in history lessons)
■ predicting events or actions that are caused by a set of conditions (e.g., predicting the effects of new seat belt laws on traffic fatalities; predicting the effects of healthier diets and exercise on body weights and fat counts)
■ speculating and wondering about interesting possibilities, and solving "what if" questions without logical evaluation (e.g., speculating about the effects of a major earthquake in California; what if historical figures had known each other)
■ visualizing, which involves creating mental images or mentally rehearsing actions (e.g., imagining yourself performing a double front flip in a diving class; imagining a battle between the immune system and an invading virus)
■ intuition or hunches about ideas are powerful strategies that are impossible to teach but worth accepting, at least as hypotheses that can be tested using other skills (e.g., guessing the worth of a painting in an art class; predicting who will win an election).

Creative thinking also involves *elaborating on information,* that is, adding personal meaning to information by relating it to personal experiences or building on an idea. Elaborating includes skills such as

■ expanding on information by adding details, examples, or other information (e.g., generating as many examples as possible of a concept such as "value"; developing a story around solving a type of math problem)
■ modifying, refining, or changing ideas for different purposes (e.g., changing a story line to have a sad ending rather than a happy one; modifying the form of a musical composition)
■ extending ideas by applying them in a different context (e.g., treating science problems like military battles from history; translating experiences from one culture to another foreign culture)
■ shifting categories of thinking by assuming a different point of view (e.g., changing from the role of a Democrat in a debate to that of a Republican; clas-

sifying food groups and nutritional values of typical meals from different countries)
- ▪ concretizing general ideas by giving examples and uses (e.g., writing a short poem in different meters; creating a voyage to the center of different atoms).

Complex Thinking Skills.   At the center of the Integrated Thinking Model are complex thinking skills. These thinking processes combine the content, critical, and creative thinking skills into larger, action-oriented processes. The three major types of complex thinking skills involve problem solving, designing, and decision making. These processes, each with a number of steps, are used in deciding whether, when, and where to use Mindtools. The Iowa Department of Education (1989) has described the critical and creative skills that are involved in each of these steps.

Problem solving involves systematically pursuing a goal, which is usually the solution of a problem that a situation presents. Problem solving is perhaps the most common complex skill. It includes the following steps and their related skills such as

- ▪ sensing the problem (intuition, visualizing, fluency, identifying assumptions)
- ▪ researching the problem (assessing information, shifting categories, classifying, recognizing fallacies)
- ▪ formulating the problem (summarizing, inferring, hypothesizing, concretizing, identifying main ideas)
- ▪ finding alternatives (expanding, extending, modifying, predicting, fluency, speculating)
- ▪ choosing the solution (assessing information, comparing/contrasting, determining criteria, prioritizing, verifying)
- ▪ building acceptance (planning, fluency, shifting categories, inferring, identifying causal relationships, predicting).

Designing involves inventing or producing new products or ideas in some form, whether artistic, scientific, mechanical, or other. It involves analyzing a need and then planning and implementing a new product. Designing includes the following steps and their related skills:

- ▪ imagining a goal (fluency, shifting categories, speculation, visualizing, intuition)
- ▪ formulating a goal (visualizing, predicting, identifying causal relationships, recognizing patterns, hypothesizing, planning, logical reasoning)
- ▪ inventing a product (fluency, planning, expanding, concretizing, shifting categories, analogical thinking, visualizing)
- ▪ assessing the product (determining criteria, assessing information, comparing/contrasting, recognizing fallacies, verifying)
- ▪ revising the product (expanding, extending, modifying)

Decision making involves selecting between alternatives in a rational, systematic way. Decision making includes awareness and manipulation of objective and subjective criteria. It involves the following steps and their related skills:

- identifying an issue (identifying the main idea, recognizing patterns, identifying assumptions, recognizing fallacies)
- generating alternatives (fluency, extending, shifting categories, hypothesizing, speculating, visualizing)
- assessing the consequences (classifying, comparing/contrasting, determining criteria, identifying causal relationships, predicting, thinking analogically)
- making a choice (summarizing, logical thinking, inferring, concretizing, intuition)
- evaluating the choices (assessing information, verifying, intuition)

The Integrated Thinking Model from the Iowa Department of Education, described above, is probably the most comprehensive model available for describing critical, creative, and complex thinking. Throughout the remainder of the book, each Mindtool will be evaluated in terms of the critical, creative, and complex thinking skills it engages and supports.

SUMMARY

In this chapter, I provided descriptions of the raison d'être of Mindtools—the engagement and fostering of critical, creative, and complex thinking in learners. When learners use Mindtools to represent their own understanding, they are necessarily engaged in different forms of critical thinking. In each Mindtool chapter (Chapters 3–13), I analyze the basic activities involved in using the tools to create personal knowledge bases in terms of the critical, creative, and complex thinking skills required to use the Mindtool. Fostering these skills should be a primary purpose of schooling. Mindtools are computer applications that, when used by students to represent their own understanding, will engage and foster these skills. I do not presume that Mindtools are the only way to engage critical thinking in schools. Skilled teachers and purposeful students have been doing that throughout the history of education. However, to the extent that you value critical thinking and computer usage, Mindtools offer a means for achieving both outcomes.

References

Ennis, R. H. (1989). Critical thinking and subject specificity: Clarification and needed research. *Educational Researcher, 18*(3), 4–10.

Gardner, H. (1983). *Frames of mind.* New York: Basic Books.

Gardner, H., & Hatch, T. (1989). Multiple intelligences go to school: Educational implications of the theory of multiple intelligence. *Educational Researcher, 18*(11), 4–10.

Iowa Department of Education (1989). *A guide to developing higher order thinking across the curriculum.* Des Moines, IA: Department of Education. (ERIC Document Reproduction Service No. ED 306 550)

Litecky, L. (1992). Great teaching, great learning: Classroom climate, innovative methods, and critical thinking. In C. A. Barnes (Ed.), *Critical thinking: Educational imperative.* San Francisco: Jossey-Bass.

Paul, R. W. (1992). Critical thinking: What, why, and how. In C. A. Barnes (Ed.), *Critical thinking: Educational imperative.* San Francisco: Jossey-Bass.

Resnick, J. B., & Klopfer, L. E. (1987). Toward the thinking curriculum: An overview. In L. B. Resnick & L. E. Klopfer (Eds.), *Toward the thinking curriculum: Current cognitive research.* Washington, DC: Association for Supervision and Curriculum Development in cooperation with the North Central Regional Educational Laboratory.

Walters, K. S. (1990). Critical thinking, rationality, and the vulcanization of students. *Journal of Higher Education, 61*(4), 448–467.

PART TWO

Semantic Organization Tools

P art 2 of this book describes a kind of Mindtool that I refer to as semantic organization tools. Semantic organization tools include databases and semantic networks, so this part consists of the following chapters:

Chapter 3   Databases as Mindtools
Chapter 4   Semantic Networks (Concept Maps) as Mindtools

In Chapter 1, I contrasted productivity tools and Mindtools. Databases were developed as productivity tools that are used to facilitate information storage and retrieval in business, government, and education. However, when used to organize and represent what learners know about content they are studying, they become Mindtools. Semantic networking tools (Chapter 4), on the other hand, were designed to function as Mindtools.

The key to databases and semantic networks is organization. They are tools that help learners to organize the ideas they are studying and learning. Why is that important? If ideas are not organized in memory, they will not be as easily retrievable. If the ideas in a knowledge domain are not organized, learners will not be as able to make inferences, draw analogies, solve problems, and perform other higher order thinking tasks as they would if their constructed knowledge were well organized. Databases and semantic networks help learners organize and visually represent what they know. These visual representations of concepts and relationships are otherwise known as structural knowledge (Jonassen, Beissner, & Yacci, 1993), cognitive structures, knowledge structures, internal connectedness, integrative understanding, or conceptual knowledge. Structure is inherent in all knowledge. The better organized personal knowledge is, the more memorable and usable it is. Consider using these Mindtools to help your students to organize what they know.

Reference

Jonassen, D. H., Beissner, K., & Yacci, M. A. (1993). *Structural knowledge: Techniques for representing, conveying, and acquiring structural knowledge*. Hillsdale, NJ: Lawrence Erlbaum Associates.

Databases as Mindtools

WHAT ARE DATABASE MANAGEMENT SYSTEMS?

Database management systems (DBMSs) are computerized record-keeping systems (see Figure 3.1). They were originally designed to replace paper-based information retrieval systems. They are, in effect, electronic filing cabinets that allow users to store information in an organized filing system and later retrieve that information, just as a secretary stores documents in organized filing drawers. The advantages offered by computerized information storage include compactness (several drawers full of paper information can be stored on a single floppy disk), speed of entering information into the system (directly via the keyboard, bar code readers, scanners, or nowadays even voice), faster and easier access to information in the system, and easier updating of information in the system.

DBMSs consist of several components: the database, a file management system, database organization tools, and reporting (printing) functions. A database consists

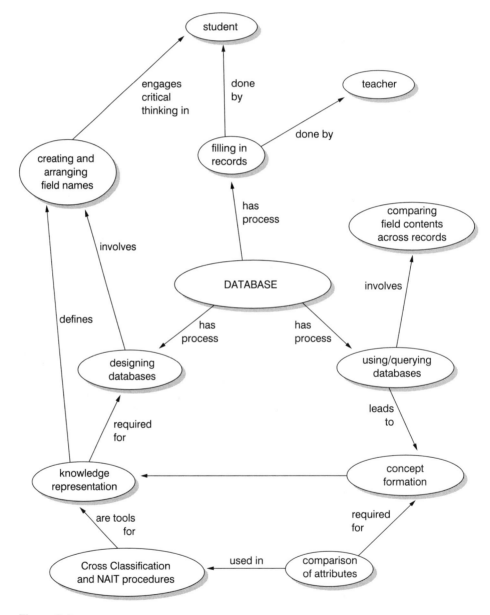

Figure 3.1
Databases as Mindtools

of one or more files, each of which contains information in the form of collections of records that are related to a content domain, event, or set of objects (e.g., an individual's account information). Each record in the database is divided into fields that describe the class or type of information contained therein. The same type of information for each record is stored in each field. For example, the address database in Figure 3.2 contains four records, each with information about a different individual. These records are systematically broken down into fields (subunits of each record) that define a common pattern of information. The database in Figure 3.2 contains six fields: one for the last name, one for the first name, one for the street address, one for the city, one for the state, and one for the zip code. The content and arrangement of each field are standardized within the records so that the computer will know which part of the record to search in order to locate a particular kind of information.

Database-manipulation tools permit the user to organize and reorganize the information in order to answer queries. The primary tools are searching, sorting, and retrieving information. For example, you can use the file management capability of the DBMS to create a file that contains the class schedule of each student in a school. You could save that file, access it, and change it to reflect changes in schedules using the file management and editing capabilities of the DBMS. For example, if a student were transferred to another class during fourth period, you would open the file, find the student's record in the database (by searching in the name field for that student's name), move across the record to the correct period, and change the information in the file.

The more important functions of DBMSs are the organization tools that will help you answer queries about students' schedules. One often-used tool is the search function, which allows you to search through the database to find specific information. For example, you may search on the name field for a particular student's name because you know that the student's record contains other information you need. For example, you could search through the name field for "Smith." Search capabilities vary with each system, although most allow you to tailor your search using different requests. You could search the name field, for example, for

Record	Field 1 Last Name	Field 2 First Name	Field 3 Address	Field 4 City	Field 5 State	Field 6 Zip
1	Smith	John	123 Maple Dr.	Columbus	Ohio	54211
2	Buchanon	Peggy	4700 Oglethorpe St.	Moose	Oregon	90202
3	Fernandez	Jose	6325 Van Buren Blvd.	Los Angeles	California	95543
4	Richmond	Aletha	321 Aspen Way	Craig	Colorado	80437
etc.						

Figure 3.2
Database Structure

records that EQUALS Smith. Such a search request would show every record that contains the word "Smith" and nothing more. Searching using CONTAINS Smith would produce every record that has the letters SMITH in it, though there could be additional letters, such as in Smith*son* or Smith*field*. EQUALS is obviously a much more limiting search term, so it would be used if you wanted to refine the search. For example, you could search the database for all students scheduled into Mr. Brown's social studies class during fourth period. This would be useful for printing grade sheets or interim reports.

Another common search feature is the NOT function. Searching a database field using NOT Smith would show every record in the database except those with Smith in the field. Most DBMSs support search methods that can search a date or number field for values greater than, equal to, or less than a particular value. Most DBMSs also permit you to identify multiple search criteria, that is, to search simultaneously on more than one field. For example, if you wanted to find all the Smiths in the eighth grade, you would make a search that identifies name field EQUALS Smith and grade EQUALS 8.

The other function that is important to the use of databases as Mindtools is the sort function, which enables you to rearrange the contents of the database in ascending or descending order according to one or more of the fields. For example, if you sorted on Field 1, Last Name, in the database shown in Figure 3.2, then the order of the records would change, with Buchanon appearing first, followed by Fernandez, Richmond, and Smith.

Essentially, DBMSs allow you to store information in an organized way and to locate or arrange the information in the database to help you answer queries about that information. The examples that I have used to illustrate the DBMS features all use the data for administrative purposes (e.g., attendance, scheduling, student records). To use DBMSs as Mindtools, students will use the same functions to analyze and enter subject-matter content into databases, which can then be searched and sorted to answer specific questions about the content or to seek interrelationships and inferences among the subject content.

DBMSs also possess file management capabilities that allow you to create and define new database files. Once the data structure is defined, information can be entered into or deleted from the file. Any database file can be saved on a disk, deleted, copied, or saved under a new name. These file management functions enable the user to make permanent copies of the information in the database.

The ease, capacity, and speed with which these activities can be accomplished varies with the system. Many databases also possess security features and the capacity to integrate with other databases.

HOW ARE DATABASES USED AS MINDTOOLS?

When used as a Mindtool, a database management system helps students integrate and interrelate content ideas, which in turn makes the ideas more meaningful and more memorable (as illustrated earlier in Figure 3.1). Building databases requires that learners organize information by identifying the underlying dimensions of the content. For example, health students studying vitamin therapy might want to set up a database in which each vitamin is a record and the characteristics of each vitamin (e.g., dietary sources, physiology, metabolic effects, etc.) are the fields. The process of searching for information and creating the database—including deciding which fields are necessary, how large they should be, and how they should be ordered (creating the data model)—can be a very meaningful instructional activity.

To build the data model, students must first decide what the appropriate content relationships are. They must then search for the information in a systematic fashion in order to fill the database. The searching and sorting of the database required to answer queries can generate a variety of comparisons and contrasts based on which fields are selected for searching and sorting. Intellectually, these processes require the organization and integration of a content domain.

There are few examples of knowledge-oriented (Mindtool-type) databases described in the literature. Goldberg (1992) recommended using databases to classify types of seashells. According to Rooze (1988–89), the value of databases to the teaching of social studies is that creating databases places students in an active as opposed to a passive role. By preparing a database, students determine which information to collect and organize seemingly unrelated bits of information into meaningful categories. However, if students are to use the database effectively, the teacher must guide (not direct) the development of categories and search procedures. Rooze recommended strategies for concept development and data interpretation in the development and use of databases.

Knight and Timmons (1986) also recommended the use of databases to meet the objectives of history instruction. Pon (1984) described the use of databases as an inquiry tool to aid higher level thinking in a fourth-grade American Indian studies course. Watson and Strudler (1988–89) described a lesson based on Taba's inductive thinking model that teaches higher order thinking using databases. Building databases involves analyzing, synthesizing, and evaluating information, according to Watson and Strudler.

The Technical Education Research Center (TERC) in Cambridge, Massachusetts, has created a simple-to-use database program called TableTop to support database construction and analysis by school-age children (Hancock, Kaput, & Goldsmith, 1992). Their approach is to provide opportunities for children to analyze authentic data, such as an elementary class's analysis of waste in school lunches.

Database construction is an analytical task that calls on a variety of critical, creative (to a lesser extent), and complex thinking skills. In the following sections, I will present a number of databases that have been constructed by teachers and students to reflect their critical thinking about content. As a product, these databases can be assessed and graded by the teacher as evidence of higher order thinking and content knowledge (rubrics for this purpose are presented later in the chapter), however, the power of any Mindtool is in the process of constructing it. So copying a database and using it as a study guide would not be particularly effective.

Constructing a database, on the other hand, is among the richest and most power-ful ways to study for an examination. There are many ways to use databases as Mindtools.

Analyzing Content Domains

Databases are tools for student analysis of content domains. While studying text-books, CD-ROMs, lecture notes, library materials, or other information sources, students must analyze the content in order to identify the underlying themes that structure it. Those themes can be used as fields with examples as records. The first example (Figure 3.3) is a simple database produced by an elementary class that includes social, political, and economic indicators from different countries. When used to analyze content domains, students experience at least two levels of analysis. The first level occurs when students seek out and organize information in the data-base. This is an analysis process. The second level is reflective and relational, when students ask questions about information in the database. In doing so, they look for relationships among the content in different fields. Understanding underlying rela-tionships in content is a higher order thinking skill that most teachers only hope that students will develop. Teachers can facilitate that kind of learning by developing complicated relational questions requiring students to search and sort the database. For instance, to answer the question "Do poorer countries have lower literacy lev-els?," students would sort the database by income or literacy rate, place the fields side by side, and compare the literacy levels with income rates. Although this method is not statistically reliable, it requires learners to compare and contrast data in a meaningful way. Ultimately, you want students to construct the same kinds of questions for their own databases, so they can play "stump the teacher" or "quiz your classmates" by generating these higher order questions and asking the teacher or classmates (technique discussed later in *Coaching the Construction of Databases in the Classroom*). For example, students who constructed the database in Figure 3.3 developed questions such as the following to ask each other about the contents of the databases:

1. What is the relationship between average income and literacy rate? Which country is different from the others with a high literacy rate? How will recent events affect that country?
2. If you knew nothing about any of these countries except for what is in the data-base, which one would you want to live in? Why?
3. How are infant mortality and literacy related to GNP?
4. Which are the most socially advanced countries? On what criteria do you base your answer?

The next database (Figure 3.4) was developed by a science teacher for the study of cells—their functions, locations, and so on. The teacher wrote questions, such as the following, that required students to search and sort on different fields in order to construct an answer:

name	population	gnp i	pop density	yrs pe	infant mort	defence bud	ave income	liter
Australia	16,646,000	220	5.4/sq.mi.	1/2.0	8.1/1000	2.7%	$14,458	99%
Brazil	153,771,000	313	47/sq.mi.	1/4.0	67/1000	.9%	$ 2,020	76%
Canada	26,527,000	486	6/sq.mi.	1/1.7	7.3/1000	2.0%	$13,000	99%
China	1,130,065,0	350	288/sq.mi.	1/12	33/1000	4.4%	$ 258	70%
El Salvador	5,221,000	4.1	671/sq.mi.	1/12	62/1000	3.9%	$ 700	62%
India	850,067,000	246	658/sq.mi.	1/62	91/1000	3.8%	$ 300	36%
Iraq	18,782,000	34	104/sq.mi.	1/18	69/1000	32.0%	$ 1,950	70%
Japan	123,778,000	1800	844/sq.mi.	1/4.1	5/1000	1.0%	$15,030	99%
Mexico	88,335,000	126	115/sq.mi.	1/8.7	42/1000	.6%	$ 2,082	88%
Saudi Arabi	16,758,000	70	15/sq.mi.	1/3.5	74/1000	12.8%		50%
Switzerland	6,628,000	111	406/sq.mi.	1/2.9	6.9/1000	2.2%	$26,309	99%
U.S.S.R.	290,939,000	2.5	33/sq.mi.	1/3.2	25.2/1000	17.0%	$ 3,000	99%
U.S.A.	250,372,000	4.8	68/sq.mi.	1/1.3	10/1000	5.7%	$16,444	99%

Figure 3.3
Database of World Statistics

1. Find all of the cell types of the connective tissue system. Which cells are involved in bone formation? What is the relationship of these cells to bone formation?
2. Find all of the cell types with cilia. Where are the cilia located within the cells, and why are they important to those locations?
3. How are erythrocytes affected within sickle cells?

cell type	location	function	shape	related cell	specialization	tissu
Astrocyte	CNS	Supply Nutrients	Radiating	Neurons, Capillaries	Half of Neural Tissu	Nerv
Basal	Stratum Basale	Produce New Cells	Cube, Columnar	Epithelial Cells	Mitotic	Epith
Basophil	Blood Plasma	Bnd hrm.E	Lobed Nuclei, Gr	Neutrophil, Eosinoph	Basic Possible Mast	Conn
Cardiac Muscle	Heart	Pump Blood	Branched	Endomysium	Intercalated discs	Musc
Chondroblast	Cartilage	Produce Matrix	Round			Conn
eosinophil	Blood Plasma	?, Protozoans, aler	Two Lobes, gran	basophil, neutrophil	acid, Phagocytize (h	conn
Ependymal	Line CNS	Form Cerebralspinal	Cube		Cilia	Nerv
erythrocytes	Blood Plasma	Transport O2, mono	Disc	Hemocytoblast, Proge	Transport	conn
Fibroblast	Connective Tissue	Fiber Production	Flat, Branched		Mitotic	Conn
Goblet	Columnar Epithelia	Secretion	Columnar	Columnar	Mucus	Epith
Keratinocytes	Stratum Basal	Strengthen other Cel	Round	Melanocytes		Epith
Melanocytes	Stratum Basale	U.V. Protection	Branched	Keratinocytes	Produce Melanin	Epith
Microglia	CNS	Protect	Ovoid	Neurons, Astrocytes	Macrophage	Nerv
Motor Neuron	CNS (Cell Body)	Impulse Away from	Long, Thin	Sensory Neuron, Ne	Multipolar, Neuroms	Nerv
Neutrophil	Blood Plasma	Inflammation, Bacter	Lobed Nuclei	Basophil, Eosinophil	Phagocytize, Neutral	Conn
Oligodendrocyte	CNS	Insulate	Long	Neurons	Produce Myelin She	Nerv
Osteoblast	Bone	Produce Organic Mat	Spider	Osteoclasts	Bone Salts	Conn
Osteoclast	Bone	Bone Restoration	Ruffled Boarder	Osteoblasts	Destroy Bone	Conn
Pseudostratified	Gland Ducts, Respi	Secretion	Varies	Goblet	Cilia	Epith
Satellite	PNS	Control	Cube	Schwann, Neurons	Chemical Env.	Nerv
Schwann	PNS	Insulate	Cube	Neurons, Satellite	Form Myelin Sheath	Nerv
Sensory Neuron	PNS (Cell Body)	Impulse to CNS	Long, Thin	Motor Neuron, Neuro	Unipolar, Action Pot	Nerv

Figure 3.4
Part of a Database on Cells

function	type	name	graph	inverse	domain	range	abs max	abs min
y = x	polynomial	linear	line	y = x	(−∞,∞)	(−∞,∞)	none	none
y = x^2	polynomial	quadratic	parabola		(−∞,∞)	[0,∞)	none	y = 0
y = x^3	polynomial	cubic	cubic	y = x^1/3	(−∞,∞)	(−∞,∞)	none	none
y = x^4	polynomial	quartic	parabola		(−∞,∞)	[0,∞)	none	y = 0
y = x^5	polynomial	quintic	cubic	y = x^1/5	(−∞,∞)	(−∞,∞)	none	none
y = x^6	polynomial	6th order	parabola		(−∞,∞)	[0,∞)	none	y = 0
y = x^7	polynomial	7th order	cubic	y = x^1/7	(−∞,∞)	(−∞,∞)	none	none
y = x^n	polynomial	nth order			(−∞,∞)		none	none
y = 2^x	exponential	base 2 – exponential	exponential	y = log2(x)	(−∞,∞)	(0,∞)	none	none
y = 10^x	exponential	base 10 – exponential	exponential	y = log10(x)	(−∞,∞)	(0,∞)	none	none
y = e^x	exponential	base e – exponential	exponential	y = log e(x)	(−∞,∞)	(0,∞)	none	none
y = n^x	exponential	base n – exponential	exponential	y = log n(x)	(−∞,∞)	(0,∞)	none	none
y = ln x	logarithmic	natural logarithm	logarithmic	y = e^x	(0,∞)	(−∞,∞)	none	none
y = log x	logarithmic	common logarithm	logarithmic	y = 10^x	(0,∞)	(−∞,∞)	none	none
y = log 7(x)	logarithmic	base 7 logarithm	logarithmic	y = 7^x	(0,∞)	(−∞,∞)	none	none
y = 1/x	rational		inverse varia	y = 1/x	(−∞,0),(0,∞)	(−∞,0),(0,∞)	none	none
y = 1/x^2	rational		volcano		(−∞,0),(0,∞)	(0,∞)	none	none
y = 1/x^3	rational		inverse varia	y = 1/x^1/3	(−∞,0),(0,∞)	(−∞,0),(0,∞)	none	none
y = 1/x^4	rational		volcano		(−∞,0),(0,∞)	(0,∞)	none	none
y = 1/x^n	rational				(−∞,0),(0,∞)		none	none
y = sin x	trigonometric	sine	sinusoidal		(−∞,∞)	[−1,1]	y = 1	y = −1
y = cos x	trigonometric	cosine	sinusoidal		(−∞,∞)	[−1,1]	y = 1	y = −1
y = tan x	trigonometric	tangent	cubic		x ≠ np2),n = 1,3,5…	(−∞,∞)	none	none
y = sec x	trigonometric	secant	sinusoidal		x ≠ np,n), n = 1,2,3…	(−∞,−1],[1,∞)	none	none
y = csc x	trigonometric	cosecant	sinusoidal		x ≠ np2), n = 1,3,5…	(−∞,−1],[1,∞)	none	none
y = cot x	trigonometric	cotangent	reciprocal		x ≠ np, n = 1,2,3…	(−∞,∞)	none	none
y = |x|	absolute value	absolute value	bird		(−∞,0)	[0,∞)	none	y = 0
y = 1/|x|	absolute value	absolute value	volcano		(−∞,0) (0,∞)	(0,∞)	none	none

Figure 3.5
Database on Mathematical Functions

The next database (Figure 3.5) was developed by a math class to describe a variety of mathematical functions, including inverse, domain, and range. Seeing these functions contrasted in a database helped the teacher, who had been teaching algebra for many years, understand the underlying structure of algebra in a different way.

Analyzing Stories

A variation on the process of analyzing content is to analyze stories and experiences for what they have to teach us. Very often, we remember and describe what we know by telling stories. Replay and analyze most any conversation, and it will probably be comprised of a series of stories. One person tells a story to make a point, which reminds other conversants of related events, so they tell the stories that they were reminded of, which in turn reminds others of stories, and so on. Why do we use stories to foster conversation? Because we remember so much of what we know in the form of stories. Stories are rich and powerful formalisms for storing and describing memories. So, one way of understanding what people know is to analyze their stories. The means for analyzing stories is called case-based reasoning (CBR).

CBR is an artificial intelligence method for representing what people know. CBR claims that what people know is stored in memory as stories (Schank, 1990). In any new situation, people examine the situation and attempt to retrieve a previously experienced situation that resembles the current situation. Along with information about the situation, we retrieve the lessons which that situation provides. New problems are solved by finding similar past cases and applying the lessons from that experience to the new case.

The database in Figure 3.6 recounts one of many stories that have been collected about the conflict in Northern Ireland. The database contains many stories that have been indexed by topic, theme, context, goal, reasoning, religion, etc. The database contains numerous topics, themes, and contexts. When students analyze stories in order to understand these issues, they better understand the underlying complexity of the content domain.

To use databases for capturing stories, you must identify cases or stories. Cases denote situations, events, experiences, problems, and so on. Cases consist of a description of the situations (context, goals, purpose, etc.), solutions that were selected, and lessons learned when the solution was carried out (Kolodner, 1993). The problem situation is defined by the goals to be achieved in solving the problem, the constraints on those goals, and any features of the problem. As stories are collected from magazines, news reports, personal interviews, or any other means and then analyzed, they must be indexed by identifying some combination of the goals, constraints, situational descriptions, themes, solutions, outcomes, and lessons in a database. Learning, from a CBR perspective, is a process of indexing and filing experience-based lessons and reusing those in similar situations in the future. In this example, students learn about the horrors of religious conflict by examining others' experiences. Databases facilitate this learning process by allowing teachers to search or sort on any field to locate similar cases or results.

topic	Peace and Reconciliation
index	Widespread monetary support from blue collar workers in Northern California for the
theme	Americans openly support IRA
Context	Northern California
goal	to get Ireland for the Irish
observation	Irish American Catholic working class supporting violence to get Ireland for the Irish
reasoning	support of IRA will get Britain out of Ireland
religion	Background of IRA supporters are Catholic

"Amerimick: I'm a third generation Irish-American, who has lost family Troubles." I find some of your commentary to be rather naive, if not ig statement as to it only being a very small portion of Irish-Americans wh to the I.R.A. is based on what empirical data? Or is it just suppose- attain Throughout Northern California, especially in the blue collar Sunset Dis Francisco, the passion that those working I-A's is backed by their wallets. Republican houses that I've been, we have drank a toast of Jameson's fo life taken by an Provisional I.R.A. action. Oh yes, we are all practicing Ca (former alter boys at that) who donate regularly to the Friends of Sinn Fe Northern Aid, and to other Irish causes. Wake up, Amerimick, you will like us in any American city that has a sizable Irish population. Ireland f Brits out now! "

Figure 3.6
Entry in Database on Northern Ireland Stories

Study Guides

Another, more traditional use for databases is as study guides or electronic worksheets. In this application, data models are given to students to guide their study of textbook or other material. The databases start out empty, and students fill in records as they study material. For example, the database in Figure 3.7 (the data model and a single record are illustrated) provides a study guide for an English student studying poetry. For each poem studied, students identify the speaker, tone, theme, symbolism, etc., that is exemplified in that poem. Study guides direct students to identify the important elements of a poem. What makes this kind of electronic worksheet powerful, though, is that when students have added a large number of poems to their database, they can begin to ask some very interesting questions of the database, such as whether poets during a certain period used particular themes or kinds of symbolism or whether different motifs were associated with certain spiritual values. This is the kind of deeper level understanding that English teachers always hope that their students will develop, although it is difficult because they do not understand the poems and their elements as well. Databases can help learners compare and contrast these elements.

| **Poem** | The World Is Too Much With Us | | **Poet** | Wordsworth | **Dates** | 1770-1850 | **Form** | Sonnet |

| **Speaker — Listener** | The Poet — himse | **Tone** | exhorting; frustrated | | **Eg of Tone** | "Great God! I'd ra |

| **Subject or Situation** | The effect of our present world view. |

| **Theme** | Comparison between our present materialist world view and its effects on our character with ear |

| **Sound Devices** | alliteration (b) | | **Rhyme Scheme** | abca abca dedede | | **Rhythm** | iambic pentameter |

| **Symbolism** | none | | **Comparative devices** | metaphors: "we are out of tune"; allusion |

| **Syntax Patterns** | apostrophizing (Gre | **Frequent Diction I Imagery** | images of nature: flowers, lea |

| **Freedom Motif** | reflected in desire for freedom from limitations of scientific world view |

| **Innocence & Inner Child Motif** | the innocent view of pagans is upheld as desirable |

| **Importance of Nature Motif** | reflected in our estrangement from natural world: "little we see in natur |

| **Glory of the Common Man Motif** | belief that Pagans lived better lives |

| **Spiritual Values Motif** | reflected in reaction against material values (getting, spending) and a time orie |

| **Immediate & Individual Experience Motif** | reflected in the importance of new individual experience |

Figure 3.7
Database Study Guide on Poems

Relational Databases

The kind of database that I have described so far in this chapter is referred to as a flat file or table, a two-dimensional organization of content into fields and records. These databases use pointers (structural computer codes embedded in the file) to connect records in the database file. Early file management systems used to store and retrieve information in these flat files were weak compared with today's powerful database management systems. For instance, the data model (organization of data into fields) could not be changed after the model was identified. If you wanted to add a new field to include a new kind of information, it was necessary to start over building a new database. In the past two decades of personal computing, database systems have become much more powerful and flexible. Most database programs have become more relational. A relational database is a collection of relations or tables of different sizes and organization that are interconnected in a network-like manner based on the kind of data contained in the fields and records, not on pointers. Information contained in different files can be interrelated through key relationships so that information does not have to be duplicated in more than one file. Also the order of rows and columns (records and field) is insignificant. Relational databases permit more sophisticated organization and queries. They enable users to combine, compare, contrast, or otherwise interrelate information in several databases (tables). This can support a higher level of content analysis by more advanced learners.

Figure 3.8 illustrates part of a group of related tables from a relational database on drugs. The bottom table describes drugs; the middle shows the presence of these drugs in natural substances; and the top table describes herbal alternatives to drugs. Additional tables, interrelating natural and artificial drugs in terms of their chemistry and pharmacology, could be added. Relational databases enable groups of students to create their own databases and combine them into a larger, classroom project. These tables are searched together in order to answer queries. Queries are formal searches of the database that can be predefined in the program. For example, Figure 3.9 shows the results of a formal query. *Access,* a database program, searched all of the tables for relevant information, showing only the records and fields necessary for answering the query.

HERBAL : Table

Herb Alternative	Source	Effects	Drug (use to replace	Toxicity	Methods -Te
Angelica	Archangelica archangelica	Stimulant	Tobacco and Caffeine	Should not be used by Pregnant	☑
Anise	Pimpinella Anisum	Stimulant	Caffeine	None	☑
Bird's-foot Trefoil	Lotus Corniculatis	Antispasmodic, Mild Sedative.	Benzodiazepines, antihistamines, and	The Flowers and leaves might be	☑

Drug-Herb : Table

Drug Name	Anise	Angelica	Bird's-foot	Black Haw	Boneset	Button Snake	Cardinal Flower	Celery	Chamomile
Alcohol	☐	☐	☐	☐	☐	☐	☑	☐	☐
Amphetamines	☐	☐	☐	☐	☐	☐	☐	☐	☐
Antidepressant	☐	☐	☐	☐	☐	☐	☐	☐	☐
Antipsychotic Tr	☐	☐	☑	☑	☐	☑	☐	☑	☑

Drug : Table

Drug Name	Derivatives/ Drugs	Medical advantages	Illegal applications
Alcohol	Ethyl alcohol or ethanol	Increases metabolic rate, thins blood, sedates, promotes sleep and is a good food source of energy.	Purching alcoholic beverages which are contraband or home brewed or selling these for profit, driving or operation machinery while intoxicated; selling alcoholic beverages to minors.
Amphetamines	Amphetamine, Dextroamphetamine	Doctors use amphetamines to treat conditions such as narcolepsy, sever depression unresponsive to	Purchasing, consuming prescribing or selling these drugs without authorization from proper authorities.
Antidepressant	Isocarbozacid. Phenelzine.	Given for relief of certain	Selling or consuming antidepressant and antimania

Figure 3.8
Tables from a Relational Database on Drugs

Figure 3.9
Formal Query from the Drug Database

What kind of abused drug could be replaced by Ginseng? : Se...

Drug Name	Derivatives/ Drugs	Ginseng
Amphetamines	Amphetamine, Dextroamphetamine	☑
Barbiturates	Amobarbital, Aprobarbital, Butabarbital, Mephobarbital¡K¡K	☑
Tobacco	Nicotine, Pyrrolidine	☑
Volatile inhalants	Products contain butyl and isobutyl nitrate. Nail polish remover, lighter fluids, cleaning fluids, ¡K.	☑
Antidepressant	Isocarbozaqid, Phenelzine, Tranylcypromine.	☑

Record: 1 of 5

The database shown in Figure 3.10 is a relational database on different pathogens, which may be studied in a health or biology class. The top table describes the various pathogens; the middle table shows their presence in different food sources; and the bottom table describes the physical and chemical conditions under which different pathogens can grow. The database supports a number of interesting queries. For example, Figure 3.11 shows the results of the query "What pathogens will grow in milk at refrigeration temperature?"

Related Mindtools

Newer databases and spreadsheets (Chapter 5) look and function very much alike. Newer databases possess more computational capabilities, whereas spreadsheets have more organizational capabilities, although spreadsheets do offer much greater arithmetic sophistication. Users frequently pass information back and forth between them. Because they can be used in conjunction with each other, information collected for one can be included in the other. Although they are becoming more similar, as Mindtools, they are different.

Conceptually, databases are similar to semantic networks (Chapter 4) in that both are used to define content domains in terms of their semantic relationships.

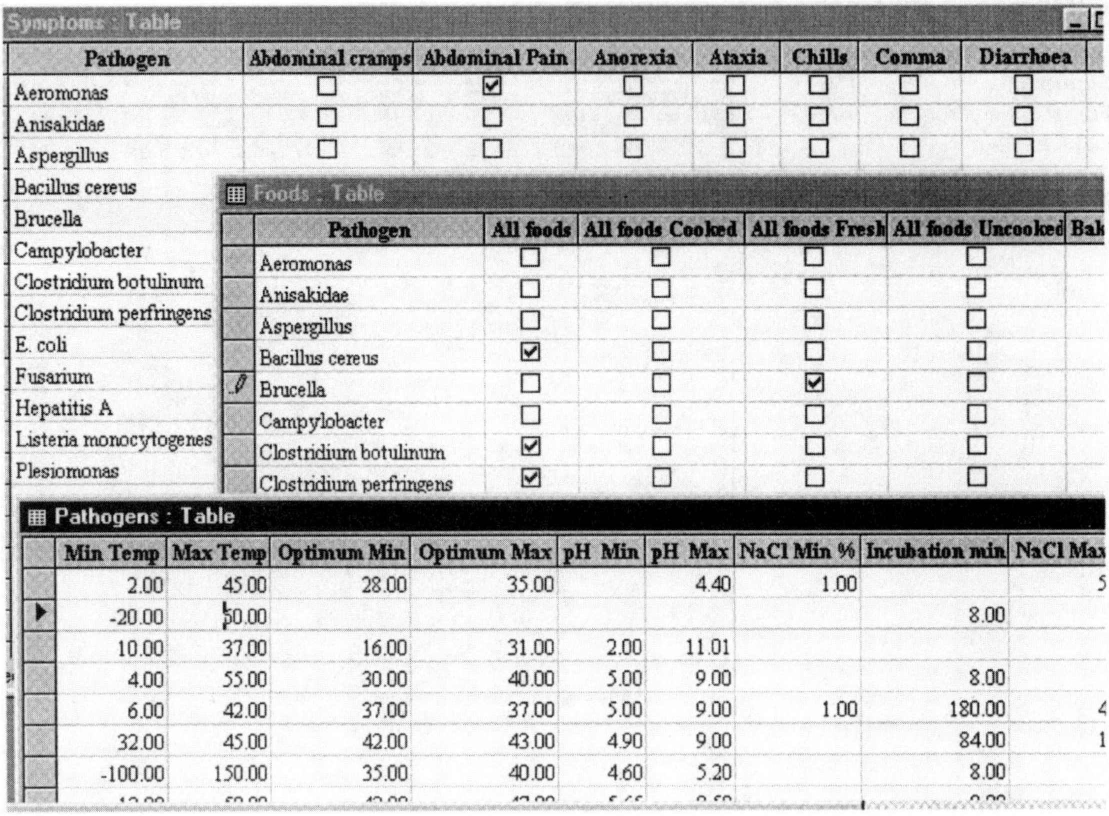

Symptoms : Table

Pathogen	Abdominal cramps	Abdominal Pain	Anorexia	Ataxia	Chills	Comma	Diarrhoea
Aeromonas	☐	☑	☐	☐	☐	☐	☐
Anisakidae	☐	☐	☐	☐	☐	☐	☐
Aspergillus	☐	☐	☐	☐	☐	☐	☐
Bacillus cereus							
Brucella							
Campylobacter							
Clostridium botulinum							
Clostridium perfringens							
E. coli							
Fusarium							
Hepatitis A							
Listeria monocytogenes							
Plesiomonas							

Foods : Table

Pathogen	All foods	All foods Cooked	All foods Fresh	All foods Uncooked	Bak
Aeromonas	☐	☐	☐	☐	
Anisakidae	☐	☐	☐	☐	
Aspergillus	☐	☐	☐	☐	
Bacillus cereus	☑	☐	☐	☐	
Brucella	☐	☐	☑	☐	
Campylobacter	☐	☐	☐	☐	
Clostridium botulinum	☑	☐	☐	☐	
Clostridium perfringens	☑	☐	☐	☐	

Pathogens : Table

Min Temp	Max Temp	Optimum Min	Optimum Max	pH Min	pH Max	NaCl Min %	Incubation min	NaCl Max
2.00	45.00	28.00	35.00		4.40	1.00		5
-20.00	50.00						8.00	
10.00	37.00	16.00	31.00	2.00	11.01			
4.00	55.00	30.00	40.00	5.00	9.00		8.00	
6.00	42.00	37.00	37.00	5.00	9.00	1.00	180.00	4
32.00	45.00	42.00	43.00	4.90	9.00		84.00	1
-100.00	150.00	35.00	40.00	4.60	5.20		8.00	
12.00	50.00	42.00	47.00	5.65	8.50		8.00	

Figure 3.10
Tables from a Relational Database on Pathogens

Figure 3.11
Results of Query in Pathogen Database

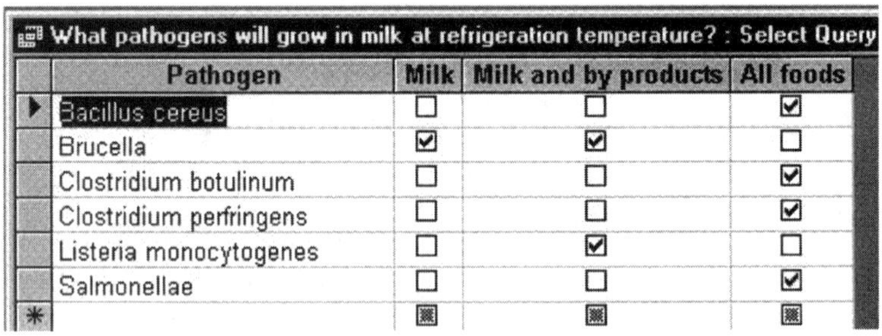

What pathogens will grow in milk at refrigeration temperature? : Select Query

Pathogen	Milk	Milk and by products	All foods
Bacillus cereus	☐	☐	☑
Brucella	☑	☑	☐
Clostridium botulinum	☐	☐	☑
Clostridium perfringens	☐	☐	☑
Listeria monocytogenes	☐	☑	☐
Salmonellae	☐	☐	☑
*			

48

Semantic networks are less structured and constrained than databases. The data model for a database constrains the kinds of information that can be included in it, whereas semantic networks can evolve in less structured ways. These reduced constraints may provide an advantage for knowledge construction by some learners, while others may profit from the structural constraints imposed by databases. I recommend learning to develop knowledge bases using databases first in order to take advantage of the more structured approach to knowledge construction.

When using computer conferences (Chapter 13), the contents of those conversations are often stored in databases in order to analyze the conversation. So, having experience in manipulating data structures is likely to transfer positively to information-retrieval processes. This transfer is likely to help in searching for any information to include in any kind of knowledge base described in this book.

Finally, databases can provide a structure (albeit rigid) for developing multimedia and hypermedia knowledge bases (Chapter 11). Many critics claim that hypermedia is nothing more than multimedia databases (which is sometimes the case). The point is that database construction provides learners the opportunity to structure information in ways that can positively affect the use of most other Mindtools.

Coaching the Construction of Databases in the Classroom

When should you use databases as Mindtools in the classroom? Databases are very useful for supplementing the learning of concept-rich content, such as that in geography, social studies, and the sciences. They are especially useful when you want students to compare and contrast different forms, styles, functions, or approaches. For example, contrasting the uses of various chemical compounds, the demographics of different countries, or the stylistic elements used by authors in various literary periods are good candidates. Databases allow learners to examine the underlying structure of most course content.

Using databases and performing the kinds of content analysis required to build them will probably require new skills for many learners. These skills should be developed carefully. The ultimate goal is for your students to be able to independently analyze a new content domain in order to determine the appropriate data model, search for the information in texts, videos, and other sources to fill in the database, and use the database to create and answer relational queries about the information it contains. To support that goal, teachers may need to guide students through some of the following learning activities and strategies in order to scaffold the development of database skills. Most students will develop database skills very quickly.

1. Students query a completed database. To introduce students to the functions and organization of a database, you may want to prompt them by having them use an existing database to answer questions about the information contained in the database. Examples of the types of questions that can be asked are presented with earlier database examples (Figures 3.3 and 3.4). Do not begin with queries as complicated as these, however. Start with a familiar database, perhaps a database of personal information about the students in the class. Require them to search for information in the database (e.g., all students over 5 feet, 5 inches tall) or sort the database (e.g., arrange the class from youngest to oldest). Initially, they will need to be coached through these experiences. These activities familiarize learners with database functions and structure. They also serve as advance organizers or overviews for lessons, and may also facilitate hypothesis generation.

2.   **Students complete existing data structures.** Begin with a partially completed database and have students fill in gaps in the database by using their textbooks or going to the library to locate the necessary information. This provides them with some existing information for comparing new data to and from which to generalize. Later, require students to complete full records; that is, provide them with a blank database in which only the fields (data model) are defined. This activity stresses purposeful searching for information, rather than general memorization of all information. If you observe textbooks that students highlight during reading, it will be obvious that students do not know how to discriminate important from trivial information. This activity provides a model for searching and identifying the more important and relevant bits of information.

3.   **Students make a plan.** Before beginning, students need to make a plan for the database. What are they interested in representing? What points do they want to make? What kinds of structure and information are required to make those points? What learning goals will they work toward?

4.   **Students adapt existing data structures or design new data structures for other students to complete.** Start with familiar content and require students to adapt existing databases, such as the classroom information database, or design new databases that they can collaboratively complete. Here you are modeling the organizational skills required to develop data structures. Topics such as local sports teams, dating patterns, and television shows are popular.

5.   **Students create and complete data structures.** Increase the complexity of the content by relating it to classroom studies. Then, starting with more concrete content, such as geographical or demographic features in social studies, have students in groups determine what fields are required. This depends on what kinds of questions people have that need to be answered, that is, what kinds of information users may want from the database. This is perhaps the most difficult part of the process. Be certain to acquire a DBMS that allows you to add or delete fields after the initial design (some file management systems do not permit this). Compare the data models in class (each group will construct a different model) and discuss them in terms of how completely and accurately they reflect the content domain and how well they facilitate access to information in them. That is, do the fields allow for efficient searching? Do they represent the content faithfully? This is the most complete activity, requiring learners to identify variables and information needs, build data structures, access information and complete the database, and search the database.

6.   **Students write queries for other students.** Have students write difficult queries that require other students to use multiple search criteria to answer the questions. Students are often challenged by the prospect of constructing queries

that are difficult for their fellow students or for teachers. The value of this activity is that it requires learners to think about relationships among and implications of the information contained in the database and the ability of the data structure to support various queries. It will very probably require a lot of coaching, because these are difficult skills to develop.

7. **Students extrapolate from databases.** Students can create new fields in existing databases to support other applications. For example, starting with a database of geographic information, adding political and economic fields of information to support geopolitical queries would be useful. Students may choose to restructure the databases or predict how others would respond to queries.

8. **Students reflect on the activity.** Reflection should not wait until the project is completed. Rather, students should continuously review their progress on the project. Are we achieving our goals? What changes are necessary? How do we compare with other groups? Are we answering questions and making the points that we set out in our plan. After the project is completed, the students should reflect on the project. What have we learned about the content? What have we learned about database construction and how we represent knowledge? What have we learned about working with each other? You may choose to provide students with some or all of the criteria for evaluating student databases (presented in the next section) to use for self-evaluation. The activity of constructing databases engages meaningful thinking. Reflection cements the knowledge that learners construct.

EVALUATING DATABASES AS MINDTOOLS

Critical, Creative, and Complex Thinking in Database Construction and Use

Several critical, creative, and complex thinking skills are required to use and construct content databases. Tables 3.1, 3.2, and 3.3 identify the skills that are required for constructing and querying a content database, adding information to a study guide, and constructing and querying a relational database. The skills in each table that are marked with an "X" are those that are employed by each process, based on an information-processing analysis of the tasks.

There are more critical and complex thinking skills required to build and query databases than there are creative skills (see Tables 3.1, 3.2, and 3.3). That is because database construction is an analytic process that makes extensive use of logical thinking. All three activities make heavy use of critical skills, such as evaluating information, (especially) analyzing information, and connecting information. Querying a database requires that learners evaluate the question and determine a strategy to answer that query in terms of searching and sorting. For example, answering question 2 given earlier about the database in Figure 3.4 requires learners to search the field of cell types for cilia cells, identify the information in the location field, and compare information in the function field. That process requires students to recognize patterns, identify assumptions and main ideas, and compare and contrast information. Filling in a database study guide such as that shown in Figure 3.4 requires the use of encyclopedias, atlases, and almanacs to assess, identify main ideas, and compare and contrast ideas.

A number of creative thinking skills are involved in constructing and using databases (see Table 3.2). Designing and using databases depends less on elaborating information than on analyzing information (a critical thinking skill). Some synthesizing is involved, but even fewer imagining skills are required, since one is essentially describing and classifying what does exist. Most of the creative skills result from writing database queries, which requires that learners hypothesize and predict responses. Answering queries effectively requires that learners develop a "feel" for the database and its contents.

Finally, a number of complex thinking skills are required for planning and constructing databases. Designing and building databases require a number of planning operations that make heavy use of designing, problem-solving, and decision-making skills (see Table 3.3). For example, deciding which attributes of cells to include in order to describe them adequately required the designer of the database shown in Figure 3.4 to design the product (the database), but first to sense the problem, conduct research, and apply that research to the product.

Table 3.1
Critical Thinking Skills Engaged by Database Construction and Use

	Analyze content domains	Study guides	Build relational database
Evaluating			
Assessing information	X	X	X
Determining criteria	X		X
Prioritizing			X
Recognizing fallacies			
Verifying		X	X
Analyzing			
Recognizing patterns	X	X	X
Classifying	X	X	X
Identifying assumptions			X
Identifying main ideas	X	X	X
Finding sequences			X
Connecting			
Comparing/contrasting	X	X	X
Logical thinking			X
Inferring deductively	X		X
Inferring inductively			X
Identifying causal relationships	X		X

Table 3.2
Creative Thinking Skills
Engaged by Database Construction and Use

	Analyze content domains	Study guides	Build relational database
Elaborating			
Expanding	X		X
Modifying			X
Extending		X	
Shifting categories	X	X	X
Concretizing	X	X	X
Synthesizing			
Analogical thinking	X	X	X
Summarizing	X	X	X
Hypothesizing	X		X
Planning	X		X
Imagining			
Fluency			
Predicting			X
Speculating	X	X	X
Visualizing			X
Intuition			

Table 3.3
Complex Thinking Skills Engaged by Database Construction and Use

	Analyze content domains	Study guides	Build relational database
Designing			
Imagining a goal			X
Formulating a goal	X		X
Inventing a product	X		X
Assessing a product	X		X
Revising the product	X		X
Problem Solving			
Sensing the problem	X		
Researching the problem	X	X	X
Formulating the problem	X		X
Finding alternatives	X		X
Choosing the solution	X		X
Building acceptance			
Decision Making			
Identifying an issue	X		X
Generating alternatives	X		X
Assessing the consequences			
Making a choice	X		X
Evaluating the choice	X		X

The process of deciding when to develop a database in order to facilitate learning probably most engages problem-solving and decision-making skills, especially sensing and formulating the problem and comparing alternatives, making the choice, and evaluating that choice (to build a database) and selling team members on the process.

Evaluating Student Databases

What makes an effective database? That depends somewhat on the age and abilities of the learners who are constructing the database. Figure 3.12 presents a number of rubrics that you may use to evaluate the databases that students construct as their knowledge and skills move from emergent to mastery. You will probably want to adapt these or add your own criteria as you evaluate your students' projects. In most cases, the quality of the database will be obvious.

Figure 3.12
Rubrics for Evaluating Student Databases

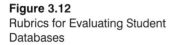

**Meaningful data model—
faithfully represents content structure**

| Fields redundant; inconsistent content in fields | Fields distinct; differentiate content |

**Completeness of data model—
all dimensions represented**

| Few fields ignore much content | Variety of fields describe all content |

Accuracy of information in records

| Data sparse, inconsistent, inaccurate | All data are included and accurate |

All instances identified

| Record incomplete; few examples included | Records are complete; all examples included |

Questions interrelate information

| Require only information or recall | Require higher order thinking (inferences, implications, etc.) |

Evaluating Database Construction Software

Database management systems are commonly available for every type of computer in use today. Many database software packages are, in fact, in the public domain, which makes them free or very inexpensive. For Windows machines, the most dominant database program is Microsoft's Access, which comes bundled with their Microsoft Office package. Other powerful packages include dBase, Rbase, Paradox, and Ability Database 98 (www.ability.com). The power of these packages is not required to implement most Mindtools strategies.

For the Macintosh, the most commonly used databases are those which are part of integrated software packages, like Microsoft Works or AppleWorks (formerly ClarisWorks) and Access in Microsoft's Office. These packages provide very adequate programs for constructing databases and spreadsheets (Chapter 5), as well as word processing and telecommunications so they represent especially good value. A number of other powerful, single-purpose database management systems are available for the Macintosh, including FoxBase or FoxPro, FileMakerPro, 4th Dimension, Helix, NuBase, Reflex, and Panorama. These programs offer database templates, flexible reporting functions, scripting, and sophisticated graphics. Some provide file compatibility between Macintosh and Windows computers, allowing users on both systems to share files.

Selecting DBMSs can be a perplexing process, so keep a few simple criteria in mind. First and most important, you should not have to spend very much for a database system that performs the functions required by activities described in this chapter. Look at the list of features and decide which ones you really need. Generally, as the number of functions and capabilities provided by a database package increases, so do the complexity of the systems and the difficulty of use. Also consider usability. How easy is it to learn the system? Most of the more sophisticated database packages have more functionality than students need in order to build content databases and are definitely more difficult to learn. If the package requires hours of practice to begin building a database, then it is probably not an effective Mindtool. That is why TERC built the TableTop package described before. If the software requires too much effort to learn, then the system will replace the Mindtool outcomes, or learners simply will not use it. One of the most serious problems with Mindtools or any computer application is the learning curve required to become an effective user. Select software that minimizes the time spent learning the software and maximizes the time spent analyzing content domains. Test any new package to see how easy it is to use. If you are a novice database user, you may want to find the simplest one.

On the other side of the complexity issue is power. For more advanced users, fully relational databases like Access can provide another level of content analysis. For those users, be sure that you have a fully relational database.

Finally, consider what other applications software you may want to use. Will you also want to perform word processing? Will you want to use other Mindtools, such as spreadsheets? If so, you may want to consider an integrated package such as Microsoft Works or Office (cross-platform).

Advantages of Databases as Mindtools

A number of advantages accrue to learners from using databases as Mindtools. The process of creating and manipulating a database is inherently constructive, which means that learners are (mentally) actively engaged in constructing representations rather than merely reading or responding to questions. They are actively building knowledge structures, because they are actively engaged in knowledge representation activities. In doing so, learners are required to define the nature of the relationships between concepts and then to construct records and fields that map those relationships. This is meaningful processing of information, as opposed to the rote recall too often required by instructional activities such as worksheets, which are designed to produce convergent thinking in learners.

Another advantage of these database learning strategies lies in the powerful searching and sorting capabilities of the DBMSs. It is here that the process of comparing concepts and relationships in the database is greatly facilitated by the speed and reporting capabilities of the DBMS. Learners can search their databases in any number of ways—to provide an overview, for example, of all of the kinds of cells, or to compare particular characteristics of different cells. They can also try to arrange the information in ways that may make more sense to them. For example, in seeking the answer to queries about what cell contributes to certain characteristics (Figure 3.5), searching two fields using common "and/or/not" logical connectors will yield the answer immediately. The ability to quickly compare and contrast relational information is tantamount to learning many different kinds of information.

A final advantage of DBMSs as Mindtools is the ease of data entry provided by most systems. Once the database has been structured, either by the student or the teacher, the program prompts learners to type in responses, which certainly takes no longer than writing notes longhand. Once the information has been entered, it can be rearranged and printed in different ways to meet various information needs.

Limitations of Content Databases as Mindtools

Critics may claim that these activities produce nothing more than a tabular summary of information, commonly available in textbooks. It is true that some textbooks do provide tabular summaries. However, using databases as Mindtools engages learners in constructing their own tables rather than trying to memorize those provided for them. Also, the table that each learner constructs will be more personally meaningful, since it will contain the learner's concepts and relationships between those concepts. This represents generative processing of information. There is a fundamental difference between this and memorizing tables.

Some teachers will be concerned that the interpretations of content produced by students may be too individualistic or idiosyncratic, and that the divergent database representations may confuse students more than enlighten them. Personal knowledge representations are individualistic. Students can compare representations that are too divergent or simply incorrect with other students' representations. The databases become a medium for socially negotiating a common understanding. For this reason, collaborative database projects will probably be more productive than individual projects.

SUMMARY

Database systems support the storage and retrieval of information in an organized manner. Structure is inherent in all knowledge, so using a tool that helps learners to structure what they know will facilitate understanding. To develop and use databases, learners must analyze and comprehend the information that they store and retrieve. This analysis requires identifying the underlying structural properties of the information. Although databases are more often used as organizational and retrieval tools in businesses, they can also function effectively as Mindtools. When students construct and query databases, they are building and exemplifying structural models of the content they are studying and are using those models to compare and contrast relationships among information contained in their models. That is the kind of meaningful processing of information that students should perform more regularly in schools. It necessarily engages higher order thinking in learners, which results in better understanding.

References

Goldberg, K. P. (1992, April). Database programs and the study of seashells. *The Computing Teacher*, pp. 32–34.

Hancock, C., Kaput, J. J., & Goldsmith, L. T. (1992). Authentic inquiry with data: Critical barriers to classroom implementation. *Educational Psychologist, 27*(3), 337–364.

Knight, P., & Timmons, G. (1986). Using databases in history teaching. *Journal of Computer-Assisted Learning, 2*(2), 93–101.

Kolodner, J. (1993). *Case-based reasoning.* New York: Morgan Kaufman.

Pon, K. (1984). Databasing in the elementary (and secondary) classroom. *Computing Teacher, 12*(3), 28–30.

Rooze, G. E. (1988–89). Developing thinking using databases: What's really involved? *Michigan Social Studies Journal, 3*(1), 25–26.

Schank, R. C. (1990). *Tell me a story: Narrative and intelligence.* Evanston, IL: Northwestern University Press.

Watson, J., & Strudler, N. (1988–89). Teaching higher order thinking skills with databases. *Computing Teacher, 16*(4), 47–50, 55.

4

Semantic Networks (Concept Maps) as Mindtools

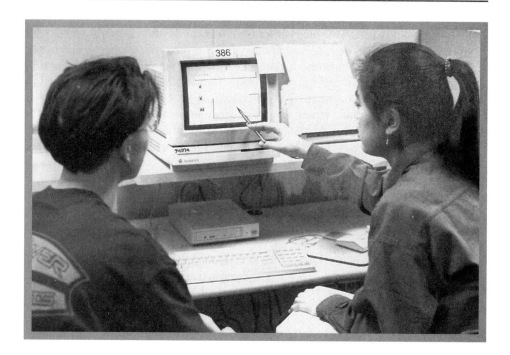

WHAT ARE SEMANTIC NETWORKS?

Semantic networks, also known as concept maps, are spatial representations of concepts and their interrelationships that are intended to represent the knowledge structures that humans store in their minds (Jonassen, Beissner, & Yacci, 1993). These knowledge structures are also known as cognitive structures, conceptual knowledge, structural knowledge, and semantic networks. Semantic networks and concept maps are graphs consisting of nodes representing concepts and labeled lines representing relationships among them (see Figure 4.1). The semantic networks in memory and the maps that represent them are composed of nodes (concepts or ideas) that are connected by links (statements of relationships). In computer-based semantic networks, nodes are represented as information blocks or cards (e.g., "structural knowledge" in Figure 4.1) and the links are labeled lines (e.g., "models" in Figure 4.1). Most semantic networking programs also provide the capability of adding text and pictures to each node in order to elaborate that concept.

Semantic networking is the process of constructing those concept maps—of identifying important concepts, arranging those concepts spatially, identifying relationships among those concepts, and labeling the nature of the semantic relationships among those concepts. These maps are used by learners to represent what they know or are learning as multidimensional networks of concepts. Semantic networks and concept maps can be drawn by hand using simple artifacts such as cards and string or paper and pencil (see Jonassen et al., 1993, for descriptions and instructions of these methods). However, a variety of computer-based semantic net-

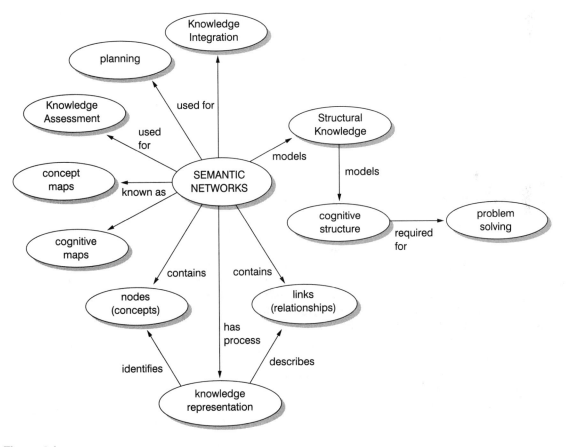

Figure 4.1
Semantic Network about Semantic Networks

working software (described later in this chapter) enables much easier (and arguably more powerful) production of concept maps. So, semantic networking programs function as Mindtools for engaging learners in critical thinking by engaging them in organizing the underlying ideas in the content being studied. That is, semantic networks or concept maps are semantic organization tools.

Why are concept mapping tools effective for learning? According to some psychological theories, knowledge is organized semantically in memory, that is, according to the meaning that defines the relationships among the ideas. Ideas, known as schemas, are arranged in networks of interconnected and interrelated ideas known as semantic networks. Semantic networking programs are computer-based visualization tools for representing these mental semantic networks as concept maps. Any tool that can externalize mental ideas has to be powerful.

Why create semantic networks? Meaningful learning refers to anchoring new ideas or concepts with previously acquired knowledge in a nonarbitrary way (Novak & Gowin, 1984). Meaningful learning requires that students connect new ideas to knowledge that they have already constructed. Concept maps help to organize learners' knowledge by integrating information into a progressively more complex conceptual framework. When learners construct concept maps for representing their understanding in a domain, they reconceptualize the content domain by constantly using new propositions to elaborate and refine the concepts that they already know. More importantly, concept maps help to increase the total quantity of formal content knowledge because they facilitate learners' ability to use the skill of relating patterns and relationships. This organizational knowledge and the total quantity of formal content knowledge facilitates meaningful learning.

HOW ARE SEMANTIC NETWORKS USED AS MINDTOOLS?

Semantic networking aids learning by requiring learners to analyze the underlying structure of the ideas they are studying. The process of creating semantic networks engages learners in an analysis of their own knowledge structures, which helps them to integrate new knowledge with what they already know. The result is that the knowledge that is constructed can be used more effectively. Kozma (1987), one of the developers of Learning Tool, believes that semantic networking tools are cognitive tools that amplify, extend, and enhance human cognition. Constructing computer-based semantic nets engages learners in

- the reorganization of knowledge
- explicit description of concepts and their interrelationships
- deep processing of knowledge, which promotes better remembering and retrieval and the ability to apply knowledge in new situations
- relating new concepts to existing concepts and ideas, which improves understanding
- spatial learning through spatial representation of concepts in an area of study.

Semantic networking tools are Mindtools for representing structural knowledge (Jonassen et al., 1993). The psychology of learning has often distinguished between declarative and procedural forms of knowledge. *Declarative* knowledge represents awareness of some object, event, or idea (knowing that). It enables learners to come to know, or define, ideas (verbal information or awareness of), and forms the basis for thinking about and using those ideas. However, merely knowing something does not mean that individuals can use that knowledge. Declarative knowledge is what you remember. *Procedural* knowledge is the knowledge of how to use declarative knowledge—how to solve problems, form plans, and make decisions and arguments (knowing how). Procedural knowledge is what you know how to do.

Declarative knowledge and procedural knowledge are interdependent. Some procedural knowledge is acquired by learning how to apply declarative knowledge, and some declarative knowledge is remembered in the context of learning how to do something. Most of us possess a considerable volume of declarative knowledge that we cannot apply and really have no use for except for answering *Jeopardy* questions (inert knowledge), while we know how to do some things that we cannot adequately declare.

Semantic networks represent an intermediate type of knowledge, *structural* knowledge, which connects declarative and procedural knowledge. Structural knowledge is the knowledge of how the ideas within a domain are integrated and interrelated (Diekhoff, 1983). Awareness of those interrelationships and the ability to describe them are essential for higher order thinking. It is not enough to know *that*. In order to know *how*, you must know *why*. Structural knowledge provides the conceptual bases for knowing why.

Structural knowledge is also known as cognitive structure, the pattern of relationships among concepts in memory (Preece, 1976) or, more specifically, the organization of the relationships among concepts in long-term memory (Shavelson, 1972). Semantic networking activities have been shown to be an accurate means for representing cognitive structure (Jonassen, 1987). That is, semantic networking, as described in this chapter, helps learners map their own cognitive structure.

Jonassen et al. (1993) describe a number of reasons for studying structural knowledge using semantic networks:

- Structure is inherent in all knowledge, so understanding the structural foundations of any content domain improves comprehension.
- Structural knowledge is essential to recall and comprehension because organization of knowledge has been shown by research to be facilitated by organization.
- When learners study, they necessarily construct structural knowledge along with declarative knowledge.
- Memory structures reflect the world; people naturally learn the underlying organization of ideas while learning.
- Structural knowledge is essential to problem solving and procedural knowledge acquisition, so semantic networking will necessarily improve problem-solving ability.

■ Experts' structural knowledge differs from novices'; understanding these differences is facilitated by semantic networking.

Semantic networking can serve many learning functions in the classroom. In this chapter, I briefly describe three ways in which semantic nets can function as a learning tool: semantic networks as study guides, knowledge integration tools, and as a planning tool. Following those, I will briefly describe how semantic nets can be used as an assessment method.

Study Guide

First and foremost, semantic networks are a learning tool—a method for focusing the process of studying in a constructive way. Most students are ineffective studiers. Students who color their textbooks with highlighters and read and reread chapters in order to memorize the contents are not actively thinking about what they are studying. They are not intellectually engaged with the ideas. Rather than trying to memorize textbooks, students would be much better served by constructing a semantic network. Rather than trying to memorize content, students should identify the most important concepts in a chapter and generate a semantic net as a review strategy. They could then compare their semantic net with other students' nets and rationalize their connections and choices, or nets from different chapters can be merged or combined when studying for a large examination. Students who study in this manner will definitely score better on almost any kind of test the teacher gives them. Semantic networking is especially effective for preparing for long essay exams. (Experience has shown semantic nets to be particularly valuable to graduate students when studying for comprehensive exams.) Some of the semantic networking tools even have built-in quizzing options.

Semantic networks can and should guide studying. The semantic network shown in Figure 4.2 is a simple, hierarchically organized net about the structure of the U.S. government created with C-Map. Although many textbooks show similar diagrams, when students figure out the relationships themselves and represent them in a semantic net, they understand and remember them better.

The semantic net shown in Figure 4.3 is one screen from a much larger net on romantic poetry. In this unit, students studied different poems. This net describes "Lines Written in Early Spring" by Wordsworth. Other screens depict other poems. And yet other screens (Figure 4.4) elaborate on the concept of nature that provides imagery in many of the poems.

It is absolutely essential for the students to construct these nets—*not* the teacher. Often teachers create semantic nets and present them to students as study guides. Students try to memorize them like they do their textbooks, which prevents them from thinking meaningfully about what they are studying. While I am sure that teachers will benefit from constructing semantic nets about whatever they teach, it is crucial for students to construct the nets if they are to do the learning. It is also important that teachers not show students "the right structure for the net" (I have witnessed this many times). There is no right net structure. The nets created by stu-

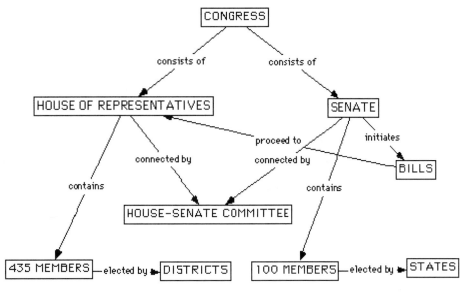

Figure 4.2
Hierarchical Concept Map Created in C-Map

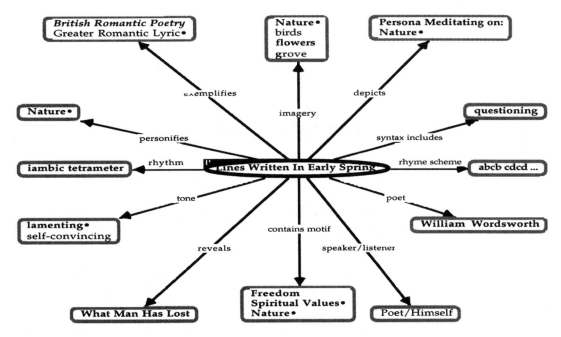

Figure 4.3
One Screen from a Semantic Network Created in SemNet

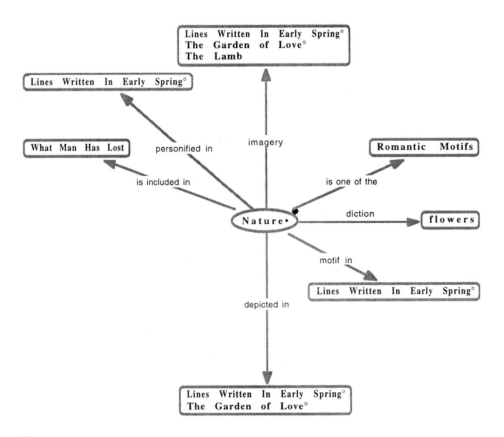

Figure 4.4
Net Elaborating the Concept of Nature in Romantic Poetry

dents will vary, because students differ in so many ways (see Jonassen & Grabowski, 1993, for a lengthy description of individual differences and learning).

Students enjoy creating semantic nets. We were working with students in a junior high school in north Denver. They loved it so much that during the winter flu season, students would come to school ilǐ on the days they were assigned to the lab to create semantic networks. A number of students have written to me:

> I was not looking forward to studying all that material. SemNet gave me an interesting and highly effective way to study some semi-boring stuff. I was surprised—it really did work. I remembered a lot of the material.

> I found that my interest level was much higher when I could utilize it, not just do it because it is an assignment for a class. I like to look at it as a tool that I can use and understand for tomorrow's problems. Thing is, I don't view them as problems I see them as opportunities waiting to be solved.

Knowledge Reflection and Integration Tool

Concept mapping provides a valuable method for learners' self-assessments of their own learning to reflect changes in their own knowledge. If concepts are accurate means for representing cognitive structure (Jonassen, 1987), then concept mapping provides learners with a powerful tool for reflecting on what they know and, more importantly, reflecting about their own lack of understanding and about the difficulties in construction of a meaningful knowledge framework.

The usefulness of semantic nets and concept maps in schools is shown by their relationship to other forms of higher order thinking, each of which requires integrated knowledge of content. For example, semantic nets have been significantly related to formal reasoning in chemistry (Schreiber & Abegg, 1991) and to reasoning ability in biology (Briscoe & LeMaster, 1991). Learners with better structural knowledge are also better problem solvers. "The students who had concept-mapping experience approached each problem by first sketching a map of the elements in the problem and were more decisive in choosing a point at which to begin their attack of the problem" (Okebukola, 1992). The concept mappers also focused more on the problem to be solved rather than irrelevant aspects of it. They were less confused about the demand of most of the problems when certain key elements appeared to be missing (Okebukola, 1992). Basconals and Briscoe (1985) found that mean scores on problem-solving tests in high school physics were much higher for students preparing concept maps when compared with students following a traditional physics program who were not using concept maps. Not only does concept mapping facilitate problem solving, but it also helps learners to transfer those skills. Robertson (1990) found that the extent to which the learner's semantic networks contained relevant structural knowledge was a stronger predictor of how well learners would solve transfer problems in physics than either aptitude or performance on a set of similar problems. The similarity of the learners' underlying cognitive structure with the expert is highly predictive of problem-solving ability (Gordon & Gill, 1989).

Thinking about the connections between concepts, evaluating their linkages by revising and reviewing the logical relationship among concepts, and planning how to organize concepts meaningfully provides valuable evidence of self-reflection and metacognitive reasoning. Thus, concept maps assist learners to become aware of and control the cognitive processes of the task (Jegede, Alaiyemola, & Okebukola, 1990).

The screen in Figure 4.5 is from a semantic network created with SemNet about mathematical functions. The teacher who constructed it had been teaching math for many years. The reflective process of constructing this net forced him to reconceptualize a lot of what and how he had been teaching. Consequently, he began teaching math in a different way. Teaching is a problem-solving process. Reorganizing what he knew helped this teacher to conceive and try out new solutions to teaching problems.

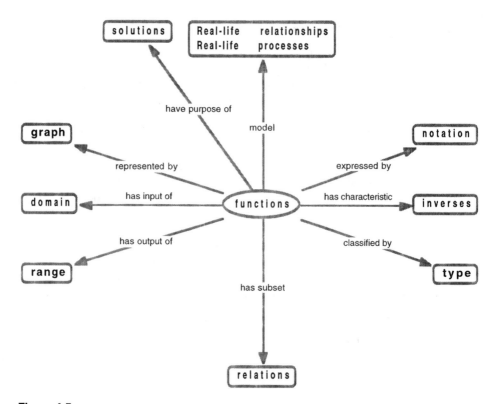

Figure 4.5
Semantic Network Reflecting Understanding of Mathematical Functions

Semantic Networking as a Planning Tool

Another classroom application is as a planning tool. When groups of students are trying to get started on solving a large and complex problem, or when individual students have to write an essay, generating a semantic net can provide the organization and impetus for completing the project. Semantic nets provide a shorthand form for organizing and sequencing ideas. Ferry (1996) reported that concept maps helped preservice teachers map their subject-matter knowledge as a precursor to lesson planning. Figure 4.6 shows a simple net that I constructed using the software program Inspiration when organizing a conference presentation. It was also useful as a graphic aid during the presentation to show the interrelationship of the ideas that I was presenting.

Semantic Networks to Assess Learning

Semantic nets can also be used as tools for assessing what learners know. If we agree that memory is organized as a semantic network, then learning can be thought of as a reorganization of semantic memory. Producing semantic networks reflects

Figure 4.6
Presentation Organizer

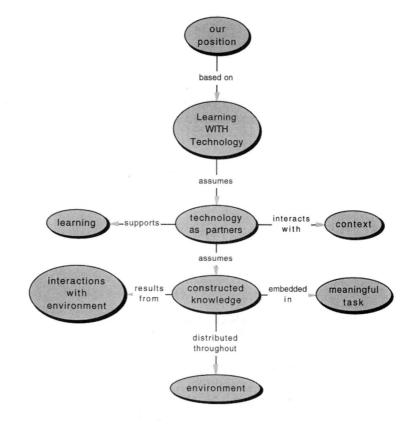

those changes in semantic memory, since the networks describe what a learner knows. So, the semantic nets learners generate after instruction reflect the growth of their knowledge structures. Semantic nets are beginning to be used to assess learning outcomes in schools and universities.

- Mansfield and Happs (1991) used concept maps to evaluate teaching outcomes and to monitor student progress in a geometry class.
- Using Pathfinder nets (Schvaneveldt, 1990), concept maps have been related to course examination performance (Goldsmith, Johnson, & Acton, 1991).
- In a study examining the use of generating computer-based concept maps in a computer programming course, Feghali (1991) found that students who built maps scored better in course tests; however the differences were not statistically significant.

Many tools are available for assessing student learning using semantic nets. Any semantic networking program that can be used to generate a concept map will work, because it is the concept map that is being assessed as a measure on knowledge. However, there are some programs, like KNOT (Knowledge Network and

Figure 4.7
Pathfinder Net of Student's
Knowledge

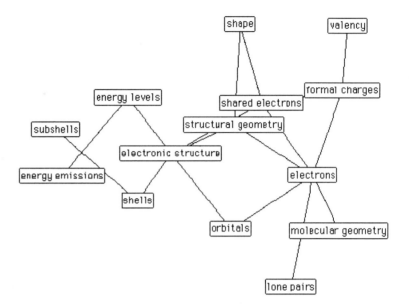

Orientation Tool available from Interlink at New Mexico State University), that are intended as assessment tools. Figure 4.7 represents a knowledge test that was generated using KNOT where students rated the similarity of each pair of concepts in Figure 4.7. The Pathfinder analysis program uses multidimensional statistical analysis to generate the map shown in Figure 4.7. This map can be statistically related to the teacher's map, the student's earlier map, or compared with the class average. The program also rates the coherence of the map.

Student maps that are generated using any semantic network can also be assessed using criteria described later in the chapter. A growing body of evidence is relating semantic networking to other learning outcomes, so educators are becoming more secure in their assessments of student nets as a learning outcome measure.

Related Mindtools

As I discussed earlier, semantic networking is often used for planning other constructions or presentations. A number of the expanded word-processing and computer-based instruction authoring systems have semantic networking functionality built in to help writers plan their documents. Semantic networking is also used for eliciting knowledge from experts when building expert systems (see Chapter 6) (Cook & McDonald, 1987). Teacher education students who build semantic networks of content domain first build more coherent expert system representations (Marra, 1995).

Conceptually, semantic nets are similar to databases. That is why they are both included in this section on semantic organization tools. They are both used to analyze and describe the structure of knowledge domains. However, semantic nets are most similar to hypertext and hypermedia knowledge bases (see Chapter 11), and they may be used as conceptual models for structuring hypertext and hypermedia systems (Jonassen, 1990, 1991). The nodes and links in the net become the nodes and links in the hypertext. In fact, a colleague at San Diego State University has developed a program called Wayfinder (distributed with the SemNet program) that automatically converts semantic nets into HyperCard stacks.

Coaching the Construction of Semantic Networks in the Classroom

Semantic nets are versatile tools that your students will learn to use quickly and want to apply in a variety of situations. The following sequence of activities will help you to integrate semantic nets in your instruction.

1. *Make* a plan and set perspective for analyzing a domain. Before beginning, students need to make a plan for the semantic net. What are they interested in representing? What points do they want to make? What kinds of information is required to make those points? What learning goals will they work toward? To answer these questions, the teacher and students must understand the perspective from which they are analyzing the content domain. For example, when studying concepts of Newtonian mechanics, such as speed, acceleration, mass, and force, unconstrained high school students are likely to immediately relate those concepts to their automobiles and the feats they dream of performing in them. Although those may be acceptable and even relevant associations, it is also important to require them to "think like physicists" when analyzing the domain. If you were to analyze the same set of concepts but asked the learners to think like poets, a substantively different set of associations would be generated. Personal knowledge structures are not static entities. They are dynamic and changeable, depending on the constructor's mood, frame of mind, recent events, and other factors. So help your learners establish the proper perspective or frame of mind while planning for the activity.

2. *Identify* important concepts. Understanding is made up of concepts. We communicate through our shared understanding of concepts, so identifying which are the important concepts in a content domain is crucial not only to understanding that content but also for collaborating on tasks. Important concepts are often highlighted for learners in textbooks. They may appear in list form at the beginning or end of textbook chapters, or they may be highlighted in the text. Initially, you may want to analyze the textbook or supplementary materials and provide a list of concepts for the learners to define in the semantic net.

As students gain experience in semantic networking, they should become responsible for highlighting important concepts in textbooks, lectures, or supplementary materials. Rather than allowing them to highlight large sections of the textbook (producing pages of colorful text), you can suggest that they highlight only single words or short phrases that are essential to understanding the content and then use those for building semantic nets. You may want to focus a discussion on evaluating the relevance and importance of different concepts that might be included in the nets. Students could vote or argue for the inclusion of different concepts in the nets. This approach would result in all learners starting with the same list of concepts. However, it will become obvious through constructing semantic nets that the beginning list will likely be amended during the construction process as students discover the need for additional concepts to adequately describe and elaborate the concepts already in the net.

3. *Create, define,* **and** *elaborate* **nodes.** Create and label a node for each concept listed in step 2. Add pictures, descriptive text, and synonyms to each node as appropriate. You may want to begin by supplying a net and requiring students to supply details about the concepts in it. Or the students may be responsible for developing the list as well as for defining the concepts in it. Each node may be embellished with graphics or a picture. Some of the semantic networking programs provide primitive graphics tools for drawing images. Most allow the learner to add descriptive text to each node. These are areas where students could relate personal interpretations or beliefs about the concepts.

4. *Construct* **links and link concepts.** Having identified the concepts in a domain that should go into the semantic net, the learner begins the more difficult and challenging part of the process: linking the concept nodes. Having to describe precisely the relationship between two ideas is much more difficult and engaging than it initially appears. Why? The process of articulating those links requires learners to search through the range of possible relationships in order to define the relationship that exists in the context in which they are studying. What does that mean? Concepts can (and typically do) relate to each other in different ways, depending on the context in which they are being used. For example, thinking about the concept "speed" in the context of physics class implies a different set of relationships than if you were studying the concept in the context of a drug education class. This variability is what contributes to the complexity of internal knowledge representations. Because concepts may be related to each other in several ways, it may be necessary to link the same two concepts with more than one relationship. Figure 4.8 presents a fairly comprehensive list of link types that may be used to connect nodes.

What characterizes a good link? First, preciseness and succinctness, but, more importantly, descriptiveness. Try to avoid using links such as "is connected to," "is related to," or "involves." They do not tell anything meaningful about the relationship. Be sure not only to link new concepts that are added to the net, but also to interlink existing concepts as much as possible. Attempt to pair each concept with every other concept in the net and decide if there is a meaningful relationship between them. If there is, create a link between them. The more interconnected your net is, the more meaningful your understanding of the content domain will be.

5. *Continue* **to expand the net.** The linking process continues among all or most of the nodes in the net. While the linking is going on, new nodes or concepts are being added to the net in order to explain some of the existing concepts. Those concepts are linked, and additional concepts are added to explain them. This process of augmentation continues in a cycle until the builder feels that the domain is explained well enough. Interestingly, this process mirrors to some degree the natural pattern of knowledge acquisition. It is theoretically (although not practically) possible for learners to build nets consisting of all of the concepts they know in which those concepts are linked together. What is also interesting and rewarding to students following the building of a large net is the realization of just how much they really know.

Symmetric Links

is opposite of	is same as
has sibling	is independent of
has synonym	is equal to
is near to	is opposed to
is similar to	

Asymmetric Links

Inclusion Relations (Typically the most common)

has part/is part of	contains/is contained in
composed of/is part in	includes/is included in
has example/is example of	has instance/is instance of

Characteristic Relations (Next most common)

has characteristic/is characteristic of	has attribute/is attribute of
has property/is property of	has type/is type of
has kind/is kind of	defines/is defined by
describes/is described by	models/is modeled by
denotes/is denoted by	implies/is implied by
has advantage/is advantage of	has disadvantage/is disadvantage of
has function/is function of	has size/is size of
is above/is below	is higher than/is lower than

Action Relations

causes/is caused by	uses/is used by
solves/is solution for	exploits/is exploited by
decreases/is decreased by	increases/is increased by
destroys/is destroyed by	impedes/is impeded by
influences/is influenced by	determines/is determined by
enables/is enabled by	absorbs/is absorbed by
acts on/is acted on by	consumes/is consumed by
converted from/converted to	designs/is designed by
employs/is employed by	evolves into/is evolved from
generates/is generated by	modifies/is modified by
originates from/is origin of	provides/is provided by
requires/is required by	regulates/is regulated by
sends to/receives from	

Process Relations

has object/is object of	has output/is output of
has result/results from	has subprocess/is subprocess of
has process/is process in	organizes/is organized by
has input/is input to	proposes/is proposed by
depends on/has dependent	concludes/is concluded by

Temporal Relations

has step/is step in	has stage/is stage in
precedes/follows	

Figure 4.8

Possible Links between Modes

Source: List adapted from Fisher, 1988.

6.   **Students *reflect* on the process.** Reflection should not wait until the project is completed. Rather, students should continuously review their progress on the project. Are we achieving our goals? What changes are necessary? How do we compare with other groups? Are we answering questions and making the points that we set out in our plan? After the project is completed, the students should reflect on the project. What have we learned about the content? What have we learned about semantic network construction and how our nets represent what we know? What have we learned about working with each other? You may choose to provide students with some or all of the criteria for evaluating student databases (presented in the next section) to use for self-evaluation. The activity of constructing semantic networks engages meaningful thinking. Reflection cements the knowledge that learners construct.

EVALUATING SEMANTIC NETWORKS AS MINDTOOLS

Critical, Creative, and Complex Thinking in Semantic Network Construction and Use

The process of constructing semantic nets requires the learner to identify important concepts in a content domain and describe the semantic relationships between them. Deciding which are the important concepts and describing relationships is not easy for novices. Experience with content (which develops procedural knowledge) is needed to become aware of which concepts are most important to describing the domain.

Tables 4.1, 4.2, and 4.3 identify the critical, creative, and complex thinking skills that are required for using semantic nets as a study guide, for knowledge reflection and integration, and for planning other constructions. The skills in each table that are marked by an "X" are those that are employed by each process, based on an information-processing analysis of the tasks.

Semantic networking engages more critical thinking skills than either creative or complex. It is a tool that focuses learners on a critical analysis of ideas in a knowledge domain. Using semantic nets to reflect on and integrate personal knowledge is the most engaging of the three uses of semantic nets in terms of critical thinking skills (see Table 4.1). Nearly every critical thinking skill is engaged when learners use semantic nets to integrate their knowledge. Using semantic nets as a study guide requires learners to evaluate and prioritize important concepts, classify them, compare and contrast them, and perhaps identify causal relationships. Using semantic nets as a planning tool engages similar evaluating and analyzing but refocuses connecting skills on developing sequential presentations.

As with critical thinking, knowledge integration engages more creative thinking skills (see Table 4.2). The primary activity is on elaborating personal knowledge structures. Most uses engage synthesis, including analogical reasoning and summarizing. The imaging skills engaged by semantic networks are more limited because of the visual constraints imposed by the programs. Learners can visualize ideas in only fairly restricted ways.

Table 4.1
Critical Thinking Skills Engaged
by Semantic Networking

	Study guide	Knowledge integration	Planning
Evaluating			
Assessing information	X	X	X
Determining criteria	X		X
Prioritizing	X	X	
Recognizing fallacies		X	
Verifying		X	X
Analyzing			
Recognizing patterns		X	
Classifying	X	X	X
Identifying assumptions		X	
Identifying main ideas	X	X	X
Finding sequences			X
Connecting			
Comparing/contrasting	X	X	X
Logical thinking			X
Inferring deductively	X	X	X
Inferring inductively		X	
Identifying causal relationships	X	X	

Table 4.2
Creative Thinking Skills
Engaged by Semantic Networking

	Study guide	Knowledge integration	Planning
Elaborating			
Expanding		X	
Modifying		X	
Extending	X	X	
Shifting categories		X	
Concretizing	X	X	X
Synthesizing			
Analogical thinking	X	X	
Summarizing	X	X	X
Hypothesizing			
Planning			X
Imagining			
Fluency	X	X	
Predicting			
Speculating		X	
Visualizing	X	X	X
Intuition			

Table 4.3
Complex Thinking Skills Engaged by Semantic Networking

	Study guide	Knowledge integration	Planning
Designing			
Imagining a goal			X
Formulating a goal			X
Inventing a product			X
Assessing a product			X
Revising the product			X
Problem Solving			
Sensing the problem			
Researching the problem	X	X	X
Formulating the problem			X
Finding alternatives		X	X
Choosing the solution			X
Building acceptance			
Decision Making			
Identifying an issue		X	X
Generating alternatives		X	X
Assessing the consequences			
Making a choice			X
Evaluating the choice			X

Very little complex thinking is engaged by using semantic nets as study guides or for knowledge integration (see Table 4.3). However, nearly every complex thinking skill is engaged when using semantic nets to plan other constructions. The construction (product) has to be conceived, and then executed, which is a problem-solving process. Finally, the planning of presentations and constructions engages a fair amount of decision making.

Evaluating Students' Semantic Nets

Criteria for Assessing Semantic Nets.   The cognitive processes engaged by concept mapping are complex and cannot be adequately assessed using a single measure. Because there is a larger research base related to semantic networks, more criteria are available for assessing nets. Rather than providing a few specific rubrics (as I do in most other chapters), I will list a large number of criteria that you can use to assess student nets:

- The number of nodes indicates the breadth of the net.
- The number of distinct propositions (node–link–node combinations) indicates completeness.

- The ratio of instances to concepts is an indicator of how well integrated the concepts in the domain are (also known as "embeddedness").
- The centrality of each node is indicated by its number of direct links (concepts linked directly to it) and indirect links (concepts linked to other concepts directly linked to it). Centrality is a measure of the importance of concepts in a domain. Look at the rank ordering of centrality for the most embedded (number of paths two nodes away). Often, the concepts that you believe are most important (typically those at the highest level of abstraction) are not very central to the net, at least according to this criterion.
- The depth (hierarchicalness) of the net is measured by the levels of nodes represented.
- Is the linking relation between nodes in each proposition valid (Novak & Gowin, 1984)?
- Is the relation in each proposition clear and descriptive?
- If the net is hierarchical, how many levels are represented? Is each subordinate concept more specific than the concept above it (Novak & Gowin, 1984)?
- Does the direction of links with arrows convey a hierarchical or causal relationship between nodes in propositions (McClure & Bell, 1990)?
- Assess the validity and synthesis of crosslinks between concepts in different propositions (Novak & Gowin, 1984).
- Assess the number and accuracy of linked concept pairs and number of insightful links between concept pairs (White & Gunstone, 1992).
- Determine the ratio of instances to concepts (integratedness or embeddedness of concepts).
- Check the centrality of each node. (How many other concepts is it linked to directly and indirectly?)
- Evaluate the number of different link types. Links should be parsimonious. The law of parsimony pertains to the economy with which you express yourself. If six different links will describe all of the relationships in the net, then do not use more than six (i.e., don't use three different links that mean the same thing, for example, "attribute of," "property of," and "characteristic of").
- On the other hand, overreliance on one or two particular types of links shows a narrowness in thinking. Use enough links to discriminate meaningful differences. These two criteria require a balancing act of sorts. Look at the proportions of link types used in the net. Calculate (roughly at least) the proportions of inclusion, characteristic, action, process, and temporal relations (see Figure 4.8).
- Evaluate the net's salience, that is, the number of valid links in the map divided by total number of links in the map (Hoz, Tomer, & Tamir, 1990).
- Determine the consistency in use of links.
- Determine the ratio of the number of links to the number of nodes.
- Use links consistently throughout the net. The meaning of any link should be the same each time it is used.
- Look at the number of "dead-end" nodes, that is, those that are only linked to one other concept. These are thought to be on the edge of the net. They

prevent the browser of the net from traveling to any node other than the one they came from.

■ The ratio of the number of types of links to the number of nodes should be low. It is not appropriate to develop a different type of link for each concept (see earlier comments on parsimony).

■ The accuracy of the information included in the net is, of course, the most important criterion. Are learners making meaningful connections? Is the text in nodes correct? That is, is the information in the net correct?

Models for Evaluating Semantic Nets.   The richness, elaborateness, and complexity of a net, as described in the assessment criteria just given, are only measures of the meaningfulness of a net. Evaluating learners' nets requires standards against which to compare them. There are a few models for evaluating the quality of nets.

    1. *Compare* **learner's net with expert's (teacher's).** Much research focuses on the expert–novice distinction, comparing student knowledge representations with teacher or expert representations. Research has shown that during the process of learning, the learner's knowledge structure begins to resemble the knowledge structures of the instructor, and the degree of similarity is a good predictor of classroom examination performance (Aidman & Egan, 1998; Diekhoff, 1983; Shavelson, 1974; Thro, 1978). Instruction, then, may be conceived of as the mapping of subject-matter knowledge (usually that possessed by the teacher or expert) onto the learner's knowledge structure. Semantic nets are a way of measuring that convergence. The closer a student's net resembles the teacher's, the more that student has (presumably) learned. This use of semantic nets represents a more traditional notion of learning (i.e., the purpose of instruction is to get the learner to think like the teacher). The constructivist ideas on which this book is based would argue that this is not an appropriate use of semantic nets. However, learners do come to think like teachers, so semantic nets are a means for evaluating that change.

    2. *Determine* **learner's knowledge growth.** The most significant problem with comparing a learner's knowledge with an expert's is that knowledge construction occurs in stages rather than in a single increment. Learners don't jump from novice to expert in a single bound. So, evaluating nets for their lack of convergence with an expert's may not be a fair comparison. Rather, evaluate a learner's net when he or she begins studying and at different points during the learning process. The net should be a visible sign of how much has been learned.

    The best semantic nets are very large. In fact, the best use of semantic networking is to spend the entire academic year contributing to a map of the ideas studied throughout an entire course. Very large nets help learners to see the complexity of knowledge and how it is all interrelated. Nets with thousands of nodes will require collaboration. The entire class can work on a net, as can a group of six or more students. From a constructivist perspective, an important goal of semantic networking is for learners to recognize that there are multiple perspectives on any content. Creating visual maps of ideas helps students compare how they think with how others think.

3. *Accept* **learner's different perspectives.** The multiple perspectives in knowledge representation often result from the variety of perspectives an individual can have on a particular content domain (for instance, thinking about Newtonian concepts "like a scientist" versus "like a race car driver"). It is useful and informative to have learners create multiple nets on the same content. Each time they begin a net, ask them to assume a different perspective, or analyze a group of ideas in different classes so learners think about the same ideas from the perspective of social scientists, mathematicians, and writers.

4. *Compare* **learner's nets to course goals.** Semantic nets have been shown to be related to examination performance (Goldsmith et al., 1991). More research is needed to verify a consistent relationship between particular criteria for evaluating nets (listed earlier) and traditional measures of course performance, such as exams, research papers, and case studies.

Evaluating Semantic Network Software

Concept mapping software, some commercial and some freeware versions, have been available for years. For the Macintosh, programs such as SemNet, C-Map, and Textvision are free. Programs such as Learning Tool and Inspiration are reasonably priced. For Windows computers, MindMan, Axon Idea Processor, VisiMap, Inspiration, and Activity Map are available for a fee, however they vary considerably in terms of functionality.

What makes a good semantic networking program? Programs must be able to represent concepts as nodes (perhaps in different forms), be able to position those nodes on the screen, provide for the hierarchical arrangement of submaps under maps, and be able to display link types on the screen. The better programs keep records of the concepts and relations and are able to output the net as a text file for assessment and transfer to other programs. Programs such as SemNet also provide assessment information about the map (see Figure 4.9). The program counts the number of nodes and measures the embeddedness and centrality of each. It also provides information about the kinds and numbers of links and propositions in the net. This information is very useful when evaluating the quality of the net.

Advantages of Semantic Networks as Mindtools

Semantic networks have these advantages:

- Semantic networking tools are easy to use. Most learners can gain proficiency within 1 to 2 hours.
- Semantic networking tools provide for spatial representations of content, which helps memory.
- Semantic networking tools enhance comprehension and retention of ideas being studied by helping learners construct structural knowledge. In addition to improving comprehension, structural knowledge improves retention of content being studied.

About Net: Geometric Optics

Net Elements	# Elements	# Synonyms	# Texts	# Pictures	# Names
Concepts	106	5	10	8	111
Relations	17	—	0	0	32
Instances	135				

Counts of Concepts Having Various Numbers of Instances

# Instances	# Concepts	% Total Concepts
0	2	1.9
1–2	69	65.1
3 or more	35	33.0
6 or more	10	9.4
10 or more	2	1.9
20 or more	0	0.0

Maximums

Most developed concept(s) with 17 instances: lens
Most embedded concept(s) with embeddedness of 39: lens
Most used relation(s) used in 42 instances: type of/has type

Figure 4.9
Information about a Semantic Net

- Semantic networks demonstrate the interconnectedness of ideas from different subjects and different courses.
- Semantic networking should improve problem-solving performance in learners.

Limitations of Semantic Networks as Mindtools

In contrast, semantic networks face these limitations:

- Semantic networks have a limited ability to represent causal relationships. One can define a causal link, but it does not provide the implications and inferences that accompany causal relations.
- Semantic networks can be too readily thought to reify the structures of the mind, implying that our semantic stores of information can be cognitively mapped and literally searched, just as a computer searches its memory stores. Semantic nets are not truly maps of the mind, but rather representations of what we think is in the mind.
- The knowledge that semantic nets represent is dynamic. It changes depending on the context and on the experiences and backgrounds of those producing the

nets. Structural knowledge also changes over time. To truly and accurately represent knowledge, semantic networking tools would need to enable minute-by-minute, context-by-context changes in the concepts, relationships, and structures that are represented in them.

■ The propositional networks in the mind, in whatever form they really exist, are far more complex than anything that can be represented in a concept map. The ideas that we know are interrelated and multiply encoded in rich, very redundant networks of ideas. These networks are multidimensional, yet n-dimensionality is a concept that is extremely difficult to grasp, and even harder to represent in two-dimensional space.

SUMMARY

Semantic networking programs provide a set of graphic conceptualization tools for creating concept maps. These concept maps represent the structure of ideas in memory or in a content domain. Semantic networking engages learners in an analysis of content domains that helps them organize their knowledge for better comprehension and retention. Semantic networking is also effective for planning other kinds of productions and knowledge bases. Semantic networks are among the most versatile of the Mindtools described in this book.

References

Aidman, E. V., & Egan, G. (1998). Academic assessment through computerized concept mapping: Validating a method of implicit map reconstruction. *International Journal of Instructional Media, 25*(3), 277–294.

Basconals, & Briscoe, (1985).

Briscoe, C., & LeMaster, S. U. (1991). Meaningful learning in college biology through concept mapping. *American Biology Teacher, 53*(4), 214–219.

Cook, N. M., & McDonald, J. E. (1987). The application of psychological scaling techniques to knowledge elicitation for knowledge-based systems. *International Journal of Man–Machine Studies, 26,* 533–550.

Diekhoff, G. M. (1983). Relationship judgments in the evaluation of structural understanding. *Journal of Educational Psychology, 75,* 227–233.

Feghali, A. A.(1991). A study of engineering college students' use of computer-based semantic networks in a computer programming language class (Doctoral dissertation, Purdue University, 1991). *Dissertation Abstracts International, 53*(3), 701.

Ferry, B. (1996). Problem understanding: The use of a computer-based tool to help pre-service teachers to map subject matter knowledge. *Research in Science Education, 26*(2), 205–219.

Fisher, K. M. (1988, April). *Relations used in student-generated knowledge representations.* Paper presented at the annual meeting of the American Educational Research Association, San Francisco, CA.

Goldsmith, T. E., Johnson, P. J., & Acton, W. H. (1991). Assessing structural knowledge. *Journal of Educational Psychology, 83,* 88–96.

Gordon, S. E., & Gill, R. T. (1989). *The formation and use of knowledge structures in problem solving domains.* Tech. Report AFOSR-88-0063. Washington, DC: Bolling AFB.

Hoz, R., Tomer, Y., & Tamir, P. (1990). The relations between disciplinary and pedagogical knowledge and the length of teaching experience of biology and geography teachers. *Journal of Research in Science Teaching, 27,* 973–985.

Jegede, O. J., Alaiyemola, S., & Okebukola, P. A. (1990). The effect of concept mapping on students' anxiety and achievement in biology. *Journal of Research in Science Teaching, 27*(10), 951–960.

Jonassen, D. H. (1987). Assessing cognitive structure: Verifying a method using pattern notes. *Journal of Research and Development in Education, 20*(3), 1–14.

Jonassen, D. H. (1990). Semantic network elicitation: Tools for structuring of hypertext. In R. McAleese & C. Green (Eds.), *Hypertext: The state of the art.* London: Intellect.

Jonassen, D. H. (1991). Representing the expert's knowledge in hypertext. *Impact Assessment Bulletin, 9*(1), 93–105.

Jonassen, D. H., Beissner, K., & Yacci, M. A. (1993). *Structural knowledge: Techniques for representing, conveying, and acquiring structural knowledge.* Hillsdale, NJ: Lawrence Erlbaum Associates.

Jonassen, D. H., & Grabowski, B.L. (1993). *Handbook of individual differences, learning, and instruction.* Hillsdale, NJ: Lawrence Erlbaum Associates.

Kozma, R. B. (1987). The implications of cognitive psychology for computer-based learning tools. *Educational Technology, 24*(11), 20–24.

Mansfield, H., & Happs, J. (1991). Concept maps. *Australian Mathematics Teacher, 47*(3), 30–33.

Marra, R.M. (1995). The effects of a concept mapping activity on expert system generation. Unpublished doctoral dissertation, University of Colorado.

McClure, J. R., & Bell, P. E. (1990). *Effects of an environmental education-related STS approach to instruction on cognitive structures of preservice science teachers.* University Park, PA: Pennsylvania State University. (ERIC Document Reproduction Service No. ED 341 582)

Novak, J. D., & Gowin, D. B. (1984). *Learning how to learn.* New York: Cambridge University Press.

Okebukola, P. A. (1992). Can good concept mappers be good problem solvers in science? *Educational Psychology, 12*(2), 113–129.

Preece, P. F. W. (1976). Mapping cognitive structure: A comparison of methods. *Journal of Educational Psychology, 68,* 1–8.

Robertson, W. C. (1990). Detection of cognitive structure with protocol data: Predicting performance on physics transfer problems. *Cognitive Science, 14,* 253–280.

Schreiber, D. A., & Abegg, G. L. (1991, April). *Scoring student-generated concept maps in introductory college chemistry.* Paper presented at the annual meeting of National Association for Research in Science Teaching, Lake Geneva, WI.

Schvaneveldt, R. W. (1990). *Pathfinder associative networks: Studies in knowledge organization.* Norwood, NJ: Ablex Publishing.

Shavelson, R. J. (1972). Some aspects of the correspondence between content structure and cognitive structure in physics instruction. *Journal of Educational Psychology, 63,* 225–234.

Shavelson, R. J. (1974). Methods for examining representations of subject matter structure in students' memory. *Journal of Research in Science Teaching, 11,* 231–249.

Thro, M. P. (1978). Relationships between associative and content structure of physics concepts. *Journal of Educational Psychology, 70,* 971–978.

White, R., & Gunstone, R. (1992). *Probing understanding.* London: Falmer Press.

PART THREE

Dynamic Modeling Tools

In Part 2 of this book, I described Mindtools that engage learners in a semantic analysis of content. That is, what are the semantic relationships among ideas in a content domain? Databases and semantic networking tools are used to represent that semantic organization. Understanding the organization of ideas in a domain is essential to understanding the domain. However, semantic relationships are only one kind of relationship. They are associative. That is, they convey the ways in which ideas are associated.

Part 3 of this book describes a group of tools that demonstrates how ideas are dynamically related. Dynamic relationships are causal, where one thing causes a change in another. Every knowledge domain is replete with dynamic relationships. Heating a substance causes a change in the activity of the molecules of that substance. Romeo loved Juliet, which caused jealousy and rage among the Capulets, which caused Mercutio to more strongly defend his friend, Romeo. Understanding the causal relationships is essential to being able to transfer those ideas to other domains.

Part 3 introduces a number of tools for representing these dynamic relationships, as described in the following chapters:

These tools are used not only to represent dynamic relationships but also to construct simulations of models of dynamic systems. These tools are perhaps the most intellectually demanding and engaging of all of the tools described in this book.

Spreadsheets as Mindtools

WHAT ARE SPREADSHEETS?

Spreadsheets are computerized, numerical record-keeping systems. They were originally designed to replace paper-based ledger systems. Accountants would enter all of the expenses and income from their business in different columns of the ledger, summing, subtracting, and balancing the assets of the company. Ledgers required that all of the accounting operations be performed by hand. If a single mistake was found, the entire ledger had to be recalculated. Spreadsheets have automated all of these processes (see Figure 5.1).

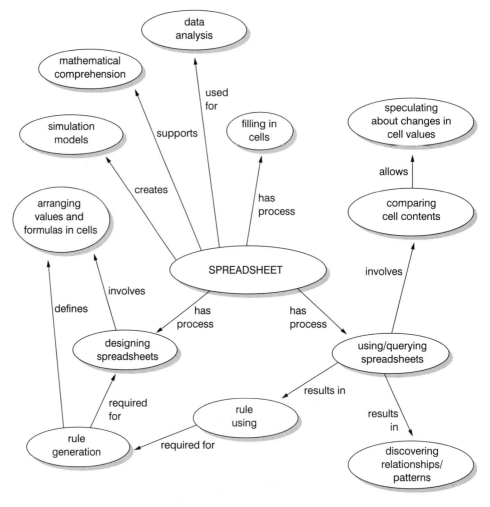

Figure 5.1
Spreadsheets as Mindtools

Essentially, a spreadsheet is a grid (or table or matrix) of empty cells, with columns identified by letters and rows identified by numbers (see Figure 5.2)—a ledger sheet spread in front of the user. The information included in any cell may be text or numbers, or cells may contain formulas or mathematical or logical functions to manipulate the numeric contents of any other cells. For example, in Figure 5.2, cells B2, B3, and B4 contain text that is used to label the contents of cells C2, C3, and C4. Cell C2 contains the number 48,000. By moving to that cell, the user can change that number by retyping it. Formulas consist of numerical relationships between the contents of different cells. For example, the formula B6+(C7/C6) would tell the program to go to cell B6, retrieve the value of the number in it, divide the contents of cell C7 by the contents of cell C6, and then add that value to the contents of cell B6. Formulas may refer to numerical values placed anywhere in the grid and may refer to any other cells by name.

Functions are mathematical or logical operations that can be performed on the values in a set of specified cells. For example, in Figure 5.2, the function in cell C6 tells the program to retrieve the values in cells C2 to C4 and SUM them. AVG (B9 . . . B12) would calculate the average of the values in cells B9 through B12. More sophisticated functions, such as ITERATE, perform operations a set number of times in a sequence. Functions are also logical, such as IF, MATCH, LOOKUP, or

	A	B	C	D	E	F	G	H	...
1		RECEIPTS				EXPENDITURES			
2		Tuition	48000			Salary	43200		
3		Public	18233			Taxes	2344		
4		Gifts	7895			Utilities	1179		
5						Rent	2365		
6		Total	SUM (C2.C4)			Misc	466		
7									
8		Profit	C6-G8			Total	SUM (G2.G6)		
...									

Figure 5.2
A Simple Profit/Loss Sheet

INDEX. These can be included in formulas, such as IF B9<E10,B9*E6 (if the value in cell B9 is less than that in E10, then multiply it by the value in E6). Other functions automatically match values in cells with other cells, look up values in a table of values, or create an index of values to be compared with other cells.

A major difference among spreadsheets is the size of the grid and the number of functions available. Small spreadsheets, such as the first VisiCalc spreadsheets, provided a grid of approximately 250 by 400 cells, whereas large spreadsheets may provide grids that are thousands of cells wide and deep. All spreadsheets provide the same basic functions, but more sophisticated ones provide more elaborate functions for interrelating content.

Spreadsheets have three primary functions: storing, calculating, and presenting information. First, information, usually numerical, can be stored in a particular location (the cell), from which it can be readily accessed and retrieved. Second, and most important, spreadsheets support calculation functions, such that the numerical contents of any combination of cells can be mathematically related in just about any way the user wishes (including logarithmic, trigonometric, etc.). Finally, spreadsheets present information in a variety of ways. All can display their contents in a two-dimensional grid, such as in Figure 5.2. All spreadsheets enable the user to display the numerical contents of any combination of cells graphically in the form of charts or graphs. The user identifies a series of cells, and the program automatically provides graphs and charts of those quantities. By merely highlighting a group of cells (such as G2 to G6 in Figure 5.2) and clicking on a chart type, the program produces a bar and line chart or multicolored pie chart (Figure 5.3). Being able to visualize data instantaneously in several ways affords new ways of thinking about numbers.

Most spreadsheets provide advanced operations as well. These include replication, in which the program fills in formulas in cells by replicating a formula in another cell. During spreadsheet construction, the author is not required to copy a

Figure 5.3

Graphic Representation of
Amounts in Figure 5.2

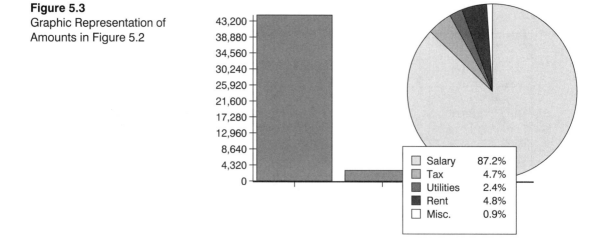

□ Salary	87.2%
■ Tax	4.7%
■ Utilities	2.4%
■ Rent	4.8%
□ Misc.	0.9%

similar formula over and over again in different cells. The spreadsheet can change the formula relative to the position of the cell. Many spreadsheet programs also allow the user to write macros, which are miniprograms that identify a sequence of operations that the program should perform when a single, special key is struck. Macros are often used in spreadsheets for collecting information from the user. A macro can be included in a cell for getting the user to input a value (e.g., his or her age), which can then be related to other cells in the spreadsheet. Finally, some spreadsheets enable the user to open several "windows," each of which provides a different view of the spreadsheet. These functions are normally reserved for the "power user" who has become skilled in spreadsheet use. Most spreadsheet programs also enable the users to produce graphic representations of data for the purpose of producing simulations (see Figure 5.6 later in the chapter). These will be described and illustrated later in the chapter.

Spreadsheets were originally developed—and are most commonly used—to support business decision making. The electronic spreadsheet was designed by a couple of graduate accounting majors as a tool to support accounting operations in their courses. Their professors assigned them problems based on balance sheets and profit and loss statements (like those shown in Figure 5.2 only much more complex) that would ask them "what if" questions, such as "What if interest rates increased by 1%?" Tired of having to recalculate all of the values that would be affected by the change, the students developed an electronic balance sheet where all of the values could be more easily manipulated. Changes would have to be made in only one location, and the spreadsheet would automatically recalculate all of the affected values. Use of this spreadsheet program, called VisiCalc, burgeoned immediately, triggering the phenomenal growth of microcomputers in business in the early 1980s.

Spreadsheets remain in common use today. Businesses use them not only for maintaining accounts but also for managing financial portfolios, determining service or interest rates, and modeling financial markets to support decision making. Spreadsheets are also commonly used for personal accounting and budgeting.

HOW ARE SPREADSHEETS USED AS MINDTOOLS?

Spreadsheets are an example of a cognitive technology that amplifies and reorganizes mental functioning (see Chapter 1). They have restructured the work of budgeting, enabling the accountant to be a hypothesis tester (playing "what if" games) rather than merely a calculator (Pea, 1985). This was the original purpose of spreadsheets, as just described. In the same way that they have qualitatively changed the accounting process, spreadsheets can change educational processes that require manipulation or speculation with numbers.

Spreadsheet construction and use engage a variety of mental processes that require learners to use existing rules, generate new rules describing relationships, and organize information (Figure 5.1). The emphasis in constructing a spreadsheet is on identifying relationships and describing those relationships in terms of higher order rules, so it is probable that if users learn to develop spreadsheets to describe content domains, they will be thinking more deeply.

So, spreadsheets are rule-using tools that require that users become rule makers (Vockell & Van Deusen, 1989). Calculating values in a spreadsheet requires users to identify relationships and patterns among the data they want to represent in the spreadsheet. Next, those relationships must be modeled mathematically using rules to describe the relationships in the model. Building spreadsheets requires abstract reasoning by the user. The Working Group for Technology of the National Curriculum Commission (1990), which helped frame the national curriculum in Great Britain, recognized the role of spreadsheets as tools that enable students to use information technology to explore patterns and relationships and to form and test sample hypotheses.

Although spreadsheets have been used most consistently in schools as management tools for accounting, they are being used increasingly as Mindtools to support higher order quantitative thinking. As Mindtools, spreadsheets can be used in at least three ways: computational reasoning tools for analyzing data, mathematics comprehension, and simulation modeling tools.

Computation, Analysis, and Reasoning Tools

First and foremost, spreadsheets are calculators that offload cognitive effort associated with computations. Whenever learners have a need to calculate, they can set up a spreadsheet to fulfill their purpose. Spreadsheets therefore support problem-solving activities. Given a problem situation with complex quantitative relationships, spreadsheets can be used to represent those relationships. Such reasoning requires learners to consider implications of conditions or options, which necessarily entails higher order reasoning. Because learners offload cognitive effort to the computer, they are able to apply more of their effort to understanding the relationships being calculated and represented graphically by the spreadsheet. So spreadsheets function as calculation and reasoning tools. They have been used to:

■ function as a calculator in order to demonstrate multiplicative relationships in elementary mathematics (Edwards & Bitter, 1989)
■ solve complex chemistry problems such as wet and dry analysis of flue gases, which may be expanded to include volumetric flow rate, pressure, humidity, dew point, temperature, and combustion temperature, in a mass and energy balances course (Misovich & Biasca, 1990)
■ calculate the force needed to lift assorted weights in various lever problems (Schlenker & Yoshida, 1991)
■ solve a number of science problems, including problems involving an incline plane and converting protein into energy (Goodfellow, 1990)
■ calculate the dimensions of a scale model of the Milky Way in order to demonstrate its immensity (Whitmer, 1990)

- solve elementary mathematical story problems (Verderber, 1990)
- support decision analysis by helping users find the best use of available information as well as evaluate any additional information that can be obtained (Sounderpandian, 1989)
- facilitate student grading of peer speech performances, providing a high level of motivation for the student (Dribin, 1985)
- estimate and compare the relative velocities of various dinosaurs (Karlin, 1988)
- implement Polya's problem-solving plan with arithmetic problems (Sgroi, 1992)
- solve rate equation chemical kinetics problems in a physical chemistry course (Blickensderfer, 1990)
- solve multiloop circuit problems (Hart, 1995).

These applications use the spreadsheet to calculate relationships among the numerical variables, allowing the learners to reason about those relationships *with* the spreadsheet. To support higher level thinking skills such as collecting, describing, and interpreting data, Niess (1992) provided students with a spreadsheet with wind data for different towns. Wind directions (NE, SW, WSW) described rows of data with the percent of days for each month of the year representing the columns. She would then ask students to use the spreadsheets to answer queries, such as the following:

- Are the winds more predominant from one direction during certain months? Why do you think this is the case?
- In which months is the wind the calmest?
- Which wind direction is the most stable throughout the year?

One of the best applications of spreadsheets is as a tool to enter and calculate the results of an experiment. They have been used to:

- analyze lunchroom trash and project annual waste for an Earth Day project (Ramondetta, 1992)
- analyze field data on ecology of tree species (Sigismondi & Calise, 1990)
- solve problems in physics laboratory experiments on time, displacement, and velocity and their interrelationships using a free-fall apparatus (Krieger & Stith, 1990)
- analyze and graphically represent data collected on the distribution and abundance of different kinds of trees in the forest (Silvius, Sjoquist, & Mundy, 1994)
- analyze the results of an experiment on microbial growth rates using simple fermentation equipment (Mills & Jackson, 1997).

The spreadsheet in Figure 5.4 supports a lab activity on blood analysis. The student is to collect the class data, arrange it by gender (this example is also arranged by descending white blood cell count), calculate averages by gender and by class, and compare his or her values with the averages for his or her gender and for the class. The data collected in this experiment were white blood count, red blood count, hematocrit, and hemoglobin.

Queries that would require students to add cells with formulas and functions might include the following:

- Are there gender differences in blood components such as red and white cells or hemoglobin?
- If white cell counts drop, what is the likely effect on red cells?
- If hemoglobin is administered to a patient, what is the likely effect on hematocrit readings?

Mathematics Comprehension

Spreadsheets support numerical thinking. When learning to perform mathematical processes, even with a great deal of practice, learners get bogged down in the manipulation of numbers and they lose sight of what they were trying to solve (Dubitsky, 1988). Spreadsheets provide a powerful manipulation tool for representing the values and developing formulas to interrelate them, which enhances learners' understanding of the algorithms used to compare them and also the mathematical models used to describe content domains. Students understand calculations (both antecedents and consequents) because they are actively involved in identifying the interrelationships between the components of the calculation. This is a substantively different activity than forcing students to sit through the countless math drill-and-practice programs, which can actually impair math performance, according to a study by the Educational Testing Service (Matthews, 1998). They concluded that simulations and real-life applications of math concepts on computers did improve math scores and improve school climate among eighth graders.

Spreadsheet construction requires learners to identify all steps of numerical solutions, showing the progression of calculations as they are performed in an algorithm. The spreadsheet models the mathematical logic that is implied by calculations, making the underlying logic obvious to learners, which should improve learners' understanding of the interrelationships and procedures. Spreadsheets have been used to:

- rootfind in precalculus using synthetic division, bisection method, and Newton's method (Pinter-Lucke, 1992)
- help children understand the meaning of large numbers (a million) by comparing quantities to everyday things (Parker & Widmer, 1991)
- implement linear system-solving algorithms, that is, advanced mathematical formulas (Watkins & Taylor, 1989)
- enable elementary students to refine estimates and see patterns while learning to solve long division problems, thus helping them to better understand numbers (Dubitsky, 1988)

	A	B	C	D	E
1	SEX	WBC	RBC(X10E6)	HCT (%)	HGB
2	FEMALE	13,760	11	42.2	15.25
3	FEMALE	9,360	11.1	41.6	14.1
4	FEMALE	9,000	1.3	43.4	17
5	FEMALE	9,000	1.3	46.1	15
6	FEMALE	7,960	3.7	34.1	15
7	FEMALE	7,680	5.5	43.2	16
8	FEMALE	7,080	4.4	41.6	14
9	FEMALE	6,720	2.18	38.6	14.2
10	FEMALE	6,600	4.5	57.1	17.5
11	FEMALE	6,400	5.5	43.4	17
12	FEMALE	6,240	3.42	52	19
13	FEMALE	5,680	5.53	60	14.5
14	FEMALE	4,980	4.74	44.6	15
15	FEMALE	4,520	8.35	44.4	15.2
16	MALE	8,968	5.79	42.2	15.5
17	MALE	7,786	5.7	51.5	16.5
18	MALE	7,760	3.4	50	15.7
19	MALE	7,520	6.7	46.3	8.9
20	MALE	6,600	3.73	49.1	19
21	MALE	6,520	4.29	47	15
22	MALE	6,450	6.5	47.2	16.5
23	MALE	6,040	11	44	14.5
24	MALE	4,600	5.7	46.2	14
25	MIN FEMALES	4,520	1.3	34.1	14
26	MAX FEMALES	13,760	11.1	60	19
27	RANGE FEMALES	9,240	9.8	25.9	5
28	AVE FEMALES	7,499	5.18	45.2	15.6
29					
30	MIN MALES	4,600	3.4	42.2	8.9
31	MAX MALES	8,968	11	51.5	19
32	RANGE MALES	4,368	7.6	9.3	10.1
33	AVE MALES	6,916	5.9	47.1	15.1
34					
35	MIN CLASS	4,520	1.3	34.1	8.9
36	MAX CLASS	13,760	11.1	60	19
37	RANGE CLASS	9,240	9.8	25.9	10.1
38	AVE CLASS	7,271	5.4	45.9	15.4

Figure 5.4
Spreadsheet to Support Lab Experiment on Blood

■ help students to develop conceptual understanding of relationships between variables while solving problems such as planning a party, holiday shopping, and calculating interest (Hoeffner, Kendall, Stellenwerf, Thames, & Williams, 1993)

■ symbolize relations and rules in algebra problems and think in general mathematical relationships by 10- and 11-year-old children in Mexico and Britain (Sutherland & Rojano, 1993).

The next spreadsheet (Figures 5.5A and B) details solutions of the quadratic equation. Through calculating the equation with the spreadsheet, learners better understood the mathematics underlying the function. It uses a variety of spreadsheet functions, especially the IF function, to analyze the values in the spreadsheet during calculation.

Simulation Modeling Tools

Simulating phenomena using spreadsheets provides a "direct and effective means of understanding the role of various parameters and of testing different means of optimizing their values" (Sundheim, 1992, p. 654). Barnes (1997) showed how a number of dynamic systems (systems that change over time as described by variables), including chaos and the butterfly effect, population growth, the ecology of predator–prey relationships, and Newton's law of cooling could all be modeled in spreadsheets. Numerous other examples of simulation modeling with spreadsheets include the following:

■ tracking portfolio performance in a stock training simulation (Crisci, 1992)
■ modeling the stoichiometric relationships in chemical reactions and calculating how many bonds are broken, the energy required to break bonds, and the new masses and densities of the products and reagents in the reactions (Brosnan, 1990)
■ representing Keynesian versus classical macroeconomic models, such as savings–investment and inflation–unemployment (Adams & Kroch, 1989)
■ interrelating demographic variables in population geography courses using population templates (Rudnicki, 1990)
■ calculating and graphing quantum mechanical functions such as atomic orbitals to simulate rotational and vibrational energy levels of atomic components in a physical chemistry class (Kari, 1990)
■ creating and manipulating economic models (e.g., balance of payments, investment appraisal, elasticity, cost–benefit analyses) in an economics course (Cashien, 1990)
■ representing different experiments on Archimedes's law and potential energy (Silva, 1998)
■ simulating electrical circuit requiring students to predict the results of changing parameters, qualitatively analyze what happens when changes are introduced, and quantitatively verify different laws (Silva, 1994)

Figure 5.5A
Quadratic Equation Spreadsheet

	A	B	C	D	E	F	G	H	I
1	problem	equation	a	check a	b	check b	c	check c	larger solution
2									
3	6	4n^2-3n+5=0	4	=IF(C3=4,4,-99999)	-3	=IF(E3=-3,-3,-99999)	5	=IF(G3=5,5,-99999)	=(-E3+Sqrt((E3^2)-(4*C3*G3)))/(2*C3)
4	14	10w^2+3-7w=1	10	=IF(C4=10,10,-99999)	-7	=IF(E4=-7,-7,-99999)	2	=IF(G4=2,2,-99999)	=(-E4+Sqrt((E4^2)-(4*C4*G4)))/(2*C4)
5	10	5=4t-2t^2	2	=IF(C5=2,2,-99999)	-4	=IF(E5=-4,-4,-99999)	5	=IF(G5=5,5,-99999)	=(-E5+Sqrt((E5^2)-(4*C5*G5)))/(2*C5)
6	13	2y^2=y-2-y^2	3	=IF(C6=3,3,-99999)	-1	=IF(E6=-1,-1,-99999)	2	=IF(G6=2,2,-99999)	=(-E6+Sqrt((E6^2)-(4*C6*G6)))/(2*C6)
7	3	x^2-3x+7=0	1	=IF(C7=1,1,-99999)	-3	=IF(E7=-3,-3,-99999)	7	=IF(G7=7,7,-99999)	=(-E7+Sqrt((E7^2)-(4*C7*G7)))/(2*C7)
8	2	9x^2-12x+4=0	9	=IF(C8=9,9,-99999)	-12	=IF(E8=-12,-12,-99999)	4	=IF(G8=4,4,-99999)	=(-E8+Sqrt((E8^2)-(4*C8*G8)))/(2*C8)
9	7	x^2-4x+4=0	1	=IF(C9=1,1,-99999)	-4	=IF(E9=-4,-4,-99999)	4	=IF(G9=4,4,-99999)	=(-E9+Sqrt((E9^2)-(4*C9*G9)))/(2*C9)
10	15	8s+9=-4s^2+5	4	=IF(C10=4,4,-99999)	8	=IF(E10=8,8,-99999)	4	=IF(G10=4,4,-99999)	=(-E10+Sqrt((E10^2)-(4*C10*G10)))/(2*C10)
11	1	2x^2+5x-3=0	2	=IF(C11=2,2,-99999)	5	=IF(E11=5,5,-99999)	-3	=IF(G11=-3,-3,-99999)	=(-E11+Sqrt((E11^2)-(4*C11*G11)))/(2*C11)
12	12	-y^2=-9y+5	-1	=IF(C12=-1,-1,-99999)	9	=IF(E12=9,9,-99999)	-5	=IF(G12=-5,-5,-99999)	=(-E12+Sqrt((E12^2)-(4*C12*G12)))/(2*C12)
13	4	t^2-6x-10=0	1	=IF(C13=1,1,-99999)	-6	=IF(E13=-6,-6,-99999)	-10	=IF(G13=-10,-10,-99999)	=(-E13+Sqrt((E13^2)-(4*C13*G13)))/(2*C13)
14	11	3x^2=5-4x	3	=IF(C14=3,3,-99999)	4	=IF(E14=4,4,-99999)	-5	=IF(G14=-5,-5,-99999)	=(-E14+Sqrt((E14^2)-(4*C14*G14)))/(2*C14)
15	8	9x^2=2x+5	9	=IF(C15=9,9,-99999)	-2	=IF(E15=-2,-2,-99999)	-5	=IF(G15=-5,-5,-99999)	=(-E15+Sqrt((E15^2)-(4*C15*G15)))/(2*C15)
16	5	3x^2-12x-10=0	3	=IF(C16=3,3,-99999)	-12	=IF(E16=-12,-12,-99999)	-10	=IF(G16=-10,-10,-99999)	=(-E16+Sqrt((E16^2)-(4*C16*G16)))/(2*C16)
17	9	16v^2=1-20v	16	=IF(C17=16,16,-99999)	20	=IF(E17=20,20,-99999)	-1	=IF(G17=-1,-1,-99999)	=(-E17+Sqrt((E17^2)-(4*C17*G17)))/(2*C17)
18									
19	Note: x^2 means [x][x] which is x squared								

93

	J	K	L	M	N	O	P
1	smaller solution	discriminant	-b/a	sum of soln's	c/a	product of solutions	
2							
3	=(-E3-Sqrt((E3^2)-(4*C3*G3)))/(2*C3)	=(E3^2)-(4*C3*G3)	=-E3/C3	=I3+J3	=G3/C3	=I3*J3	
4	=(-E4-Sqrt((E4^2)-(4*C4*G4)))/(2*C4)	=(E4^2)-(4*C4*G4)	=-E4/C4	=I4+J4	=G4/C4	=I4*J4	
5	=(-E5-Sqrt((E5^2)-(4*C5*G5)))/(2*C5)	=(E5^2)-(4*C5*G5)	=-E5/C5	=I5+J5	=G5/C5	=I5*J5	
6	=(-E6-Sqrt((E6^2)-(4*C6*G6)))/(2*C6)	=(E6^2)-(4*C6*G6)	=-E6/C6	=I6+J6	=G6/C6	=I6*J6	
7	=(-E7-Sqrt((E7^2)-(4*C7*G7)))/(2*C7)	=(E7^2)-(4*C7*G7)	=-E7/C7	=I7+J7	=G7/C7	=I7*J7	
8	=(-E8-Sqrt((E8^2)-(4*C8*G8)))/(2*C8)	=(E8^2)-(4*C8*G8)	=-E8/C8	=I8+J8	=G8/C8	=I8*J8	
9	=(-E9-Sqrt((E9^2)-(4*C9*G9)))/(2*C9)	=(E9^2)-(4*C9*G9)	=-E9/C9	=I9+J9	=G9/C9	=I9*J9	
10	=(-E10-Sqrt((E10^2)-(4*C10*G10)))/(2*C10)	=(E10^2)-(4*C10*G10)	=-E10/C10	=I10+J10	=G10/C10	=I10*J10	
11	=(-E11-Sqrt((E11^2)-(4*C11*G11)))/(2*C11)	=(E11^2)-(4*C11*G11)	=-E11/C11	=I11+J11	=G11/C11	=I11*J11	
12	=(-E12-Sqrt((E12^2)-(4*C12*G12)))/(2*C12)	=(E12^2)-(4*C12*G12)	=-E12/C12	=I12+J12	=G12/C12	=I12*J12	
13	=(-E13-Sqrt((E13^2)-(4*C13*G13)))/(2*C13)	=(E13^2)-(4*C13*G13)	=-E13/C13	=I13+J13	=G13/C13	=I13*J13	
14	=(-E14-Sqrt((E14^2)-(4*C14*G14)))/(2*C14)	=(E14^2)-(4*C14*G14)	=-E14/C14	=I14+J14	=G14/C14	=I14*J14	
15	=(-E15-Sqrt((E15^2)-(4*C15*G15)))/(2*C15)	=(E15^2)-(4*C15*G15)	=-E15/C15	=I15+J15	=G15/C15	=I15*J15	
16	=(-E16-Sqrt((E16^2)-(4*C16*G16)))/(2*C16)	=(E16^2)-(4*C16*G16)	=-E16/C16	=I16+J16	=G16/C16	=I16*J16	
17	=(-E17-Sqrt((E17^2)-(4*C17*G17)))/(2*C17)	=(E17^2)-(4*C17*G17)	=-E17/C17	=I17+J17	=G17/C17	=I17*J17	
18							
19							

Figure 5.5B
Quadratic Equation Spreadsheet (continued)

■ identify factors affecting growth and determining the factors and their interrelationships that should be included in a simulation of population growth (Wells & Berger, 1985–86)

■ modeling planetary orbits (Bridges, 1995)

■ modeling a thermostatted water bath and graphing heat distributions (Sundheim, 1992).

Erich Neuwirth maintains a web site (http://SunSITE.univie.ac.at/Spreadsite/) where he illustrates many spreadsheet models and applications for math, science, and statistics education, including a series of batteries, as shown in Figure 5.6. When the voltages on the left side of the model are reset the values of the other variables in the figure change. This is a simple model; others are more complex.

Figure 5.7 simulates an internal combustion engine, where students can experiment with the effects of changing the angle and direction of the crank. Figure 5.8 illustrates a simple experiment on growth of pathogens that a student constructed. To run the experiment, you set the temperature and temperature change factor and see the effects on the growth of pathogens illustrated in the graph. Constructing

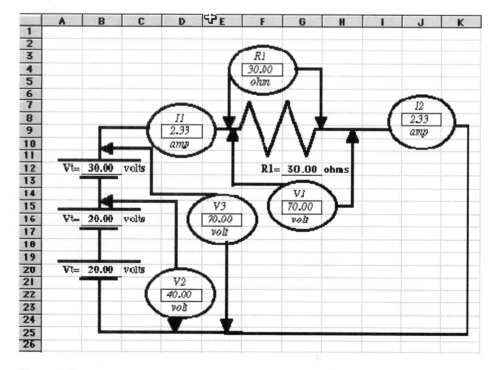

Figure 5.6
Battery Series Spreadsheet Model
Courtesy of Eric Neuwirth.

	A	B	C	D	E	F	
10							
11	Theta (deg)	Theta (rad)	Position	Speed	Accel	Volume	
12			(mm)	(m/s)	(m/s^2)	(liters)	
13	-4	-0.070	22.03			75.78	
14	-2	-0.035	22.05	1.73		75.12	
15	0	0.000	22.05	0.58	-17269	74.90	
16						75.12	
17						75.78	
18						76.87	
19						78.39	
20						80.34	
21						82.72	
22						85.52	
23						88.73	
24						92.36	
25						96.39	
26							
27							
28	26	0.4					
29	28	0.4					
30	30	0.5					
31	32	0.5					
32	34	0.5					
33	36	0.6					
34	38	0.6					
35	40	0.6					

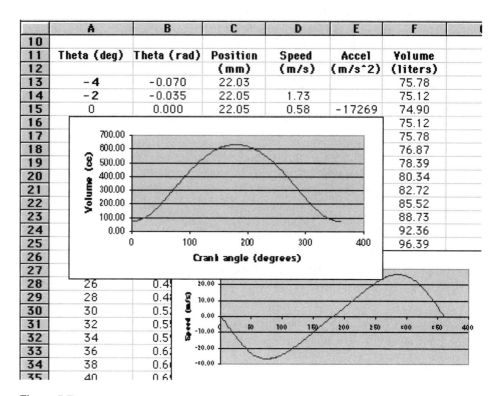

Figure 5.7
Slider Crank Experiment
Courtesy of Tom Litzinger.

simulations of dynamic systems is one of the most complete intellectual activities in which students can engage. Modern spreadsheets make this activity relatively easy.

Who should build spreadsheet simulations, teachers or students? Teachers can create simulations of experiments which their students can use as microworlds (Chapter 8) to explore and manipulate. This is an effective use of spreadsheets. However, when students produce their own simulations, they are engaged in the most meaningful, deep-level learning possible with or without computers. This should be the goal to work toward.

Related Mindtools

Spreadsheets and databases (Chapter 3) look and function very much alike. They both display information in a matrix of rows and columns, and information can even be passed back and forth between them. Also, powerful spreadsheet programs have many database features, so these tools are often used in conjunction with each other.

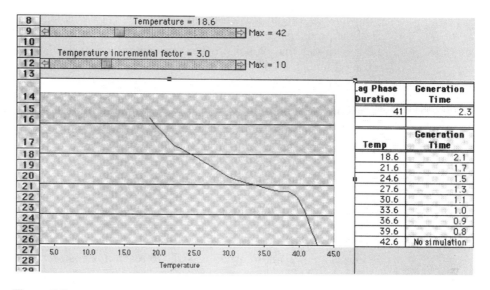

Figure 5.8
Pathogens Experiment
Courtesy of Julian Hernandez-Serrano.

Spreadsheets provide a lot of the same functionality as systems modeling tools (Chapter 7) when they are used to construct simulation models of systems. The graphical output of spreadsheets resembles the graphical output of those tools. There may be little intellectual difference between using spreadsheets and systems modeling tools to build simulation models. The simulations that learners create with spreadsheets are clearly a kind of microworld (Chapter 8), a simplified model of the world that learners can manipulate. The simulation capabilities of spreadsheets have made them much more powerful as Mindtools.

Spreadsheets also provide much of the functionality of statistical analysis programs, which, like word-processing and graphics programs, are not discussed in depth in this book but could be used as Mindtools. Many researchers collect data with computers and then load that data into spreadsheets where the data are massaged and preprocessed before being loaded into a statistical analysis program. Newer spreadsheet programs, like Excel, have sophisticated statistical analysis programs built into them. Spreadsheets are versatile programs for mathematically manipulating almost any kind of computerized information.

Coaching the Construction of Spreadsheets in the Classroom

Imagine that for Earth Day this year, your students want to calculate and represent the impact of a new recycling policy on the county they live in. Identifying all of the disposable and recyclable products, the quantities discarded in each part of the county, and the costs (short term and long term) of burying or recycling those products would require extensive investigation. Then building a model to interrelate all of the products, costs, and savings on a spreadsheet would require extensive synthesis activities that would provide your students with feelings of satisfaction and accomplishment. Rather than having your elementary science students read about experiments in their science books, have them conduct the experiments and use spreadsheets to record and analyze the results. Or have your students construct a survey about the attitudes of students in different grades, administer the survey, and use spreadsheets to record and analyze the results. There are so many applications of spreadsheets that could be used by all grades.

Performing the kinds of content analysis required to set up and describe such problem situations for building spreadsheets will require many new skills. The ultimate goal is for your students to be able to independently analyze a new problem situation by identifying the problem variables and interrelationships among those variables and creating formulas and using functions to calculate and manipulate the quantities in those variables. The ability to create quantitative models of problem situations is a powerful, transferable skill. To reach this goal, several stages of learning must occur. This section recommends a series of stages and learning activities for preparing your students to achieve that goal.

1. **Provide a spreadsheet template.** To introduce students to the structure and functions of spreadsheets, you may want to begin by having them complete some exercises using an existing spreadsheet. Begin with a spreadsheet template (a spreadsheet with formulas entered but no values) and require students to fill in gaps in the spreadsheet. For example, complete a simple science experiment and have students enter the data collected in particular cells. Or start with a familiar spreadsheet—perhaps a spreadsheet of personal information (height, weight, shoe size, age, parent data) about the students in the class—and require them to input their personal information in the spreadsheet and then calculate high, low, and averages of these values and other quantities, such as density (weight/height). Later, use a content spreadsheet that contains the formulas and have them look up information from almanacs, tables, or other reference materials to enter into the spreadsheet. Make sure that students trace all of the calculations that are completed by the spreadsheet. These activities familiarize learners with spreadsheet functions and structure.

2. **Students make a plan.** Before beginning, students need to make a plan for their spreadsheet. What are they interested in representing? Do they want to build a simulation? What points do they want to make? What kinds of structure and information are required to make those points? What learning goals will they work toward? Are they interested in understanding mathematics better?

3. **Students adapt existing spreadsheets or design new spreadsheets for other students to complete.** Start with familiar content and require students to adapt existing spreadsheets, such as adding nutritional information and relationships to the personal variables in the classroom information spreadsheet. Or design new spreadsheets that they can collaboratively fill in. Topics such as local sports

teams, dating patterns, and television shows are popular. Students can add data, construct graphs and charts to represent that data, and then add some variables.

4. Students create and complete a problem-oriented spreadsheet. Increase the complexity of the spreadsheet content by relating it to classroom studies. Starting with more concrete activities—such as geographic or demographic features in social studies or mathematical formulas in algebra—and working in small, collaborative groups, have students determine what values, formulas, and functions are required. Have them start with small phenomena first. For example, model the output of a single farm or business before trying to develop models of national economies. What gets modeled depends on what kinds of questions people want answered, that is, what kinds of relationships should be compared in the spreadsheet. This is perhaps the most difficult part of the process. Compare the spreadsheets in class and discuss the relationships in terms of how completely and accurately they reflect the content domain. This is the most complete activity, requiring learners to identify variables and information needs, develop formulas and functions, complete the spreadsheet, and then use the spreadsheet to answer questions.

5. Students extrapolate from spreadsheets. Students can create new formulas, variables, and graphs in an existing spreadsheet to support other applications. For example, starting with a spreadsheet on geographic information, adding political and economic variables and relationships to support geopolitical relationship questions would be useful.

6. Students reflect on the activity. Reflection should not wait until the project is completed. Rather, students should continuously review their progress on the project. Are we achieving our goals? What changes are necessary? How do we compare with other groups? Are we answering questions and making the points that we set out in our plan? After the project is completed, the students should reflect on the project. What have we learned about math? What have we learned about spreadsheet construction that can be used to represent knowledge? What have we learned about working with each other? You may choose to provide students with some or all of the criteria for evaluating student spreadsheets (presented in the next section) to use for self-evaluation. The activity of constructing spreadsheets engages meaningful thinking. Reflection cements the knowledge that learners construct.

EVALUATING SPREADSHEETS AS MINDTOOLS

Critical, Creative, and Complex Thinking in Spreadsheet Construction and Use

A variety of critical, creative, and complex thinking skills are required to construct and reason with knowledge-oriented spreadsheets. Tables 5.1, 5.2, and 5.3 identify the skills that are engaged when students analyze and reason with data, comprehend mathematical functions, and build dynamic simulations with spreadsheets. The skills in each table that are marked by an "X" are those that are employed by each process, based on an information-processing analysis of the tasks.

As is the case with most other Mindtools, building and reasoning with spreadsheets engages more critical and complex thinking skills than creative thinking skills (see Table 5.1). That is because spreadsheet construction and use are analytic processes that make heavy use of logical thinking. When spreadsheets are to collect, analyze, and reason about data from experiments used (as in Figure 5.4), designing a spreadsheet to reflect the data-collection needs of an experiment requires a variety of evaluating and connecting skills and fewer analyzing skills. Building spreadsheets to understand mathematical functions, on the other hand, stresses analysis and connecting skills. For example, having students speculate about the change in products from altering one of the factors in the quadratic equations represented in Figure 5.5 requires inferences, logical thinking, comparing and contrasting quantities, and looking for causal relationships. Constructing dynamic simulations, such as those demonstrated in Figures 5.6, 5.7, and 5.8, engages nearly every kind of critical thinking skill.

A smaller portion of creative thinking skills are engaged by spreadsheet construction (see Table 5.2). All three applications of spreadsheets use nearly all of the

Table 5.1
Critical Thinking Skills Engaged by Spreadsheet Construction and Use

	Computation/ analysis/ reasoning	Mathematical functions comprehension	Constructing simulations
Evaluating			
Assessing information	X		X
Determining criteria	X		X
Prioritizing	X		X
Recognizing fallacies		X	X
Verifying	X	X	X
Analyzing			
Recognizing patterns	X	X	X
Classifying	X	X	X
Identifying assumptions		X	X
Identifying main ideas		X	X
Finding sequences		X	X
Connecting			
Comparing/contrasting	X		X
Logical thinking	X	X	X
Inferring deductively		X	X
Inferring inductively	X	X	
Identifying causal relationships	X	X	X

Table 5.2
Creative Thinking Skills Engaged by Spreadsheet Construction and Use

	Computation/ analysis/ reasoning	Mathematical functions comprehension	Constructing simulations
Elaborating			
Expanding			X
Modifying		X	
Extending		X	X
Shifting categories			X
Concretizing	X	X	X
Synthesizing			
Analogical thinking		X	
Summarizing	X		X
Hypothesizing	X	X	X
Planning	X		X
Imagining			
Fluency		X	X
Predicting	X		X
Speculating	X	X	X
Visualizing	X	X	X
Intuition	X	X	X

synthesizing and imagining skills, especially hypothesizing, speculating, and visualizing with graphs and charts.

Complex thinking skills are engaged more by using spreadsheets to analyze and reason about data sets but especially by constructing simulations (see Table 5.3). Designing and building databases requires a number of planning operations that make heavy use of designing, problem-solving, and decision-making skills (see Table 3.3). With spreadsheets, on the other hand, heavier use of problem solving and decision making takes place during speculating. This makes sense, because the purpose of using spreadsheets is to help users make decisions about what actions to take if a particular set of conditions evolves. Problem solving is an important outcome of using spreadsheets.

Evaluating Student Spreadsheets

What makes an effective spreadsheet? That depends on the kind of spreadsheet that students are constructing and the age and abilities of the learners who are constructing the spreadsheet. Figure 5.9 presents a number of rubrics that you may use to evaluate the spreadsheets that students construct as their knowledge and skills move from emergent to mastery. You will probably want to adapt these or add your own criteria as you evaluate your students' projects.

Table 5.3
Complex Thinking Skills Engaged by Spreadsheet Construction and Use

	Computation/ analysis/ reasoning	Mathematical functions comprehension	Constructing simulations
Designing			
Imagining a goal	X		X
Formulating a goal	X		X
Inventing a product	X	X	X
Assessing a product			X
Revising the product			X
Problem Solving			
Sensing the problem	X		X
Researching the problem		X	X
Formulating the problem	X	X	X
Finding alternatives			X
Choosing the solution	X		X
Building acceptance			X
Decision Making			
Identifying an issue	X		X
Generating alternatives			X
Assessing the consequences	X		X
Making a choice	X		X
Evaluating the choice	X		X

Evaluating Spreadsheet Software

Spreadsheet programs are commonly available for every type of computer in use today. Many spreadsheet software packages are in the public domain and thus very inexpensive. A search of the World Wide Web will turn up a number of shareware spreadsheet programs. These are not as powerful, but they are typically inexpensive (users copy the program for free, and if they choose to keep it, they send in a nominal registration fee). For users who seek more powerful spreadsheets, Microsoft's Excel has become the industry standard.

For PCs, VisiCalc was the referent standard until Lotus bought and retired it, which made Lotus 1-2-3 the referent. After IBM acquired Lotus, Microsoft's Excel became the market leader for Windows and Macintoshes. For Windows machines, Quattro Pro is number three. Less powerful programs, such as Lucid 3-D, can be purchased very inexpensively. Spreadsheets are also a part of many integrated programs for Windows machines, including Microsoft Works, StarOffice including CalcStar (www.ability.com), and Ability Office 98.

For the Macintosh, spreadsheets are part of most integrated packages, such as AppleWorks (formerly ClarisWorks) or Microsoft Works. Other less expensive

**Accuracy of variables
in experiment or simulation**

No variables identified;
data are random/out of range

All important variables identified;
variables have proper range of values

Accuracy of formulas

Formulas are inconsistent;
formulas are inaccurate

Formulas characterize inherent
mathematical relationships among
variables and values

**Graphs/charts enhance
understanding of values**

Graphs/charts inappropriate;
confuse or misrepresent
relationships

Appropriate graph/chart types
selected; show important
relationships

Organization of data

Values presented randomly,
not grouped; data are
difficult to access

Values classified and organized in
similar groups; data are accessible

**User-controlled variables
(if used) enhance causal reasoning**

Illustrate noncausal
relationships; incorrectly
sequence or predict values

Explicate causal relationships
among variables

Figure 5.9
Evaluation Rubrics for Assessing Student-Constructed Spreadsheets

spreadsheet programs include Spreadsheet 2000 (www.emer.com/s2k/), Storeys (www.profunda.dk/spreadsheet_storeys/spreadsheet_storeys.html), and Sum-It, a simple spreadsheet program (www.xs4all.nl/~hekkel/SumIt.html).

Selecting a spreadsheet can be a perplexing process, so keep a few simple criteria in mind. The most important one is cost. It should not be necessary to spend very much for the kinds of functionality described in this chapter, except for building simulations, which will require more powerful programs, like Excel.

As with databases, you should consider what other applications software you want to use. Will you also want to perform word processing and use databases? If so, you may want to consider an integrated package such as AppleWorks (ClarisWorks), Microsoft Works, or Microsoft Office.

Whichever software you purchase, it is always a good idea to try it out and spend some time using it. A potential problem with Mindtools or any computer application is the learning curve required to become an effective user. Generally, as the number of functions and capabilities afforded by a package increases, so does the complexity of the system and the difficulty of use. Test any new package to see how easy it is to use. If you are a novice spreadsheet user, you may want to select the simplest system, with the expectation that you will upgrade later if the program proves to be inadequate. Try to select software that minimizes the time spent learning how to use the software and maximizes the time spent solving quantitative problems.

Advantages of Spreadsheets as Mindtools

A spreadsheet will always perform the calculations that are embedded into its cells, so if one value in the grid is changed, all of the values in the spreadsheet that are related to it are also automatically recalculated. This capability frees the user from reentering all of the values in a formula if one value changes, as is required by most calculators. Perhaps the major logistical advantage of spreadsheets is that they are easy to adapt and modify.

A spreadsheet is, in essence, a computer program for making multiple calculations. But since spreadsheets do not require the use of a complex programming language, they reduce the proliferation of syntax and logical errors that are common with these programming languages (Misovich & Biasca, 1990). If you like computer languages, many of the more powerful spreadsheet packages provide simple programming languages to enhance the capabilities of the spreadsheet, but you can access the power of spreadsheets without learning to program.

Spreadsheets support speculation, decision-making, and problem-solving activities. Given a problem situation with complex quantitative relationships, the experienced spreadsheet user can quickly create a spreadsheet to represent those relationships. Spreadsheets are perhaps best used for supporting "what if" analyses (e.g., "What will be the effect on accounts payable and debt ratio if interest rates increase 1%?" or "What will happen if the population of an emerging country increases at 7% rather than 5%?"). This type of thinking is best supported by spreadsheets and is essential to decision analysis (Sounderpandian, 1989). Such questioning requires learners to consider the implications of various conditions or options, which entails higher order reasoning.

Spreadsheets explicitly demonstrate values and relationships in any problem or content domain in numerical form. Identifying values and developing formulas to interrelate them enhance learners' understanding of the algorithms used to compare them and of the mathematical models used to describe content domains. Students understand calculations (both antecedents and consequents) because they are actively involved in identifying the interrelationships among the components of the calculation. Spreadsheet construction and use demonstrate all steps of problem solutions and show the progression of calculations as they are performed. The spreadsheet process models the mathematical logic that is implied by calculations.

Making the underlying logic obvious to learners should improve their understanding of the interrelationships and procedures.

Finally, spreadsheets integrate graphics with computation. What makes modern spreadsheet programs so powerful is their ability to visualize quantitative relationships in different ways. Early spreadsheets could only show the grid of cells, but modern spreadsheets can easily create graphs, charts, and models of phenomena. Research has shown that even children as young as 6 years are able to enter and graphically display information (Goodfellow, 1990). This characteristic enables spreadsheets to be used as simulation modeling (Chapter 7) and visualization (Chapter 10) tools.

Limitations of Spreadsheets as Mindtools

Although the spreadsheet is a versatile tool, it is most effective in solving quantitative problems. Although modern spreadsheets are able to represent a variety of data types, they are intended primarily to manipulate and represent quantitative information. Therefore, they are most useful in mathematics and science, and in some social science applications (e.g., economics, psychology, and sociology). Spreadsheets are generally not as useful for humanities instruction, although there are a few types of analyses in this area that can be quantified and are therefore amenable to spreadsheet use (e.g., metric analysis of poems).

SUMMARY

Spreadsheets are versatile tools for identifying, manipulating, and visualizing quantitative relationships between entities and creating simulations of dynamic, quantitative phenomena. On the simplest level, they are programmable calculators that eliminate the need for time-consuming manipulation and calculation of numbers. They allow users to effectively organize a variety of calculations on a simple grid structure, using almost any kind of mathematical relationship. Spreadsheets are also effective problem-solving tools. While they are more often used as productivity tools, they can also function well as Mindtools. When students create spreadsheets, they are building quantitative models of the real world and using those models to speculate about changes in the phenomena contained in their models. Those are powerful skills to acquire.

References

Adams, F. G., & Kroch, E. (1989). The computer in the teaching of economics. *Journal of Economic Education, 20*(3), 269–280.

Barnes, J. A. (1997). Modeling dynamical systems with spreadsheet software, *Mathematics and Computer Education, 31*(1), 43–55.

Blickensderfer, R. (1990). Learning chemical kinetics with spreadsheets. *Journal of Computers in Mathematics and Science Teaching, 9*(4), 35–43.

Bridges, R. (1995). Fitting planetary orbits with a spreadsheet. *Physics Education, 30*(5), 266–271.

Brosnan, T. (1990). Using spreadsheets in the teaching of chemistry: Two more ideas and some limitations. *School Science Review, 71*(256), 53–59.

Cashien, P. (1990). Spreadsheet investigations in economics teaching. *Economics, 26*(Part 2, 110), 73–84.

Crisci, G. (1992, January). Play the market! *Instructor,* pp. 68–69.

Dribin, C. I. (1985, June). Spreadsheets and performance: A guide for student-graded presentations. *The Computing Teacher,* pp. 22–25.

Dubitsky, B. (1988, November). Making division meaningful with a spreadsheet. *Arithmetic Teacher,* pp. 18–21.

Edwards, N. T., & Bitter, B. G. (1989, October). Changing variables using spreadsheet templates. *Arithmetic Teacher,* pp. 40–44.

Goodfellow, T. (1990). Spreadsheets: Powerful tools in science education. *School Science Review, 71*(257), 47–57.

Hart, F.X. (1995). Solving multi-loop circuit problems with a spreadsheet. *The Physics Teacher, 33,* 542.

Hoeffner, K., Kendall, M., Stellenwerf, C., Thames, P., & Williams, P. (1993, November). Problem solving with a spreadsheet. *Arithmetic Teacher,* pp. 52–56.

Kari, R. (1990). Spreadsheets in advanced physical chemistry. *Journal of Computers in Mathematics and Science Teaching, 10*(1), 39–48.

Karlin, M. (1988, February). Beyond distance = rate * time. *The Computing Teacher,* pp. 20–23.

Krieger, M. E., & Stith, J. H. (1990, September). Spreadsheets in the physics laboratory. *The Physics Teacher,* pp. 378–384.

Matthews, J. (1998, September). http://www.washingtonpost.com/wpsrv/washtech/daily/sept98/tech093098.htm.

Mills, J., & Jackson, R. (1997). Analysis of microbial growth data using a spreadsheet. *Journal of Biological Education, 31*(1), 34–38.

Misovich, M., & Biasca, K. (1990). The power of spreadsheets in a mass and energy balances course. *Chemical Engineering Education, 24,* 46–50.

National Curriculum Commission. (1990). *Technology in the national curriculum.* London: Author.

Niess, M. L. (1992, March). Winds of change. *The Computing Teacher,* pp. 32–35.

Parker, J., & Widmer, C. C. (1991, September). Teaching mathematics with technology. *Arithmetic Teacher,* pp. 38–41.

Pea, R. D. (1985). Beyond amplification: Using the computer to reorganize mental functioning. *Educational Psychologist, 20*(4), 167–182.

Pinter-Lucke, C. (1992). Rootfinding with a spreadsheet in pre-calculus. *Journal of Computers in Mathematics and Science Teaching, 11,* 85–93.

Ramondetta, J. (1992). Learning from lunchroom trash. *Learning Using Computers, 20*(8), 59.

Rudnicki, R. (1990). Using spreadsheets in population geography classes. *Journal of Geography, 89*(3), 118–122.

Schlenker, R. M., & Yoshida, S. J. (1991). A clever lever endeavor: You can't beat the spreadsheet. *The Science Teacher, 58*(2), 36–39.

Sgroi, R. J. (1992, March). Systematizing trial and error using spreadsheets. *Arithmetic Teacher,* pp. 8–12.

Sigismondi, L. A., & Calise, C. (1990). Integrating basic computer skills into science classes: Analysis of ecological data. *The American Biology Teacher, 52*(5), 296–301.

Silva, A. A. (1994). Simulating electrical circuits with an electronic spreadsheet. *Computers in Education, 22*(4), 345–353.

Silva, A. A. (1998). Archimedes' law and potential energy: Modelling and simulation with a spreadsheet. *Physics Education, 33*(2), 87–92.

Silvius, J. E., Sjoquist, D. W., & Mundy, D. D. (1994). Vegetation analysis using a computer spreadsheet, *The American Biology Teacher, 56*(1), 41–43.

Sounderpandian, J. (1989). Decision analysis using spreadsheets. *Collegiate Microcomputer, 7*(2), 157–163.

Sundheim, B. R. (1992). Modelling a thermostatted water bath with a spreadsheet. *Journal of Chemical Education, 69*(8), 650–654.

Sutherland, R., & Rojano, T. (1993). A spreadsheet approach to solving algebra problems. *Journal of Mathematical Behavior, 12*, 353–383.

Verderber, N. L. (1990). Spreadsheets and problem solving with AppleWorks in mathematics teaching. *Journal of Computers in Mathematics and Science Teaching, 9*(3), 45–51.

Vockell, E., & Van Deusen, R. M. (1989). *The computer and higher order thinking skills.* Watsonville, CA: Mitchell Publishing.

Watkins, W., & Taylor, M. (1989). A spreadsheet in the mathematics classroom. *Collegiate Microcomputer, 7*(3), 233–239.

Wells, G., & Berger, C. (1985–86). Teacher/student-developed spreadsheet simulations: A population growth example. *Journal of Computers in Mathematics and Science Teaching, 5*(2), 34–40.

Whitmer, J. C. (1990). Modeling the Milky Way. *The Science Teacher, 57*(7), 19–21.

Expert Systems as Mindtools

WHAT ARE EXPERT SYSTEMS?

Expert systems are artificial intelligence programs designed to simulate expert reasoning in order to facilitate decision making for all sorts of problems (see Figure 6.1). The early expert system, MYCIN, was developed to help physicians diagnose bacterial infections with which they were unfamiliar. Expert systems have also been developed to help geologists decide where to drill for oil, firefighters decide how to extinguish different kinds of fires, computer sales technicians configure computer systems, bankers to decide on loan applications, and employees to decide among a large number of company benefits alternatives. Problems whose solutions include recommendations based on a variety of decisions are good candidates for expert systems.

Expert systems evolved from research in the field of artificial intelligence. *Artificial intelligence* (AI) is a specialty in computer and cognitive science that focuses on the development of both hardware innovations and programming techniques that enable machines to perform tasks that are regarded as intelligent when done by people. *Artificial* means simulated, and *intelligence* is the capacity to learn, reason, and

Figure 6.1
Expert Systems as Mindtools

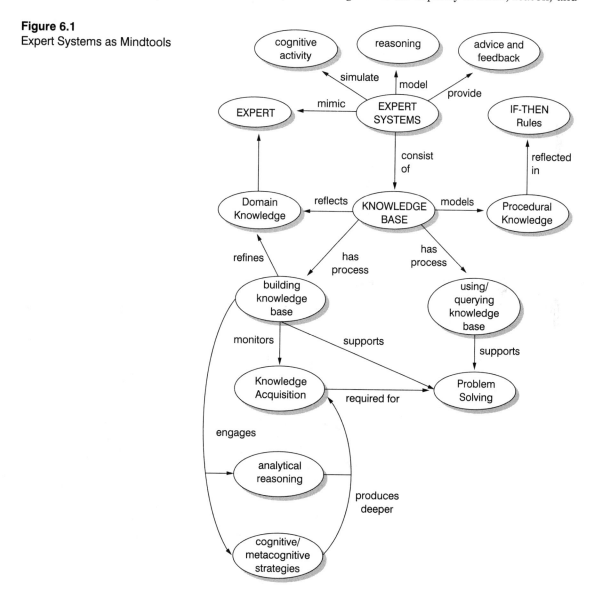

understand, so AI researchers and expert system builders attempt to develop programs that simulate the human capability to reason and to learn. *Simulated* means only imitating a real object or event. For example, flight simulators look real and feel real to flight trainers; however, a flight simulator is an *artificial* airplane that never actually flies and could not replace an airplane's primary function—to fly.

AI programs, including expert systems, may perform functions that resemble human thinking, such as decision making. In reality, though, AI programs are just *programs* that imitate what we believe to be human mental activity in a certain situation. Human intelligence is generalizable and transferable to new situations, but most forms of computer intelligence are not, and that includes expert systems. For example, a computer that is programmed to play chess cannot transfer that capability to playing Monopoly.

An expert system, then, is a computer program that attempts to simulate the way human experts solve problems—an artificial decision maker. For example, when you consult an expert (e.g., doctor, lawyer, teacher) about a problem, the expert asks for current information about your condition, searches his or her knowledge base (memory) for existing knowledge to which elements of the current situation can be related, processes the information (thinks), arrives at a decision, and presents a solution. Like a human expert, an expert system (computer program) is approached by an individual (novice) with a problem. The system queries the individual about the current status of the problem, searches its knowledge base (which contains previously stored expert knowledge) for pertinent facts and rules, processes the information, arrives at a decision, and reports the solution to the user.

Components of Expert Systems

Figure 6.2 diagrams the integration of the components of an expert system. I will describe each component briefly.

User.   Like a human expert, an expert system cannot put its knowledge and skills to use unless a need arises. The computer must await input from a user with a need or problem. For example, imagine that a novice loan officer in a bank is asked by an individual for a personal, unsecured loan. There are many factors to consider when making the decision (e.g., applicant's income and past credit record, amount of loan, reason for the loan, size of monthly payment, etc.)—so many factors that it may take months or years of training to prepare the loan officer to consider all of the parameters involved. An alternative is to build an expert system that asks the loan officer to input all data necessary for making an informed decision. The expert system, which is composed of facts and rules that an experienced or expert loan officer uses in making a decision, relates the information provided by the loan applicant to the rules and presents a decision that provides valuable advice to the loan officer. In this way, the expert system increases productivity because it saves both analysis time and training time.

Figure 6.2
Components of an Expert System

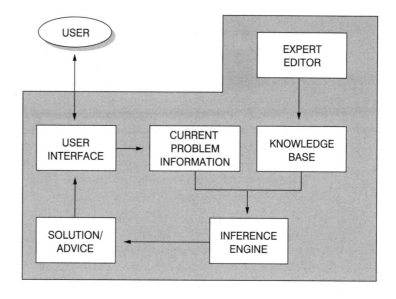

Current Problem Information.   Because an expert system is based on programming techniques derived from AI, it is designed to deal with changing conditions in the problem situation it was designed to help. To handle these changing conditions, data about the current situation are collected from the user and entered into computer memory to help guide the expert system to a solution. For example, an expert system designed to help an undergraduate select courses for the current semester might ask the student the following questions:

> What is your major?
> What courses have you completed?
> Do you have a job that prevents you from taking classes at certain times?
> When do you expect to graduate?
> Do you plan to take summer school courses?

The questions asked by the expert system through the *user interface* assemble information that may change with each individual situation. The answers to these questions are integrated within an existing knowledge base of information (facts and rules) that remains relatively stable.

User Interface.   The user interface is built by the expert system designer (also known as a knowledge engineer) to facilitate the program's communication with the user. This communication process gathers current problem data from the user, explains the expert's reasoning, and presents the solution or advice for the problem being solved. The user interface gathers information from the user through questions and answers that define the conditions that will be evaluated by the rules in the knowledge base (discussed next). The interface also provides explanations about the questions being asked and the decisions being made. Typically, the interface allows users to ask why they were asked for information or why the program made a particular decision, and the expert system will retrieve that information from the knowledge base and display it for the user.

Finally, the *inference engine* evaluates all of the available information and presents its solution to the user through the interface. As in other computer programs, the interface is a critical feature. The program must carry on a dialogue with the user, so the nature of the dialogue, as well as the format of the presentation, must be developed and tested carefully to ensure easy input of the information sought.

Knowledge Base.   Information placed in the knowledge base (analogous to long-term memory) is relatively stable. It is composed of facts about objects and rules about the relationships among those objects that represent knowledge structures used by a human expert to reach a decision. Facts simply state given conditions (e.g., Calculus 1 is offered at 8 A.M., 10 A.M., and 2 P.M. on Monday, Wednesday, and Friday), and rules consist of conditions and decisions. That is, rules state that IF a set of conditions exists, THEN some decision is reached. Conditions can be combined in a number of ways into sets. Sets of IF conditions can be combined using conjunctions (condition 1 AND condition 2 must exist), disjunctions (condition 1 OR condition 2 must exist), and negations (condition 1 but NOT condition 2 must exist) in order for a decision to be reached. A decision may be an action or it may state another condition, which is then combined with other conditions to reach another decision. In the previous situation, the knowledge base would have stored lists of required courses for every major, as exemplified by the following rules:

IF student's major is mechanical engineering, THEN Differential Equations is required.
IF student's major is mechanical engineering OR student's major is electrical engineering, THEN Calculus 2 is required.
IF Differential Equations is NOT taken AND Calculus 2 is complete AND Differential Equations is offered at a time student is available, THEN advise student to sign up for Differential Equations.

Variables may be used to carry current problem information or to carry a preliminary decision value on through the process. The knowledge base also may contain explanations for why questions are being asked and why certain rules are activated, that is, why certain decisions are reached.

Expert Editor.   Most expert system programs provide an editor that enables the expert or the knowledge engineer to enter information into the knowledge base. Editors consist of text editors and parsers. The text editor allows the engineer to input facts and rules into the knowledge base in a prespecified format. The parser will check the syntax of the information that is input, as well as the validity or logic of the information that is entered. For example, the parser will usually decide if the rules are consistent and mutually exclusive or whether any redundancy exists.

Inference Engine. The inference engine is the part of an expert system that functions intelligently while querying the knowledge base. This component is not usually accessible to an expert system designer; instead, it is built into the system that the designer uses. It is constructed of AI programming techniques that act on the knowledge base and current problem data to generate solutions. In an expert system, the inference engine does its work when the user poses a specific problem and enters current problem information. The inference engine contains the logical programming to examine the information provided by the user, as well as the facts and rules specified within the knowledge base. It evaluates the current problem situation and then seeks rules that will provide advice about that situation.

Inference engines are usually of two types: *backward chaining* and *forward chaining.* The backward-chaining engine (goal-driven model) starts with a solution or decision and then searches the knowledge base for rules containing the conditions necessary to fulfill that solution. If sufficient conditions are not found, it asks the user to supply information or searches the knowledge base for subgoals that contribute to the solution. The forward-chaining engine (data-driven model) starts by trying to match existing data with a condition or conditions stated in the rules and examines the knowledge base to see if a solution is viable with only that information. It successively acquires information in an effort to be able to make a decision.

Solution/Advice. The final feature of an expert system is its presentation of a solution generated by the inference engine based on the permanent knowledge base and current problem information. The student advisor example considers all of the data entered by the student, relates those data to the rules in the knowledge base, and presents a solution, such as the following:

Recommend Calculus 1, Section 2, 10–11, MWF

HOW ARE EXPERT SYSTEMS USED AS MINDTOOLS?

Expert systems have primarily been used in business to control manufacturing processes and assist people with decision making. However, there are also many applications of expert systems in education. Jonassen, Wilson, Wang, and Grabinger (1993) described a range of uses of expert system shells, including providing advice on demand, expert and student models for intelligent tutoring systems, structuring and guiding personal feedback, simulating cognitive processing, and engaging critical thinking as Mindtools.

A good deal of research has focused on developing expert systems to provide advice to help educators or psychologists clinically diagnose students with learning disabilities or other special needs. They have also been used to model experts' and students' thinking in intelligent tutoring systems. Expert system advisors have also been developed to guide novices through the instructional development process (Tennyson & Christensen, 1991) and to assist students in selecting the correct statistical test (Karake, 1990; Saleem & Azad, 1992). In all of these applications, the user assumes a passive role when consulting the expert system in order to receive advice.

Expert systems can also function as computer-based cognitive amplification tools (see Figure 6.1), that is, as Mindtools. Trollip, Lippert, Starfield, and Smith (1992) believe that the development of expert systems results in deep understanding because they provide an intellectual environment that demands the refinement of domain knowledge, supports problem solving, and monitors the acquisition of knowledge.

Building expert systems is a knowledge modeling process that enables experts and knowledge engineers to construct conceptual models (Adams-Webber, 1995). This requires identifying declarative knowledge (facts and concepts), structural knowledge (knowledge of interrelationships among ideas), and procedural knowledge (how to apply declarative knowledge) that an expert (or at least a knowledgeable person) possesses. The expert system is one of the few formalisms for depicting procedural knowledge. Psychologists usually represent procedural knowledge as a series of IF–THEN rules (Gagné, 1985), just as in expert systems. As learners identify the IF–THEN structure of a domain, they tend to understand the nature of decision-making tasks better, so this deeper understanding should make subsequent practice opportunities more meaningful. This is not to suggest that the mere development of an expert system necessarily leads learners to acquire the compiled procedural knowledge of a domain. For example, a student project may correctly identify many of the IF–THEN rules involved in flying an airplane, but actually acquiring the procedural expertise would require extended practice opportunities in realistic performance settings.

Trollip et al. (1992) believe that learning environments, whether computer based or not, should provide a mechanism for helping learners monitor their own knowledge growth. This involves metacognitive awareness of their knowledge, which is a necessary component of problem solving (Flavell & Wellman, 1977). Clearly, building expert systems requires learners to synthesize knowledge by making explicit their own reasoning, thereby improving retention, transfer, and problem-solving ability. While all of this sounds complex and beyond the grasp of most school-age students, experience has indicated otherwise. Using a simple shell, most students are able to begin building simple rule bases within an hour.

The use of expert systems as Mindtools is relatively new and unresearched. Lippert (1987) found that the analysis of subject matter that is required to develop expert systems is so deep and so incisive that learners develop a greater comprehension of the subject matter. Building expert system rule bases engages learners in analytical reasoning, elaboration strategies such as synthesis, and metacognitive strategies. Among the early advocates of expert systems as Mindtools, Lippert (1988) argued that having students construct small knowledge bases is a valuable method for teaching problem solving and knowledge structuring for students from sixth grade to adults. Learning is more meaningful because learners evaluate not only their own thinking processes but also the product of those processes, the resulting knowledge base. Developing the knowledge base requires learners to isolate facts, variables, and rules about the relationships in a domain.

Expert system shells may be used in at least three different ways to engage learners in critical thinking: providing advice and feedback, engaging meta-reasoning, and providing a medium for constructing cognitive simulations.

Advice and Feedback

As I pointed out before, the primary use of expert systems is to provide intelligent advice to novices when requested. For this application, knowledge engineers work with subject matter experts to record their expertise about a knowledge domain. Users then query the knowledge base in order to get help in making a decision. For instance, a novice teacher might query a knowledge base to help make a diagnosis about the nature of a student's problems. The expert system would ask questions of the teacher about the student. Based on the information provided by the teacher and the knowledge that was programmed into the expert system, it will provide a recommended classification and course of treatment. In this application, users are relying on the intelligence of the program to help them make decisions. Consulting an expert system knowledge base does not necessarily engage users as deeply as building a knowledge base that reflects their own thinking. Querying a knowledge base to help solve a problem primarily involves comprehension of the problem and its factors and application of some predetermined rules for solving it. The program is replacing the knowledge and abilities that the user does not possess.

An important issue in expert system use is that of how much knowledge and intelligence users can gain from repeatedly using expert systems in this way. Surprisingly little research has been reported about this issue. Students who used an expert system to select the most appropriate statistical analysis procedure were more accurate in their selections and also retained the information better than students who used traditional computer-assisted instruction (Marcoulides, 1988). In another study, students who followed expert systems queries for deducing research hypotheses learned to break the task into small steps, helping them to better understand the process. If the expert system questions model the kind of thinking that users need to learn, and they practice that sequence consistently, how much will they learn about the process? Is it enough to follow questions in order to make decisions?

Negative consequences can result from relying on the expertise of expert systems. When using expert systems to resolve chemical spill scenarios, operators tended to overestimate their performance capabilities when using the expert system (Su & Lin, 1998). Such overconfidence could prove to be very dangerous if the operators were required to solve problems in real time without the use of the expert system.

What are the limitations of expert system use for learning? We do not know. Some promising results may help to extend the limits. Grabinger and Pollock (1989) used expert systems to guide students through a self-evaluation of their own projects. This form of feedback was as effective at enhancing learning as instructor-provided feedback. It is possible that using expert systems as a feedback method may be more useful than using expert systems to walk learners through required decision-making sequences. More research is needed before we will know.

Meta-Reasoning: Modeling Others' Reasoning

The preferred use of expert systems, from the perspective of this book, is to have learners create their own expert systems. *Building* an expert system knowledge base necessarily involves deeper thinking than when *using* an expert system. Expert system builders must analyze a knowledge domain and synthesize rules and rule sequences that knowledgeable performers use to make decisions. That is, the goal of meta-reasoning expert systems is to attempt to simulate the way in which experts think. To do so, learners must identify and analyze outcomes, factors, and values that experts use when solving problems. Restructuring that information into IF–THEN rules requires builders to synthesize that knowledge into a form that models causal reasoning. Anyone who has attempted to build even a simple rule base realizes how engaging this process is. The research on the effects of this application of expert systems is consistent.

- Lai (1989) found that when nursing students developed medical expert systems to perform diagnoses, they developed enhanced reasoning skills and acquired a deeper understanding of the subject domain.
- Six first-year physics students who used an expert system to create questions, decisions, rules, and explanations pertaining to classical projectile motion developed more refined, domain-specific knowledge due to greater degrees of elaboration during encoding and greater quantity of material processed in an explicit, coherent context, and therefore in greater semantic depth (Lippert & Finley, 1988).
- High school students with hearing impairments who constructed rule bases in current events and geographical continents learned significant amounts of content and spontaneously used categorization and conditional reasoning while building the expert systems (Wilson, 1997).
- Lippert (1988) described physics students' development of rule bases to solve problems about forces. Students identified factors such as kind of force acting on an object (gravitational, centripetal, etc.), motion of the object (free fall, circular, sliding, etc.), velocity of the object, and so on. The decisions that students

reached included the laws that affect the motion, the formulas that should be applied, and so on. Students reported meaningful learning from evaluating their own thought processes, more enthusiasm for learning, and the learning of content that they were not expected to master.

■ Knox-Quinn (1992) reported that MBA students who developed knowledge bases on tax laws in an accounting course were consistently engaged in higher order thinking, such as classifying information, breaking down content, organizing information, and integrating and elaborating information. All of the students who developed rule bases showed substantial gains in the quantity and quality of declarative and procedural knowledge and improved their problem-solving strategies. Students who built expert systems reasoned more similarly to experts.

The following examples of expert systems as Mindtools represent very divergent goals in very divergent curricula. The first knowledge base (Figure 6.3) was developed by a student using a simple shell called PC Expert (Starfield, Smith, & Bleloch, 1990). It attempts to represent the reasoning that Truman may have used in deciding whether or not to drop an atomic bomb on Hiroshima. Although the content is gruesome and many factors were not considered, it describes a deeper reflection on historical events than the typical memorization of names, dates, and places. In this kind of rule base, the decisions are usually stated first. This requires that the designers identify the goals before clarifying any of the decision factors. Next the designer identifies the decision factors in the form of questions that will be asked of the user. This is the essence of the design process. Writing questions that are simple enough for any novice user to be able to answer is difficult. With this expert system shell, the designer next writes the rules, using IF–THEN (Boolean) logic to relate the decisions to the decision factors or questions. This rule base consists of 20 rules that comprise the heart of the knowledge base. For example, the first rule states that IF the answer to question 1 is yes AND the answer to question 2 is also yes AND the answer to question 5 is also yes, THEN the atomic bomb should be used as quickly as possible, primarily on military targets. The remainder of the rules specify alternative conditions that may have existed at that time.

The next set of rules is selected from a knowledge base developed by students in a home economics class for advising classmates or the public on how to order from a fast-food menu (Figure 6.4). It was developed using a shell called McSmarts, which uses a different syntax from the previous rule base. In each rule, the advice is presented first, followed by the conditions that will lead to that advice.

The next example of student-produced expert systems, shown in Figure 6.5, is excerpted from a knowledge base on predicting severe weather in a meteorology class. Only the decisions and factors are shown here because there are too many rules to display.

These rule bases are simple examples of how students can think about the causal relationships in content they are studying. When students become expert system designers, they have to become the authorities (a role reversal that they enjoy), and this engages deeper thinking about the subject.

Decision 1: 'Atomic fission should only be used for peaceful purposes.'
Decision 2: 'The atomic bomb should be used as quickly as possible, primarily on military targets.'
Decision 3: 'Only knowledge of the weapon's existence should be used as a threat to induce Japan to surrender.'
Decision 4: 'The atomic bomb should not be used, but research should be made known after the war ends.'

Question 1: 'Do you want to encourage the Japanese to surrender as quickly as possible?'
Answers   1 'Yes'
  2 'No.'

Question 2: 'Do you want to limit the loss of Allied and Japanese lives?'
Answers   1 'Yes'
  2 'No.'

Question 3: 'Do you want to use the weapon against the Germans?'
Answers   1 'Yes'
  2 'No'
  3 'Unsure.'

Question 4: 'Do you want to use the atomic fission research ONLY to create alternate sources of energy?'
Answers   1 'Yes'
  2 'No'
  3 'Unsure.'

Question 5: 'Do you want to increase the political power of the Allies during and after the war?'
Answers   1 'Yes'
  2 'No'
  3 'Unsure.'

Question 6: 'Do you believe the Japanese will surrender with continued conventional bombing of Japanese cities?'
Answers   1 'Yes'
  2 'No'
  3 'Unsure.'

Question 7: 'Was the Manhattan Project (development of atomic fission) initially begun primarily for future military use?'
Answers   1 'Yes'
  2 'No'
  3 'Unsure.'

Question 8: 'Do you want to end the Japanese march through Asia?'
Answers   1 'Yes'
  2 'No'
  3 'Unsure.'

Question 9: 'Do you want to use atomic fission as only a psychological weapon?'
Answers   1 'Yes'
  2 'No'
  3 'Unsure.'

Question 10: 'How much longer should the war continue (from Spring 1945)?'
Answers   1 '3 months'
  2 '6 months'
  3 '1 year'
  4 'indefinitely.'

Figure 6.3
Expert System Rule Base for Hiroshima Scenario

Rule 1:
IF Question1=Answer1 & Question2=Answer1 & Question5=Answer1 THEN Decision2.
Rule 2:
IF Question3=Answer2 THEN Decision4.
Rule 3:
IF Question4=Answer1 THEN Decision3.
Rule 4:
IF Question4=Answer2 THEN Decision2.
Rule 5:
IF Question5=Answer1 & Question6=Answer2 THEN Decision2.
Rule 6:
IF Question6=Answer1 THEN Decision4.
Rule 7:
IF Question6=Answer2 & Question1=Answer1 & Question8=Answer1 THEN Decision2.
Rule 8:
IF Question6=Answer3 THEN Decision3.
Rule 9:
IF Question7=Answer1 & Question1=Answer1 THEN Decision2.
Rule 10:
IF Question7=Answer2 THEN Decision1.
Rule 11:
IF Question7=Answer3 THEN Decision4.
Rule 12:
IF Question8=Answer1 & Question6=Answer2 & Question1=Answer1 THEN Decision2.
Rule 13:
IF Question8=Answer2 THEN Decision3.
Rule 14:
IF Question9=Answer1 THEN Decision3.
Rule 15:
IF Question9=Answer2 & Question8=Answer1 & Question7=Answer1 &
Question1=Answer1 THEN Decision2.
Rule 16:
IF Question4=Answer1 & Question5=Answer1 & Question7=Answer3 THEN Decision4.
Rule 17:
IF Question10=Answer1 & Question2=Answer1 & Question6=Answer3 THEN Decision2.
Rule 18:
IF Question10=Answer2 & Question3=Answer1 & Question5=Answer1 THEN Decision2.
Rule 19:
IF Question10=Answer3 & Question6=Answer1 & Question8=Answer3 THEN Decision4.
Rule 20:
IF Question10=Answer4 & Question4=Answer1 & Question6=Answer3 THEN Decision4.

Figure 6.3
Continued

2 Eat: Chunky chicken salad, diet soft drink, and low-fat yogurt cone
  IF YES: Question 1 Do you want a balanced, nutritious meal? (Meal will represent all of the basic four food groups)
  IF YES: Question 2 Do you desire a low-fat meal? (<30% calories come from fat)
  IF YES: Question 3 Do you desire a low-cholesterol meal? (>84 mg)
  IF YES: Question 4 Do you desire a low-carbohydrate (sugar and starch) meal? (<30% calories come from carbohydrates)
  IF NO: Question 5 Do you desire a low-salt meal? (<650 mg)

6 Eat: Chunky chicken salad and 2% milk
  IF YES: Question 1 Do you want a balanced, nutritious meal? (Meal will represent all of the basic four food groups.)
  IF YES: Question 2 Do you desire a low-fat meal? (<30% calories come from fat)
  IF NO: Question 3 Do you desire a low-cholesterol meal? (>84 mg)
  IF YES: Question 4 Do you desire a low-carbohydrate (sugar and starch) meal? (<30% calories come from carbohydrates)
  IF NO: Question 5 Do you desire a low-salt meal? (<650 mg)

9 Eat: Garden salad and a diet drink
  IF YES: Question 1 Do you want a balanced, nutritious meal? (Meal will represent all of the basic four food groups.)
  IF NO: Question 2 Do you desire a low-fat meal? (<30% calories come from fat)
  IF YES: Question 3 Do you desire a low-cholesterol meal? (>84 mg)
  IF YES: Question 4 Do you desire a low-carbohydrate (sugar and starch) meal? (<30% calories come from carbohydrates)
  IF YES: Question 5 Do you desire a low-salt meal? (<650 mg)

12 Eat: Hamburger, sm. fries, and dairy drink OR 6ct. McNuggets, sm. fries, and van. shake OR Filet-o-fish, sm. fries, and van. shake
  IF YES: Question 1 Do you want a balanced, nutritious meal? (Meal will represent all of the basic four food groups.)
  IF NO: Question 2 Do you desire a low-fat meal? (<30% calories come from fat)
  IF YES: Question 3 Do you desire a low-cholesterol meal? (>84 mg)
  IF NO: Question 4 Do you desire a low-carbohydrate (sugar and starch) meal? (<30% calories come from carbohydrates)
  IF NO: Question 5 Do you desire a low-salt meal? (<650 mg)

14 Eat: McDLT and diet soft drink OR 6ct. McNuggets, side salad, and 2% milk OR Chunky chicken salad and 2% milk
  IF YES: Question 1 Do you want a balanced, nutritious meal? (Meal will represent all of the basic four food groups.)
  IF NO: Question 2 Do you desire a low-fat meal? (<30% calories come from fat)
  IF NO: Question 3 Do you desire a low-cholesterol meal? (>84 mg)
  IF YES: Question 4 Do you desire a low-carbohydrate (sugar and starch) meal? (<30% calories come from carbohydrates)
  IF NO: Question 5 Do you desire a low-salt meal? (<650 mg)

17 Eat: Any food menu item of your choice
  IF NO: Question 1 Do you want a balanced, nutritious meal? (Meal will represent all of the basic four food groups.)

Figure 6.4
Selected Rules from an Expert System on Dietary Recommendations

---

SEVERE WEATHER PREDICTOR

This module is designed to assist the severe local storms forecaster in assessing the potential for severe weather using soundings. The program will ask for measures of instability and wind shear, as well as other variables important in the formation of severe weather. Instability and wind shear parameters are easily calculated using programs such as SHARP, RAOB, and GEMPAK. The other variables can be found on surface and upper-air charts.

ADVICE

The following output indicates the potential for severe weather in the environment represented by the sounding you used. A number between 1 and 10 indicates the confidence of the guidance. A higher number indicates a greater confidence

Severe Weather (Tornadoes, Hail, and/or Straightline Winds)
Severe Weather Possible
Severe Weather Not Likely
Severe Weather Likely
Severe Weather Potential

QUESTIONS (Decision Factors)

What is the value of CAPE (J/kg)? < -6, -2 to -6, 0 to -2, > 0
What is the Lifted Index (LI) value (C)? 0, 0-25, 25-75, > 75
What is the Convective Inhibition (CIN) (J/kg)? 0, 1-3, > 3
What is the Lid Strength Index (LSI) (C)? > 450, 250-449, 150-249, 0-150, <150, < 0
What is the value of storm-relative helicity? > 6, 4-6, 2-4, < 2
What is the value of 0-6 km Positive Shear (s-1)?
What is the value of storm-relative helicity (m^2 s^{-1})?, Left Entrance, Right Entrance, Left Exit, Right Exit, None
Which quadrant of the jet streak is the area of interest in? Cold Front, Dryline, Convergence Zone, Outflow Boundary, Nothing Significant
Is there likely to be a significant trigger mechanism? Yes, No

---

Figure 6.5
Advice and Factors from an Expert System Predicting Severe Weather

Cognitive Simulations: Simulating Your Own Thinking

In a class that I taught some years ago, we were studying metacognitive decision making that learners use. After studying many papers and chapters, we all knew what metacognition was but still did not fully understand how people came to use metacognitive strategies. So, Jonassen, Dallman, Wang, and Hamilton (1991) experimented with having the class develop an expert system to simulate that reasoning process. The purpose of the project was to model how learners employ metacognitive reasoning when learning in a defined context, specifically the seminar itself. So, we reflected on the processes that we all used to study for the course.

The procedure for building this rule-based cognitive simulation included identifying the range of learning strategies that can be used by learners (the outcomes). These include information-processing strategies such as recall, organizing, integration, and elaboration strategies. The factors or variables that are needed to represent metacognitive decision making were identified next. Based on this analysis, the cognitive simulation began as two rule bases: an executive control base and a comprehension monitoring rule base. We used a commercial expert system shell, VP-Expert, to enter, debug, and refine the rule bases. The development process was highly iterative, involving extensive discussions and very intense self-reflections about our own methods. Development of the rule bases indicated the need for several overlapping or redundant factors, so we eventually combined the two rule bases into one. The merged rule base modeled the initial phases of engaging metacognitive processes, most of which normally take place before studying begins. Crucial elements of metacognition identified through the rule base construction (see Figure 6.6) included the identification of the depth of processing required by the subject matter, taking into account learner characteristics (prior knowledge, preferred learning style, etc.) and task variables (level of mastery required, difficulty of the material, time available, etc.). Another integral component included the kinds of support strategies that would facilitate maximum efficiency in studying. This included exploring issues such as comfort of the studying environment, the learner's energy level, attitude toward the task, and perceived self-efficacy. After eliciting this information from a user, the expert system describes the results—a set of study, metacognitive, and support strategies that would best facilitate the learning outcomes desired. This description represented a simulation of the thought processes that we believed (based on reading, understanding, research, and a whole lot of self-reflection) learners think about when studying for a seminar. It is inevitable that different groups of developers would generate different outcomes, factors, and rules, given the same task. When constructing simulations, there is no single right answer. It would be very instructive to contrast the knowledge bases produced by different groups, given the same topic.

The process of a system of rules is very complex. We originally began with 6 primary factors, which later grew to more than 20 in order to represent the complexity of the personal decision-making process. Because the personal processes of each participant in the knowledge base construction process was represented in the discussions, many different perspectives had to be accommodated in the rule base. Initially, we intended to build an abstract model of metacognitive reasoning that could represent metacognition in different contexts. It became obvious that such a goal was not only impossible but also meaningless, because metacognition could only be thought of in the context of a particular learning need.

The results of this process of using an expert system to represent thinking processes were varied. Only half of the members of the seminar participated in the construction of the cognitive simulation. Subsequent classroom discussions about the topic were documented. Students' comments were logged and later classified. The students who participated in constructing the cognitive simulation made significantly more contributions to the seminar discussion. Those contributions were more

ASK Purpose:"Why am I studying this material?"
    Assigned = Material was assigned by professor.
    Related = Material is useful to related research or studies.
    Personal = Material is of personal interest.
ASK Depth: "How well do I need to know this material?"
    Gist = I just need to comprehend the main ideas.
    Discuss = We will discuss and interrelate the issues.
    Evaluate = I have to judge the importance or accuracy of these ideas.
    Generate = I have to think up issues, new ideas, hypotheses about the material.
ASK Reading: "How fast a reader am I?"
    CHOICES: slow, normal, fast.
ASK Hours: "How many hours do I have to study?"
    None = Less than an hour.
    Few = 1–3 hours.
    Several = 4–8 hours.
ASK Days: "How many days until class?"
    CHOICES Days: more_than_7, 2_to_6, less_than_2.
ASK Comparison: "How do I compare with the other students in the class?"
    Superior = I think that I am better able than my classmates to comprehend the material.
    Equal = I am equivalent to the rest of the class in ability.
    Worse = I am not as knowledgeable or intelligent as the rest of the class.
ASK Instructor: "What intellectual orientation does the instructor have?"
    Theoretical = The professor likes to focus on theoretical issues and comparisons.
    Applied = The professor is interested in applications and implications for practice.
    Argument = The professor likes to argue about the ideas.
ASK Topic: Can I identify important terms or major issues related to this topic?"
    CHOICES: yes, no.
ASK Previous: "Have I studied this topic before?"
    CHOICES: yes, no.
ASK Author: "Have I previously read articles, reports, or books by the listed author(s)?"
    CHOICES: yes, no.
ASK Context: "Do I have a useful context (information need or situation in which I can apply this topic) for assimilating this content?"
    CHOICES: yes, no, do_not_know.
ASK STSupport: "Have I set short term goals for this study session?"
    CHOICES: yes, no.
Ask LTSupport: "Have I set long term goals for all of the study sessions until the class?"
    CHOICES LTSupport: yes, no.
Ask ConcenStrat: "Am I feeling relaxed and confident that I can study effectively?"
    CHOICES ConcenStrat: yes, no.
Ask Tension: "Am I feeling overly tense or anxious about studying?"
    CHOICES: yes, no.
Ask NegSelf: "Am I engaging in negative self-talk about this study session or the course?"
    CHOICES: yes, no.
Ask SelfEff: "Do I feel confident that I can master the material?"
    CHOICES: yes, no.

Figure 6.6
Selected Factors Used in a Simulation of Metacognitive Reasoning

assertive and argumentative than those of students who did not participate in the simulation, indicating a deeper level of understanding of the issues being studied. The students who participated in the simulation construction had stronger opinions about the material.

A few people have experimented with constructing cognitive simulations.

■ Kersten, Badcock, Iglewski, and Mallory (1990) demonstrated the use of rule-based expert systems for simulating how negotiations progress.
■ Law (1994) had high school students use expert systems to simulate common sense reasoning.

Having students reflect on their own thinking is the essence of metacognition. Expert systems provide a powerful formalism for thinking about and simulating how we think.

Related Mindtools

As indicated in Chapter 4, building semantic networks is sometimes used as a process for identifying the ideas that will go into an expert system knowledge base. This is a process known in the AI literature as knowledge elicitation. Identifying the issues and their relationships is important to expert system construction.

Another related Mindtool is the database management system. As will be described in the next section, some expert system shells are able to induce rules from a database, so an easy approach to building expert system rule bases is to create a database of instances and let the program generate the rules. This approach limits the kind of logic that can be used, but it is valuable for demonstrating the interrelated nature of Mindtools.

Expert systems may complement simulation modeling tools (Chapter 7). While expert systems use IF–THEN reasoning to represent meaning, simulation modeling tools show the relationships of variables on others mathematically.

Coaching the Construction of Expert Systems in the Classroom

Expert system rule bases are reflective tools that can be used in a variety of classroom situations. Imagine that you have just completed a science lab. As a way of reviewing what was learned, have the students construct a rule base that reflects the decisions they had to make in order to complete the lab. In social studies, have students create a rule base that will predict who will win an election, or whether a health care reform bill will pass through Congress, and why. For any content that you ask your students to remember and think about, expert systems require you to consider how you could have them use that information to predict outcomes, explain results, or infer reasoning. This probably will represent a new way of thinking that will have to be modeled for students.

1. **Students *make* a plan.** Before beginning, students need to make a plan for their expert systems. What are they interested in representing? What points do they want to make? What kinds of structure and information are required to make those points? What learning goals will they work toward?

2. ***Identify* the purpose for building the expert system and the problem domain.** This will determine the overall approach students take in seeking information to fill in the knowledge base. If your goal is to understand students' current mental models, then they will do very little outside research to create the knowledge base (Knox-Quinn, 1988). However, if your goal is student mastery and problem solving of new content, then research may be very integral to the process. This decision will depend, to a large degree, on students' current level of knowledge about the subject domain.

Regardless of learners' age or amount of prior subject knowledge, it will be necessary to help them develop the skills needed for constructing expert systems. Getting them to understand the IF–THEN logic of rules and the syntax of even simple expert system shells is not easy, so it is desirable to start with familiar content. Have students develop rule bases on which fast-food restaurant to eat in, what kind of person to ask out on a date, or which popular music groups are best. They will be surprised by how much they know, how much they don't know, and how difficult it is to articulate what they do know.

3. ***Specify* problem solutions or decisions.** Once students have determined the problem domain, they work to identify the solutions, decisions, or outcomes the expert system is expected to provide. In the atomic bomb example (see Figure 6.3), there are only four decisions (threaten to drop the bomb, drop the bomb, don't drop the bomb, and a general statement of advice about using fission for peaceful purposes). Decisions are not necessarily mutually exclusive; that is, you may want to provide more than one recommendation to the same individual.

There are several reasons for beginning with the solutions or decisions. Most problems suitable for implementation in an expert system have many alternative solutions, so the first part of the goal-identification stage involves generating all possible solutions *within the defined problem area.* "All possible solutions" refers to all those you can think of. It is important that you not make judgments about the feasibility or value of each solution (brainstorming can help here). It is critical that you identify as many alternative solutions as possible so that none are overlooked.

Having identified all possible solutions, you may want to limit the options, because in most cases it is neither practical nor necessary to deal with each one. You can identify the most probable solutions or develop classes of solutions that have common attributes. For example, you could decide to reject any goal with less than a 25% likelihood of happening. You have to decide how important any particular solution is and whether it is worth including in the knowledge base.

4. ***Isolate* problem attributes, factors, or variables.** The *problem attributes* provide the set of factors an expert considers when making a decision. They are decision points used during the problem-solving process to determine the most appropriate solution. The expert gathers and analyzes information and then decides

what other information is needed in order to solve the problem. Each decision point adopts a value that is called an *attribute value*. In other words, each problem attribute used in an expert system must have at least two alternatives or options to help direct the process to a solution. For example, in the student scheduling advisor described earlier, the goal was to schedule each student into appropriate classes. The problem attributes in this case are the required courses for the student's curriculum, courses completed, available times, etc. Problem attributes, then, are those arguments used by an expert when arriving at a decision (you need this course; it is available at 8:00, so take it).

The three major steps to identifying the primary problem attributes used in an expert system are (1) identify the problem factors or attributes used when making the decision (the questions that will be asked by the expert system), (2) separate the critical problem attributes from the trivial attributes, and (3) assign the significant values for each attribute (i.e., the answers to the questions).

5. **Generate rules and examples.** Rules represent the knowledge or expertise in an expert system. They are used to arrive at a decision. For example, "IF the consumer makes $1,200 per month and has a job and has a good credit rating and is over 24, THEN a loan of $10,000 is permitted." Rules are a series of IF–THEN statements that describe the means of reaching a specific decision in narrative form. They set forth the conditional relationships among the problem attribute values.

Rules consist of two essential elements: the premise (antecedent) and the conclusion (consequent). The premise begins with the word *if* and states the conditions that are compared with the situation or the desires of the user. Conditions are combined logically using the logical operators *and* and *or.* If conditions are connected by *and,* both conditions must be met in order for the rule to be true. If the conditions are connected by *or,* one or both conditions must be true in order for the rule to be true. Conclusions are signaled by the word *then.*

Rules in expert systems vary in complexity and certainty (confidence levels). Rule complexity refers to the number of premises that must be satisfied before reaching a decision for solving the problem. The number of antecedents may vary, as well as the number of consequents. For example, a rule that must meet only one condition is simple, such as

IF the subject in a picture is more than 40 yards away
THEN use a 400-millimeter lens.

The only condition in that rule is the subject's distance from the camera. A rule that meets more than one condition or a rule that contains alternative solutions is complex, such as

IF the purpose of the car is commuting
AND IF number of commuters is less than 4
AND IF distance to work is greater than 25 miles
OR IF more than one return trip per day is made
THEN buy a 2-door sedan
ELSE take the bus.

The conditions or attributes in this rule for helping consumers to select an appropriate car to buy include the purpose of use, number of commuters using the car, distance to work, and number of trips per day. Given a particular combination of these conditions, the alternative solutions include either buying a two-door sedan or taking the bus. You will probably want to use complex rules with a number of conditions and alternatives. A few simple rules do not warrant the development time involved in creating an expert system, nor will they be able to provide advice on any significant problem.

6. *Refine* logic and efficiency of decision making. To make construction of the rule base easier, you may want to generate interim decisions and use those as factors rather than writing very complex rules with eight or more factors. For example, in the car selection example you may want to make an interim decision about the size of car (compact, midsize, luxury) and use section factors to first determine the size of the car needed:

IF the purpose of the car is commuting
AND IF number of commuters is less than 3
AND IF distance to work is greater than 25 miles
AND IF the roads are good
THEN size needed is compact.

This conclusion can then be combined with other factors to make the final decision:

IF size needed is compact
AND IF price must be below $8,000
AND IF status need is low
THEN buy a Yugo.

Interim decisions help the flow of knowledge base development by preventing long, complex rules. You can also collaborate with others by breaking the final decision up into a set of subdecisions and assigning the subdecisions to different groups.

7. *Test* the system. Although the purpose of a Mindtool knowledge base is not absolute fidelity of the knowledge base to real-world occurrences, it is useful to ensure that the system works. Have different people query the system and note any improper conclusions or sets of conditions that do not produce a conclusion. As the number of factors increases, the number of possible combinations of rules increases geometrically. Writing a rule for every possible combination of circumstances may not be feasible or even desirable. However, if users' queries lead to dead-ends, you should probably generate a rule for those combinations.

8. Students *reflect* on the activity. Reflection should not wait until the project is completed. Rather, students should continuously review their progress on the project. Are we achieving our goals? What changes are necessary? How do we compare with other groups? Are we answering questions and making the points that we set out in our plan? After the project is completed, the students should reflect on the

project. What have we learned about the content? What have we learned about expert systems and causal relationships among variables? What have we learned about working with each other? You may choose to provide students with some or all of the criteria for evaluating student expert systems (presented in the next section) to use for self-evaluation. The activity of constructing expert systems engages meaningful thinking. Reflection cements the knowledge that learners construct.

EVALUATING EXPERT SYSTEMS AS MINDTOOLS

Critical, Creative, and Complex Thinking in Expert System Construction and Use

Tables 6.1, 6.2, and 6.3 identify the critical, creative, and complex thinking skills that are required to consult an expert system rule base for advice or feedback, to design and construct a meta-reasoning rule base, and to design and construct a cognitive simulation. The skills in each table that are marked by an "X" are those that are employed by each process, based on an information-processing analysis of the tasks.

Clearly there are more critical, creative and complex thinking skills required to build a rule base than simply to consult one. Consulting a rule base requires only that the user senses a problem, realizes that she or he does not know enough to solve it, and responds to questions from the rule base in order to render a decision. This activity does not require many kinds of critical thinking. Therefore, I will concentrate on building expert system rule bases, which is an analytic process that engages nearly every kind of critical thinking (Table 6.1), creative thinking (Table 6.2), and complex thinking (Table 6.3). Building the rule base on the atomic bomb in Figure 6.3, for example, required assessing the information available, determining the criteria for using it, verifying the information, and, in particular, making inferences. Building rule bases probably requires learners to make more inferences than any other Mindtool. You should note that the critical thinking requirements of building meta-reasoning rule bases and cognitive simulations are nearly identical. The intellectual processes required for both are quite similar.

Under creative thinking skills, building rule bases engages a lot of hypothesizing, planning, predicting, and speculating about causal relations (see Table 6.2). Few creative thinking skills are required to consult an expert system.

Finally, nearly every type of complex thinking skill is required for designing knowledge bases. Designing and building knowledge bases requires the use of almost every kind of designing, problem-solving, and decision-making skill (see Table 6.3). Keeping the potential user in mind (imagining and formulating the goal) and then balancing the goals of the rule base against the factors and the rules requires students to research and formulate the problem, find alternatives, and choose a solution. Decision making is at the heart of expert systems, so identifying issues and alternatives, assessing them, and making choices are essential to con-

Table 6.1
Critical Thinking Skills Engaged by Expert System Construction and Use

	Guidance and feedback	Meta-reasoning	Cognitive simulations
Evaluating			
Assessing information	X	X	X
Determining criteria		X	X
Prioritizing		X	X
Recognizing fallacies		X	X
Verifying		X	X
Analyzing			
Recognizing patterns		X	X
Classifying	X	X	X
Identifying assumptions		X	X
Identifying main ideas	X	X	X
Finding sequences		X	X
Connecting			
Comparing/contrasting			X
Logical thinking		X	X
Inferring deductively		X	X
Inferring inductively	X		
Identifying causal relationships		X	X

Table 6.2
Creative Thinking Skills Engaged by Expert System Construction and Use

	Guidance and feedback	Meta-reasoning	Cognitive simulations
Elaborating			
Expanding			X
Modifying		X	X
Extending		X	X
Shifting categories		X	X
Concretizing	X		
Synthesizing			
Analogical thinking		X	X
Summarizing	X		
Hypothesizing		X	X
Planning		X	X
Imagining			
Fluency		X	X
Predicting	X	X	X
Speculating		X	X
Visualizing			
Intuition	X	X	X

Table 6.3
Complex Thinking Skills Engaged by Expert System Construction and Use

	Guidance and feedback	Meta-reasoning	Cognitive simulations
Designing			
Imagining a goal		X	X
Formulating a goal		X	X
Inventing a product		X	X
Assessing a product		X	X
Revising the product			
Problem Solving			
Sensing the problem	X	X	X
Researching the problem		X	X
Formulating the problem		X	X
Finding alternatives		X	X
Choosing the solution	X	X	X
Building acceptance			
Decision Making			
Identifying an issue		X	X
Generating alternatives		X	X
Assessing the consequences		X	X
Making a choice	X	X	X
Evaluating the choice		X	X

structing rule bases. Building a knowledge base is a complex process consisting of cycles of hypothesizing and testing.

Evaluating Student Expert Systems

What makes a meaningful expert system simulation? That depends on the kind of expert system that students are constructing and the age and abilities of the learners who are constructing it. As I will discuss later, learners younger than high school may have problems building expert systems. So you must consider the age and ability of your students. Figure 6.7 presents a number of rubrics that you may use to evaluate the expert systems that your students construct as their knowledge and skills move from emergent to mastery. You will probably want to adapt these or add your own criteria as you evaluate your students' projects.

Evaluating Expert System Software

Expert system rule bases are built using either a procedural language, such as BASIC, Pascal, or C; an AI-oriented language, such as Lisp or Prolog; or an expert system shell program. Building expert system knowledge bases in a language

---

Quality of decisions/solutions/advice

◄───►

Advice would never be
given (implausible); solutions
missing or not elaborated;
conclusions not useful

Advance is plausible; all solutions
identified; provide meaningful
solutions

Explanations meaningful

◄───►

Explanations of results are
vague; do not explain
reasoning or enhance learning

Explanations of advice explains
reasoning, enhances user's
understanding

Sensitivity of factors (questions)

◄───►

Factors don't discriminate
solutions; variables and factors
missing; factors overlap

Ask important questions; identify
all variables that pertain to solution;
each factor elicits different information

Rules logical and complete

◄───►

Running system results in
dead ends; combinations not
anticipated; not enough rules;
rules poorly organized

All combinations of factors
represented by a rule; all dead ends
blocked; rules well organized

Meaningful representation of thinking

◄───►

Poorly simulates thought;
poor models of activity;
represents associative thinking

Simulates coherent thinking; models
meaningful activity; represents causal/
predictive reasoning

Figure 6.7
Rubrics for Evaluating Student-Constructed Expert Systems

requires that the expert system builder understand the language and its syntax. Computer languages are complex to learn. Computer languages are often compiled, so knowledge bases constructed in them typically run faster than expert system shells can run them. This is not a problem with most small rule bases that are built as Mindtools, but large rule bases with hundreds or thousands of rules run more efficiently when composed in a computer language.

When using expert systems as Mindtools, everyone uses an expert system shell program, which typically consists of a knowledge input editor, an inference engine, and an output generator—all of the components necessary for building and running an expert system rule base. Be careful, though. Shells differ dramatically in capability. For example, some shells permit the builder to use only binary, yes–no options to questions. This would prevent the builder from asking a question such as "How full is the tank? Empty, Half Full, Full." This question would have to be rephrased as a series of binary questions, such as "Is the tank empty?" "Is the tank half full?" and "Is the tank full?" (yes or no to each). Such a limitation can be very restrictive.

A variety of expert system shells is available. For Windows computers, ACQUIRE from Acquired Intelligence, Knowledge Seeker from Angoss Software, GOLDWORKS from Gold Hill Computers, GURU from Micro Data Base Systems, Icarus, Level 5 from Information Builders, XpertRule from Attar Software, Personal Consultant from Texas Instruments, M4 from Techknowledge, and EXSYS are available. Other shells, such as NEXPERT and GURU cost several thousands of dollars, so they are not useful as Mindtools. A less expensive alternative is VP-Expert from Wordtech Systems. A number of shells are also available for the Macintosh, including Super Expert, Instant Expert, Expert Ease, and PowerSmarts. They vary in capability and price, ranging from a few dollars to hundreds or even thousands of dollars. PC Expert is probably the easiest to learn and most flexible freeware available. A web search will turn up many more options.

A shell may provide many other features besides the basic components of an expert system, such as the following.

Induction.   Many expert system shells are able to induce rules automatically from examples. To do this, the user creates a database (some shells provide for database construction; others read a variety of files created by database programs) of examples, with each of the factors designated by a field and each example consisting of a record. The shell reads these examples and creates rules automatically.

Chaining.   Some shells enable the inference engine to use a backward-chaining or forward-chaining sequence of rule firing when searching the knowledge base. These sequences will produce a different sequence of queries for the users, emphasizing different factors within the knowledge base.

Confidence Factors.   Confidence factors state a level of certainty in the rule decisions or in the input. The knowledge engineer designing the rule base can identify the degree of certainty in the THEN portion of the rule. For example, in the rule stated earlier, the conclusion is to buy a Yugo. The builder could state the conclusion, "THEN purchase = Yugo CNF = .40," indicating that the conclusion has a 40% chance of being correct. Many shells also allow the user to enter levels of confidence when answering queries from the inference engine. For example, if the program asked "What is the primary purpose for this car?," users could enter "commuting CNF = 70." This means either that the users are 70% certain of their answer or that they intend to use the car for commuting 70% of the time.

Explanatory Support.   Many shells enable linking decisions or questions to hypertext, graphics, or a web browser. That is, when a rule is fired, rather than merely presenting the solution in text, the program interfaces to authoring systems in order to produce elaborate explanations. Some shells also display graphics along with the text. For example, if the rule base were supporting identification of bacteria from microscopic displays, the program could display graphics and ask the user which most closely resembled what they were seeing in the microscope.

Advantages of Expert Systems as Mindtools

Advantages of expert systems include the following:

- More than other Mindtools, except for simulation modeling tools (Chapter 7), expert systems focus thinking on causal reasoning and problem-solving activities.
- Expert systems engage learners in metacognitive reasoning. Reflecting on and representing the thinking involved in problem solving provides valuable insights to learners.
- Expert systems emphasize inferential and implicational reasoning. Few activities in schools stress going beyond existing information to infer why something happened or to consider the implications of what might happen if a set of conditions exists. Building expert systems engages learners in this form of deeper level processing.
- Expert systems highlight the natural complexity that exists in most problem-solving situations. Becoming aware of how complex problems can really be is also enlightening.

Limitations of Expert Systems as Mindtools

In contrast, expert systems have these disadvantages:

- The process of building coherent knowledge bases requires novel thinking for many learners, so the work is difficult.
- Formal operational reasoning is probably required. Even though Lippert (1988) reports that expert systems may be used as Mindtools for children as young as sixth grade, my experience has shown that it may be very difficult for students who have not yet achieved formal operational reasoning. Wideman and Owston (1991) found that expert system development most benefited learners with higher abstract reasoning ability and that students with lower abstract reasoning ability were not affected as much or as capable. However, in an earlier study (Wideman & Owston, 1988), they found that while the task was complex, seventh graders built rule bases enthusiastically, even though it was necessary to use rigorous, systematic thinking and metacognitive skills. The ability of students to construct expert systems will depend on their intellectual development and motivation to perform.

SUMMARY

Expert system knowledge bases represent causal, procedural knowledge about content domains. They are especially effective in representing problem-solving tasks that require decision making. Expert systems represent inferential thinking about the implications of findings. Building expert system rule bases engages learners in reflective thinking about the dynamic, causal relationships among concepts in any knowledge domain. The thinking required to build expert systems may be the most difficult of any Mindtool because of the formal, logical reasoning. They are perhaps the most intellectually engaging and challenging of all of the Mindtools.

References

Adams-Webber, J. (1995). Constructivist psychology and knowledge elicitation. *Journal of Constructivist Psychology, 8*(3), 237–249.

Flavell, J. H., & Wellman, H. M. (1977). Metamemory. In R. V. Kail & J. W. Hagen (Eds.), *Perspectives on the development of memory and cognition.* Hillsdale, NJ: Lawrence Erlbaum Associates.

Gagné, E. (1985). *The cognitive psychology of school learning.* Boston: Little, Brown.

Goodall, A. (1985). *The guide to expert systems.* Oxford: Learned Information.

Grabinger, R. S., & Pollock, J. (1989). The effectiveness of internally-generated feedback with an instructional expert system. *Journal of Educational Computing Research, 5*(3), 299–309.

Jonassen, D. H., Dallman, B., Wang, S., & Hamilton, R. (1991, November). Modeling metacognitive skills in an expert system: A cognitive simulation. In *Proceedings of the 34th Annual Conference of the Association for the Development of Computer-based Instructional Systems.* Columbus, OH: ADCIS.

Jonassen, D. H., Wilson, B. G., Wang, S., & Grabinger, R. S. (1993). Constructivistic uses of expert systems to support learning. *Journal of Computer Based Instruction, 20*(3), 86–94.

Karake, Z. A. (1990). Enhancing the learning process with expert systems. *Computers and Education, 14*(6), 495–503.

Kersten, G. E., Badcock, L., Iglewski, M., & Mallory, G. R. (1990). Structuring and simulating negotiation: An approach and an example. *Theory & Decision, 28*(3), 243–273.

Knox-Quinn, C. (1988). A simple application and a powerful idea: Using expert systems shells in the classroom. *Computing Teacher, 16*(3), 12–15.

Knox-Quinn, C. (1992, April). *Student construction of expert systems in the classroom.* Paper presented at the annual meeting of the American Educational Research Association, San Francisco, CA.

Lai, K. W. (1989, March). *Acquiring expertise and cognitive skills in the process of constructing an expert system: A preliminary study.* Paper presented at the annual meeting of the American Educational Research Association, San Francisco, CA. (ERIC Document Reproduction Service No. ED 312986)

Law, N. (1994). Students as expert system developers: A means of eliciting and understanding common sense reasoning. *Journal of Research on Computing in Education, 26*(4), 497–513.

Lippert, R. (1987). Teaching problem solving in mathematics and science with expert systems. *School Science and Mathematics, 87,* 407–413.

Lippert, R. C. (1988). An expert system shell to teach problem solving. *Tech Trends, 33*(2), 22–26.

Lippert, R., & Finley, F. (1988, April). *Students' refinement of knowledge during the development of knowledge bases for expert systems.* Paper presented at the annual meeting of the National Association for Research in Science Teaching, Lake of the Ozarks, MO. (ERIC Document Reproduction Service No. ED 293872)

Marcoulides, G. A. (1988). An intelligent computer-based learning program. *Collegiate Microcomputer, 6*(2), 123–126.

Sacks, J.G. (1990). Teaching students by having them emulate an expert system. *Computers in Human Services, 7*(3/4), 307–325.

Saleem, N., & Azad, A. N. (1992). Expert systems as a statistics tutor on call. *Journal of Computers in Mathematics and Science Teaching, 11,* 179–191.

Starfield, A. M., Smith, K. A., & Bleloch, A. L. (1990). *How to model it: Problem solving for the computer age.* New York: McGraw-Hill.

Su, Y. L., & Lin, D. Y. (1998). The impact of expert-system-based training on calibration decisions confidence in emergency management. *Computers in Human Behavior, 14*(1), 81–194.

Tennyson, R. D., & Christensen, D. L. (1991). Automating instructional systems development. Proceedings of selected research presentations at the annual convention of the Association for Educational Communications and Technology. (ERIC Document Reproduction Service No. ED 335018)

Trollip, S., Lippert, R., Starfield, A., & Smith, K. A. (1992). Building knowledge bases: An environment for making cognitive connections. In P. Kommers, D. H. Jonassen, & T. Mayes (Eds.), *Cognitive tools for learning.* Heidelberg, Germany: Springer-Verlag.

Wideman, H. H., & Owston, R. D. (1988). Student development of an expert system: A case study. *Journal of Computer-Based Instruction, 15*(3), 88–94.

Wideman, H. H., & Owston, R. D. (1991, April). *Promoting cognitive development through knowledge base construction.* Paper presented at the annual meeting of the American Educational Research Association, New Orleans, LA.

Wilson, L.M. (1997). *The effects of student created expert systems on the reasoning and content learning of deaf students.* Unpublished doctoral dissertation, University of Minnesota.

CHAPTER 7

Systems Modeling as Mindtools

WHAT ARE SYSTEMS MODELING TOOLS?

Systems Thinking

The tools described in this chapter are based on systems dynamics theory (see Figure 7.1). Systems dynamics attempts to show the causal interrelatedness of components in systems. Systems are dynamic when their components are related to changes in other system components. The components of systems can be modeled using causal loops or feedback loops (see Figure 7.2), the normal parlance of systems dynamics. Causal loops are used to describe the influences of system components on each other. They do not assume that, for instance, hunger causes eating. Rather, hunger has a causal relationship to eating, which then feeds back to influence hunger. The influences of system components on each other can be positive or negative. Positive influences are those in which a directional change in one component causes a similar change in another. The relationships are reciprocal. Eating influences the habit of eating, which influences hunger, which influences eating. However, dynamic changes result from the interplay of factors, both positive and negative. Negative influences are regulatory. Eating influences fullness, which negatively influences (or regulates) hunger. A system in which positive factors and negative factors increase or decrease a factor equally is in balance. For instance, eating habit and fullness counterbalance each other. If these forces are equal, there will be no change in eating and therefore weight. When one force exerts a greater influence, eating and weight will rise or fall.

Causal loops provide a formalism for diagramming relationships in dynamic systems. However, causal loops have limitations when used to represent systems. They may specify relationships and specify predictions, but they do not describe the operations of the system and they lack quantitative information, so they cannot be used to simulate the systems they describe (Mandinach & Cline, 1994). An underlying assumption of the tools described in this chapter is that most systems can be

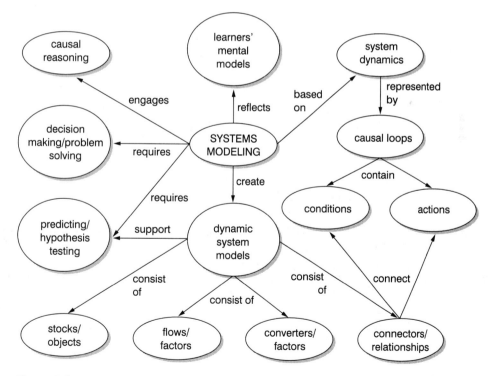

Figure 7.1
Systems Modeling as a Mindtool

Figure 7.2
Causal (Feedback) Loop Diagram

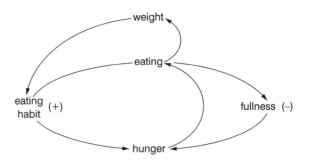

modeled by causal loops (Steed, 1992) but that those systems need more powerful tools to simulate them. Those tools are the subject of this chapter.

Systems Modeling/Dynamic Simulation Construction Tools

Complex learning requires that students solve complex and ill-structured problems and develop complex mental models of the world in order to do so. Mental models are mental representations, including metaphorical, visual-spatial, and structural knowledge, that enable learners to build runnable models of the phenomena to test their understanding (Jonassen & Henning, 1999). Because systems thinking is so important to understanding complex, real-world systems and for building mental models of those systems, a number of tools for simulating systems are now available, as described in this chapter.

Building models of real-world phenomena (representations that are abstracted from the details of a situation but grounded in the particulars of phenomena) is at the heart of scientific thinking and requires diverse mental activities such as planning, data collecting, collaborating and accessing information, data visualizing, modeling, and reporting (Soloway, Krajcik, & Finkel, 1995). The process for developing the ability to model phenomena requires defining the model, using the model to understand some phenomena, creating a model by representing real-world phenomena and making connections between its parts, and finally analyzing the model for its ability to represent the world (Spitulnik, Studer, Finkel, Gustafson, Laczko, & Soloway, 1995).

This chapter describes computer tools for developing dynamic simulations of systems. What the students construct are referred to in different places as dynamic models, dynamic simulations, or systems models. What are they? A *model* is a conceptual representation of something, described verbally, visually, or quantitatively. A *simulation* is a resemblance of a phenomenon that imitates the conditions and actions of it. These are sometimes referred to as computer models. *Dynamic* is characterized by action or change in states. So a dynamic simulation model is one that conceptually represents the changing nature of system phenomena in a form that resembles the real thing. These simulations are only abstractions or models of reality. They are not faithful, actual simulations of things. There is a class of computer tool now available that helps learners to build these dynamic simulation models of systems that elaborate causal loops. They are the topic of this chapter.

The most popular systems modeling tool to date is Stella from High Performance Systems. Stella is a powerful and flexible tool for building simulations of dynamic systems and processes. It uses a simple set of building block icons to construct a map of a process: stocks, flows, converters, and connectors (see Figure 7.3). Stocks illustrate the level of some thing in the simulation. In Figure 7.3, *people*, *forest*, and *buildings* are stocks. Flows control the inflow or outflow of material to stocks. *Birth*, *new trees*, and *trees used* are flows. Flows often counterbalance each other, like positive and negative influences in causal loops. For example, *new trees* and *trees used* are positive and negative influences on the number of trees. Converters convert inputs into outputs. They are factors or ratios that influence flows. *Birth rate*, *death rate*, and *fuel rate* are converters. Converters are used to add complexity to the models to better represent the complexity in the real world. Finally, connectors are the lines that show the directional effect of factors on each other by the use of arrows. Students generate equations in the stocks and flows for numerically representing relationships between the variables identified on the map. Once a model has been built, Stella enables learners to run the model that they have created and observe the output in graphs, tables, or animations. That is, Stella enables students to create physical runnable models of their own mental runnable models. At the run level, students can change the variable values to test the effects of parts of a system on the other. This kind of what-if logic is similar to those afforded by many microworlds (described in Chapter 8), only with Stella, students create the models themselves.

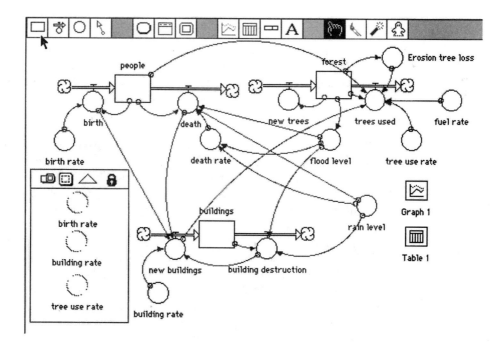

Figure 7.3
Student Model of Film *Mahenjo Daro*

HOW ARE SYSTEMS MODELING TOOLS USED AS MINDTOOLS?

Not a lot of systematic research is available on the effects of building dynamic systems models on learning and thinking, although there has been plenty of experience. The Cross-Curriculum Systems Thinking and Dynamics Using Stella (CC-STADUS) project (http://www.teleport.com/~sguthrie/cc-stadus.html), funded by the National Science Foundation, has trained a couple of hundred junior high and high school teachers to use Stella in their classrooms. All of their experience indicates that developing systems models significantly enhances learning.

- Niedderer, Schecker, and Begthe (1991) show how Stella can be used in physics classes.
- Hopkins (1992) developed a Stella model that analyzes Hamlet's motivation to avenge the death of his father by killing Claudius. Students used the model to follow the action and to speculate about a variety of possible responses. Hopkins goes on to show how Stella could be used for literary analysis and for writing short stories and plays.
- Blankenship and Tumlinson (1995) show how Stella can be used to represent action potentials (eating doughnuts, drinking milk, writing a story). Building simulation models makes action theory come alive.
- Using case study analysis, Steed (1995) showed how Stella modeling portrayed diverse dimensions of information and helped high school students shift their thinking by allowing them to compare different representations (different models).

The Stella model illustrated in Figure 7.3 was based on a film that students saw entitled *Mahenjo Daro*. It was part of a yearlong course on global studies organized by Scott Guthrie. Students used Stella to model a range of political, ecological, and social phenomena around the world. Not only do students think systemically in this course, they also gain empathy and understanding of issues faced by people in different countries.

The Stella model illustrated in Figure 7.4 was developed by an English teacher in conjunction with his 10th-grade students to describe how the boys' loss of hope drives the increasing power of the beast in William Golding's novel, *The Lord of the Flies*. The model of beast power represents the factors that contributed to the strength of the beast in the book. The resulting model can be run (Figure 7.5) by changing the values of *Faith building, Fear,* and *Memory of home* experienced by the boys while assessing the effects on their belief about being rescued and the strength of the beast within them. While Stella is most frequently used to model scientific phenomena, this application illustrates that Mindtools can be used across the curriculum.

Systems modeling tools provide a powerful suite of tools for representing the complexity of dynamic systems. Students can build models of those systems and test them. Observing the systems that students create is perhaps the most powerful way to assess the viability and comprehensiveness of learners' knowledge. These are very probably the most powerful Mindtools available to students.

Figure 7.4
Conceptual Map of the Beast

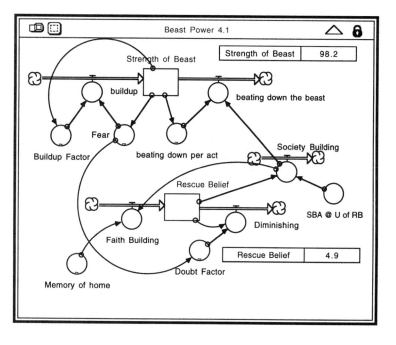

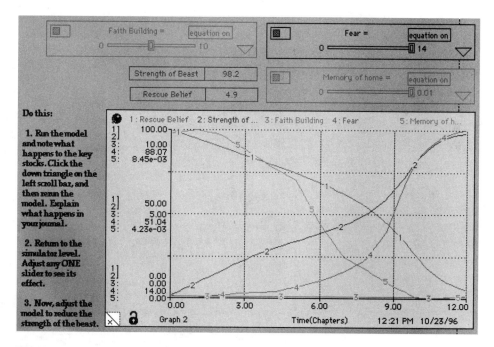

Figure 7.5
Runnable Version of the Strength of the Beast

Students can use systems modeling tools to model scientific, literary, or any kind of content. Perhaps the most powerful use of these tools is for modeling experiments and real-world phenomena. The model illustrated in Figure 7.6 was developed in PowerSim to simulate a fish tank. The population of the fish in the tank was shown to be a function of temperature, amount of water, frequency of cleaning, amount of food, and so on. Just as expert systems (Chapter 6) can be used to reflect on and represent the results of experiments, simulation modeling tools provide an even more powerful formalism for representing the factors and results of experiments.

In the fish tank simulation, users can reset the values of all of the variables (Figure 7.7) and run the simulation with results shown in a graph (Figure 7.8) to test various hypotheses about the interaction of causal factors in the environment. These activities are the embodiment of the scientific process.

Although simulation modeling tools like Stella and PowerSim are extremely powerful Mindtools, they require more intensive effort to learn than any of the other Mindtools discussed. Students will need more practice to master these tools. In an effort to afford students the ability to model systems while reducing the difficulty of the modeling process, the Highly Interactive Computing (HI-C) group at the University of Michigan developed a simpler modeling tool called Model-It.

To build a model in Model-It, students are required to identify the measurable, quantifiable factors that are used to predict the outcome they are simulating, in this

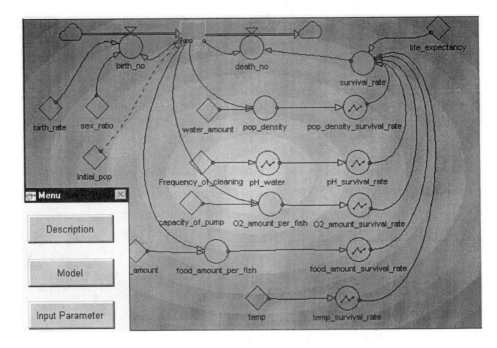

Figure 7.6
Simulation Model of a Fish Tank

Figure 7.7
Setting Values in the Fish Tank
Simulation

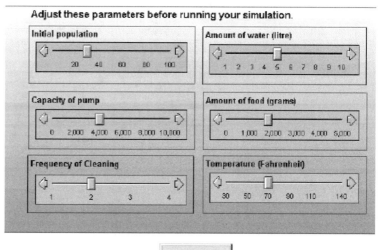

Figure 7.8
Results of the Fish Tank Simulation

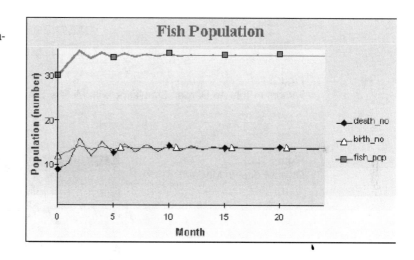

case a tomato garden. The factors in Figure 7.9 show the beginnings of a simulation of a tomato garden. Each object in the simulation can be described using the Object Editor (Figure 7.10). In the Object Editor, the type of object is defined and the factors affecting and affected by the object are defined. Each factor may be further described in terms of its measurement units, initial values, minimum, average, and maximum values in the Factor Editor (Figure 7.11). Students then build factor maps (Figure 7.9) showing the interactive effects of factors on each other. Students then must define the relationships between those factors using the Relationship Editor (Figure 7.12). When the model is complete, it may be tested, with the results shown either by meters (Figure 7.9) or in a graph (Figure 7.13). Model-It is very easy to use, usually requiring no more than 1 hour to learn.

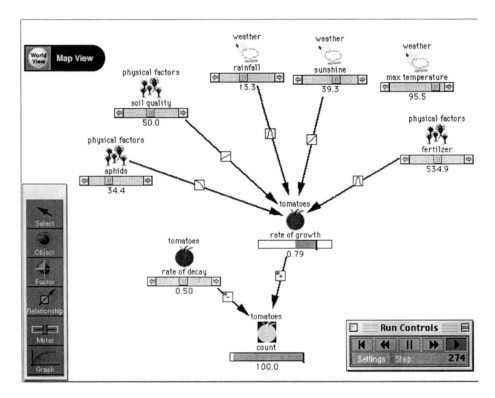

Figure 7.9
Factors in Tomato Garden Simulation with Meters Turned On

Figure 7.10
Object Editor in Model-It

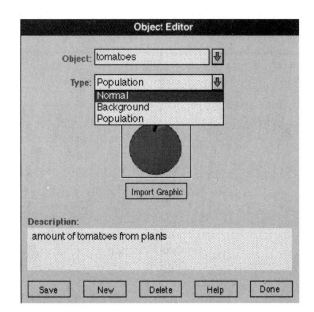

Figure 7.11
Factor Editor in Model-It

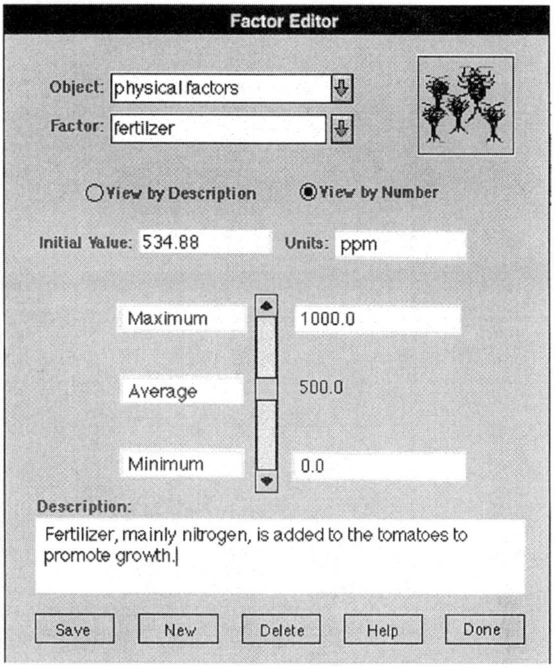

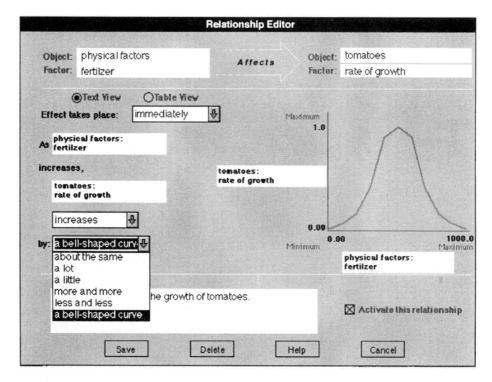

Figure 7.12
Relationship Editor in Model-It

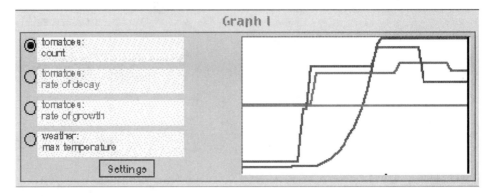

Figure 7.13
Graph of Model-It Output

Since Model-It, the modeling program built by HI-C, was designed to be used with middle school students who have not mastered advanced mathematics, the Relationship Maker in Model-It scaffolds their use of mathematics by providing a range of qualitative relationships that describe the quantitative relationship between the factors or allows them to enter a table of values that they have collected. So, students use pull-down menus to describe relationships such as "As fertilizer use increases, the number of tomatoes decreases/increases by about the same/a lot/a little/more and more/less and less, or (as in this case) a bell-shaped curve." Through inferring and speculating about the effects of variables on each other, these students are thinking like scientists, that is, building working models of phenomena and testing them against the real world.

Systems modeling enables students to engage in scientific decision making, treating science as a process, as opposed to facts and concepts to memorize. Providing students with the responsibility of making decisions should be the goal of scientific literacy. To make a decision, a student must determine his or her own opinion and state a position based on scientific knowledge; comprehend the implications, advantages, and disadvantages of that position; and also understand the effects of such a position (Spitulnik et al., 1995).

Related Mindtools

The model building screen in most systems modeling programs resembles semantic networks (Chapter 4). However, the similarity is limited. In semantic networking programs, concepts are linked with words that convey the semantic relationship between them. In systems models, those links are mathematical formulas that describe the dynamic, causal relationship of one component on the other.

Systems modeling is conceptually similar to expert systems. Both represent causal reasoning, though expert systems typically do not permit the use of mathematical formulas to describe the nature of the relationships.

Functionally, systems modeling tools are most similar to spreadsheets. As shown in Chapter 5, spreadsheets can be used to create simulations as well. While these simulations are quite similar, the advantage of systems modeling tools over spreadsheets is the ease of use. Systems modeling tools are designed to do just that, model systems. With spreadsheets, most of the operations are more difficult to achieve.

Coaching the Construction of Systems Models in the Classroom

Diane Fischer, the director of the CC-STADUS project mentioned earlier, recommends that students be introduced to modeling by having the teacher demonstrate how to develop a model and then allow the students to manipulate the model and make predictions. Later, students develop models as a classroom activity while being guided by the teacher. As they become more independent, students select a topic that interests them, identify the system parameters, work with a resource person to develop a model, and present it to their class. Coaching the development of modeling skills in learners may include these steps. The rate of progress depends on the age, intelligence, and interest of your students.

1. **Students run and test an existing model.** Provide simulation templates with predefined components and connections that work. Students make predictions and generate hypotheses, testing their predictions using the model while they test the model.

2. **Students manipulate existing model.** Create a diagram but leave some of the "between" variables left unspecified. Students would be required to deduce their own relationships. The models in step 1 and this step could represent an experiment that students have conducted. Or they could represent a local phenomenon with which the students would be familiar.

3. **Students create a group model.** Working as a class, with the guidance of the teacher, students work together to create a model of some familiar phenomenon. This is especially useful if you have only one computer in your classroom. Students are supported by the teacher and by each other. The teacher probes students' understanding, asks leading questions to help the students articulate their model, and encourages students to make predictions and hypotheses about the results before running it. When the students test their model, the teacher will need to provide hints about why the model may not be producing the output expected by the learners.

4. **Students make a plan for their own models.** Before developing their own model, students need to make a plan for their system models. What are they interested in representing? What points do they want to make? What kinds of structure and information are required to make those points? What learning goals will they work toward?

5. **Students create their own models.** Working in groups, students attempt to model an experiment, a chapter, some real-world phenomenon, or some other system being studied. They must test their own model.

6. **Students demonstrate their models to the class.** The class discusses and evaluates their models or helps their peers to troubleshoot difficulties.

7. **Students create their own theories.** Based on their working models, students should attempt to generalize their results into a theory that describes the behavior of a larger class of objects or events.

8. **Students reflect on the activity.** Reflection should not wait until the project is completed. Rather, students should continuously review their progress on the project. Are we achieving our goals? What changes are necessary? How do we compare with other groups? Are we answering questions and making the points that we set out in our plan? After the project is completed, the students should reflect on the project. What have we learned about the content? What have we learned about model building and about our own mental models? What have we learned about working with each other? You may choose to provide students with some or all of the criteria for evaluating student models (presented in the next section) to use for self-evaluation.

EVALUATING SYSTEMS MODELING TOOLS AS MINDTOOLS
Critical, Creative, and Complex Thinking in Systems Modeling

Steed (1992) argues that model building addresses higher levels of thinking, such as evaluation synthesis, and analysis. Specifically, the building of models requires students to predict behavior of system components, develop and test hypotheses, reason analytically in order to interpret results, and explain phenomena through the model.

As indicated in Table 7.1 nearly every critical, creative, and complex thinking skill is engaged by building systems models. It is among the most complete intellectual activities that students can perform in a classroom. I believe that building systems models requires deeper thinking and understanding about the content being studied than just about any other kind of learning activity. Because it is so complex, learning to build systems models will require more time than learning to use other Mindtools. The intellectual results will justify the effort.

Evaluating Student Systems Models

What makes an effective systems model? That depends on the kind of model that students are constructing and the age and abilities of the learners who are constructing the model. Viewing a student model created with a systems modeling tool provides perhaps the clearest and most definitive evidence of student intellectual activity available. I have experienced considerable excitement viewing student models. Some of the criteria that you might use to evaluate those models include the following:

Table 7.1
Critical, Creative, and Complex Thinking Skills Engaged by Building Dynamic Systems Models

Evaluating Assessing information Determining criteria Prioritizing Verifying	**Imagining** Predicting Speculating Visualizing
Analyzing Recognizing patterns Identifying assumptions Identifying main ideas Finding sequences	**Designing** Imagining a goal Formulating a goal Inventing a product Assessing a product Revising the product
Connecting Logical thinking Inferring deductively Inferring inductively Identifying causal relationships	**Problem Solving** Sensing the problem Researching the problem Formulating the problem Finding alternatives Choosing the solution
Elaborating Expanding Shifting categories Concretizing	**Decision Making** Identifying an issue Generating alternatives Assessing the consequences Making a choice Evaluating the choice
Synthesizing Hypothesizing Planning	

■ Does the model include all of the important components or objects?
■ Are the values of each component appropriately defined?
■ Are the direction and dimension of the relationships between components viable or accurate?
■ Do the graphical outputs of the model convey viable relationships?
■ Are the important variables represented as graphs?

Figure 7.14 presents a number of rubrics that you may use to evaluate the models that students construct as their knowledge and skills move from emergent to mastery. You will probably want to adapt these or add your own criteria as you evaluate your students' projects.

Evaluating Systems Modeling Software

Only a few systems modeling programs are available. The most prominent, as described earlier, is Stella from High Performance Systems. A very similar albeit less

Quality of factors	
Factors are irrelevant; insufficient factors identified; important factors are missing	Factors are important; enough factors identified to represent complexity of system

Relationship quality	
Relationships associative; use incorrect mathematic functions; connected to incorrect objects	Relationships are causal; use appropriate mathematic functions; flow between appropriate objects

Quality of model	
Inaccurately simulates systems; represents naive student understanding; makes incorrect assumptions; cannot support predictions or hypotheses	Simulates real-life system; simulates appropriate student understanding of system; makes appropriate assumptions; supports predictions/ hypotheses

Appropriate objects	
Objects(concepts) too advanced or too simple for target audience	Objects (concepts) appropriate for target audience (challenging but not impossible)

User testing	
Provides restricted range of tests; enables manipulation of limited variables/values	Enables users to test a range of hypotheses by manipulating appropriate variables or values

Figure 7.14
Possible Rubrics for Evaluating Student Models

expensive version of Stella is called PowerSim (www.powersim.com). With both of these modeling tools, students build icon-based models using stocks, flows, converters, and connectors. Both enable students to test and refine their models. Both are complex and more difficult to learn than most Mindtools. However, the effort is justified with both in terms of the thinking outcomes.

A simpler, cheaper, but less powerful tool is available for younger students in the form of Model-It, developed by the HI-C group at Michigan but refined and marketed now by Cogito Media (www.cogito.com). The interface on Model-It is friendlier, making it preferable for less experienced modelers.

The primary criteria for selecting a modeling tool are cost, power, and ease of use. Model-It is much cheaper and easier to use. However, experienced modelers will be limited by its lack of mathematical capacity. For more experienced users, especially high school and college students, Stella or PowerSim will permit them to go farther.

Advantages of Systems Modeling as Mindtools

Diane Fischer suggests a number of advantages of systems modeling, including these:

- Affords students the ability to visualize functional relationships among system components, illustrating all of the components and their dependent relationships (the Stella manual refers to this as "laying out the plumbing").
- Requires mathematical rigor by defining the dynamic relationships between components.

Steed (1992) identifies a number of advantages and benefits of systems modeling:

- Building dynamic simulations is useful when performing the real experiments would be impossible, too dangerous, or require too long a time.
- Simulations allow you to manipulate one variable at a time, which is often impossible in the real world.
- Students are required to make explicit their assumptions, generate hypotheses, and make predictions about how their model will perform.
- Models reflect the mental models that learners have of the systems that they are studying.
- Systems modeling tools are laboratories for scientific inquiry, exploration, explanation, and testing.
- Models are highly symbolized, using meaningful icons to represent ideas.
- Modeling makes fuzzy causal relationships less ambiguous. By explicitly diagramming the connections between system components, understanding is clarified.
- Modeling makes concrete the relationship between a system's processes and its structure.
- Models enable real-world phenomena to be explored without sophisticated mathematical knowledge.
- Simulations can help to identify hidden, causal factors in systems.
- Modeling engages metacognitive reasoning.

Joy and Zaraza (1997), experienced CC-STADUS teachers, have provided perhaps the most eloquent description of the power of systems modeling in classrooms:

As the modeling reaches deeper realms, the teacher and student explore together—a student's curiosity and imagination teamed with a teacher's wisdom and experience. This intellectual intimacy, brief on a daily basis, but profound over time, conjures the master-apprentice models of earlier times. For the students of average ability, this relationship bears much fruit. Many of these students have languished through course work, doing what's required but retaining little over time, just enough to pass or a bit better; many of these students are lost in the vast crowds of American education. But the visual aspect of system dynamics engages students both conceptually and pragmatically so that many more students are drawn into this question-rich learning. This dialectic mode of instruction is far more endearing to these students for whom teachers were oft viewed as authoritarians rather than mentors. Because the computer model makes explicit what heretofore was unknown in a student's mind, the teacher and student now have very clear venues for questions and suggestions. The best teaching and the best learning still take place at this primary level—the intellectual intimacy of teachers and students breeds trust, curiosity, imagination. It is not that this didn't happen before; it was just rare. System dynamics creates more possibilities for this as it enjoins minds in deep ways: students solve complex problems and teachers instruct directed minds.

Limitations of Systems Modeling as Mindtools

Numerous implementation issues arise when moving toward systems modeling. Based on longitudinal case studies, Mandinach and Clive (1994) identified several concerns, including these:

- administrative support (most principals were supportive)
- adequate and appropriate hardware (newer software demands more powerful computers)
- technical expertise (supporting Stella and the hardware)
- relatively expensive software
- orientation of the curriculum (accommodating systems modeling)
- expertise and training
- the changing role of teachers (constructivist perspective; more to follow).

Systems modeling, like all Mindtools, requires new approaches to teaching. Teachers must relinquish some of their intellectual authority to students and allow them to explore the limits of their own understanding. Joy and Zaraza (1997) identify some of the obligations:

The nature of system dynamics demands some measure of independence for its devotees. If we wish students to fully study, then we must grant them some intellectual independence and allow their curiosity to lead them. In this new setting, the teachers grant the questioners primacy. A teacher might introduce some conceptual material on acceleration, and then allow students to work through a series of increasingly difficult models that test some of the conceptual material as well as some equations and precise data. More advanced students are free to experiment and test their own well-educated notions, each time receiving immediate feedback that redirects their personal search. Likewise, the struggling student can receive such thoughtful, prolonged attention from the teacher who knows the other students are well engaged. No longer one question for the many, but a myriad of questions, each appropriate, for the multitude.

It is not easy for many teachers to teach this way. Before systems modeling can be successfully implemented in classrooms, teachers must adopt a more constructivist pedagogy.

SUMMARY

Systems modeling is the most complex and engaging of the dynamic modeling tools described in this section of the book. Because of that, learning to model systems will require more effort on the part of your students. It is learnable, however. Systems modeling has been accomplished successfully and regularly with junior high school and high school students. Little, if any experience, has been recorded with elementary students.

Because of its complexity, model building is a clear indicator of the depth and breadth of student understanding. If your students can build reasonable models of the systems that you are studying, then you may rest assured that they understand the content very deeply. Systems modeling, like most Mindtools, is an antidote to the mindless regurgitation of ideas in textbooks. However, as with most other Mindtools, systems modeling will not allow you to "cover" as much of the curriculum. This is one of the major issues related to constructivist pedagogies: is it better to learn a little bit about a lot, or to learn a lot about less? It's your choice.

References

Blankenship, V., & Tumlinson, J. (1995). A Stella-II teaching simulation of the dynamics of action model. *Behavior Research Methods, Instruments, and Computers, 27*(2), 244–250.

Fisher, D. M. (1994). *Teaching system dynamics to teachers and students in 8–12 environment.* Paper presented at the International Systems Dynamics Conference, Scotland.

Hopkins, P. L. (1992). Simulating Hamlet in the classroom. *Systems Dynamics Review, 8*(1), 91–98.

Jonassen, D. H., & Henning, P. (1999). Mental models: Knowledge in the head and knowledge in the world. *Educational Technology, 39*(3).

Joy, T., & Zaraza, R.(1997). *Fundamental changes in how we teach: A narrative about teaching systems dynamics and the art of learning.* Paper presented at the International Systems Dynamics Conference, Turkey.

Mandinach, E. B., & Cline, H. F. (1994). *Classroom dynamics: Implementing a technology-based learning environment.* Hillsdale, NJ: Lawrence Erlbaum Associates.

Niedderer, H., Schecker, H., & Begthe, T. (1991). The role of computer-aided modelling in learning physics. *Journal of Computer-Assisted Learning, 7*, 84–95.

Richmond, B., Peterson, S., & Vescuso, P. (1987). *An academic user's guide to Stella.* Lyme, NH: High Performance Systems.

Soloway, E., Krajcik, J., & Finkel, E. A. (1995). *Science project: Supporting science modeling and inquiry via computational media and technology.* San Francisco: American Educational Research Association.

Spitulnik, J., Studer, S., Finkel, E., Gustafson, E., Laczko, J., & Soloway, E. (1995). The RiverMUD design rationale: Scaffolding for scientific inquiry through modeling, discourse, and decision making in community based issues. In T. Koschman (Ed.), *Proceedings of Computer Support for Collaborative Learning.* Hillsdale, NJ: Lawrence Erlbaum Associates.

Steed, M. (1992). Stella, a simulation construction kit: Cognitive process and educational implications. *Journal of Computers in Science and Mathematics Teaching, 11*(1), 39–52.

Steed, M. (1995). *Effects of computer simulation construction on shifts in cognitive representation: A case study using Stella.* Unpublished doctoral dissertation, University of Massachusetts.

Microworlds as Mindtools

WHAT ARE MICROWORLDS?

Logo-Based Microworlds

The term *microworld* was coined by Papert (1980) to describe explorative learning environments that used Logo turtles to learn principles of geometry. Logo provides learners with simple commands to direct turtles to create their own personal, visual worlds. Learners enter commands to manipulate a turtle on the screen in an effort to create more elaborate renderings, thus becoming familiar with the "powerful ideas" underlying the turtle's operations; ideas such as variables, procedures, and recursion. The computer should be an "object to think with," according to Papert. Logo is, Papert argued, an ideal environment for creating microworlds, which are "constrained problem spaces that resemble existing problems in the real world." These microworlds are generated by learners so they are inherently interesting (experimenting to "see if I can do that").

An example of a Logo microworld was the POLYSPI (for poly-spiral) procedure, which requires learners to use variables in a procedure to create a spiral (Lawler, 1984). By manipulating the values of the variables, the spiral changes form. Another, the beach microworld, uses the turtle to draw a beach scene, replete with bird, boat, house, kid, man, sun, and many other objects. The beach is a visual model for testing hypotheses about the placement and movement of objects in a scene. Because the ideas and methods are simple and grounded in a visual reality, they become useful to learners in their experimentation.

Thompson and Wang (1988) used Logo to create a microworld where learners could explore concepts by plotting points in a Cartesian coordinate system. Students created pictures (as in the beach microworld) by placing objects in the picture using *x* and *y* coordinates. Students in the microworld treatment not only outperformed a control group on a post-test of coordinate problems, but, more importantly, they performed substantially better on a test of transfer of the ideas to real-world coordinate problems. The key here is creating an environment in which students can explore the ideas being learned.

Not all of the research and experience with Logo has been positive. There are at least two significant limitations of Logo-based microworlds:

1. Logo microworlds typically represent very constrained and circumscribed problems that engage a limited set of skills. The procedures used to create Logo microworlds and the skills they require are not very generalizable. They are powerful, but learners cannot practice a range of exploratory skills, which is an important criterion for Mindtools.
2. The generalizability of Logo microworlds can certainly be enhanced if learners create their own microworlds using Logo rather than using those created by a teacher, but that entails that students learn Logo. Although Logo is a syntactically simple language, it still requires several months of practice to develop skills sufficient for easily creating microworlds.

The idea of microworlds as problem exploration and experimentation spaces is indeed a powerful idea. Many other microworld environments have been created that offer the exploratory advantages of Logo without the requirement of learning a programming language. They are constrained versions of reality that enable learners to manipulate variables and experiments within the parameters of some system. Although this kind of microworld does not always allow students to construct their own exploration spaces, as Logo and most other Mindtools do, they do enable learners to represent their own thinking in the ways that they explore, manipulate, and experiment with the environment. Ergo, they are Mindtools. Such environments are the subject of this chapter.

Microworld Learning Environments

Notwithstanding my concerns about Logo, the concept of microworlds remains a "powerful idea." Microworlds can assume many forms in different knowledge domains (see Figure 8.1); however, they are primarily exploratory learning environments, discovery spaces, and constrained simulations of real-world phenomena in which learners can navigate, manipulate or create objects, and test their effects on one another. "Microworlds present students with a simple model of a part of the world" (Hanna, 1986, p. 197). Microworlds allow learners to control those phenomena and construct deeper level knowledge of the phenomena they are manipulating. Microworlds replicate the functionality that is needed to explore phenomena in those parts of the world. That is, they provide learners with the observation and manipulation tools necessary for exploring and testing objects in those parts of the world. They have proven extremely effective in engaging learners in higher order thinking such as hypothesis testing and speculating.

Video-based adventure games are microworlds that require players to master each environment before moving onto more complex environments. They are compelling to youngsters, who spend hours transfixed in these adventure worlds. Microworlds are perhaps the ultimate example of active learning environments, because the users can exercise so much control over the environment.

Microworlds are composed of objects, relationships among objects, and operations that transform the objects and their relationships (Thompson & Wang, 1988). As learners interact with the microworld, they manipulate objects (or variables) in order to reach a goal state. For example, in CHANCE, a simulation-oriented computer microworld that runs using Object Logo, the goal state is that of accurately predicting the probability of an occurrence given a certain set of conditions. The student will predict the number of times a coin will land heads up out of 10 tosses, 100 tosses, and so on. Other goal states are much more complex. For example, in a microworld developed at Wright State University, the goal state is the process of conducting psychological research (Colle & Randall, 1996).

The ideal associated with this approach is the feeling of "direct engagement," the feeling that the computer is invisible, not even there; what is present instead is the world we are exploring, be that world music, art, words, business, mathematics, literature, or whatever your imagination and task provide you (Draper & Norman, 1986, p. 3).

Microworlds are not necessarily computer based. They can exist in the classroom, the kitchen, or anywhere. And they are relative to the learner's age and interests. When I was a child, a chemistry set and later a crude darkroom became microworlds that occupied much of my time. A cabinet full of pots and pans can be an engaging microworld for a toddler to learn about measurement, shape, hardness, gravity, and other concepts.

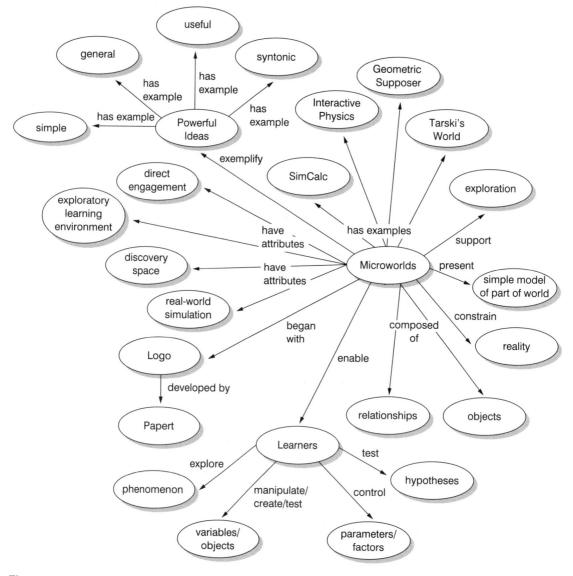

Figure 8.1
Microworlds as Mindtools

Burton, Brown, and Fischer (1984) use skiing instruction as a pretext for developing a model for designing increasingly complex, skill-based microworlds. They believe that a microworld is a controlled real-world learning environment where a student is able to try out new skills and knowledge. It is important to their definition of microworlds that skills be practiced in the real environment with skills "isomorphic in [their] most important components to the final form of the skill" (p. 143).

In microworlds, instruction proceeds from simple to complex skills. Knowledge, skills, and attitudes are integrated through problem-solving activities, and instruction is situated in rich, meaningful settings. There are only a few factors involved in microworld design. For example, with skiing, complexity is learner controlled by manipulating the equipment (e.g., the length of the skis), the task (e.g., gliding downhill, making easy turns, making more difficult turns), and the environment (e.g., steepness of slope, presence or absence of moguls). Initially, these decisions are coached to ensure that the learner has challenging but attainable goals and practices an appropriate set of necessary subskills.

Microworlds are exploration environments that exploit the interest and curiosity of the learner, so they must contain phenomena that learners are interested in. They incorporate instructional strategies such as modeling, coaching, reflecting, exploring, and encouraging the learner to debug his or her knowledge rather than apply principles attained during direct instruction. But they also rely on the learner. Self-regulated learning is an important component of microworld use. Learners need to identify their own goals and use the microworld to satisfy those goals.

Microworlds are based on powerful ideas. Powerful ideas are major building blocks in children's mental models, so they should be foundational for microworlds as well. Powerful ideas have powerful criteria (Lawler, 1984). If microworlds are based on powerful ideas, they should have the following characteristics:

- *simple,* so they can be understood
- *general,* so they apply to many areas of life
- *useful,* so the ideas are important to learners in the world
- *syntonic* (resonant with one's experience), so learners can relate them to prior knowledge and experience.

Most important, microworlds are experiential. Learners learn by doing, instead of just watching or listening to a description of how something works. Because of this, microworlds tend to be intrinsically more motivating than traditional descriptions of activities.

HOW ARE MICROWORLDS USED AS MINDTOOLS?

There are many other fine examples of microworlds, such as Boxer (diSessa & Abelson, 1986), Writing Partner (Salomon, 1993), ThinkerTools (White, 1993), and Bubble Dialogue (McMahon & O'Neill, 1993) that are not described in this chapter. These environments share at least two important characteristics. They usually provide multiple representations of phenomena, and they provide immediate feedback when learners try something out. The learner manipulates the objects in the environment and runs the simulation. The microworld shows how the object behaves based on that manipulation. The system performance functions as feedback that the learners must interpret and use to revise their conceptual model of the domain. It is important for this feedback to come about as a natural consequence of using the microworld. Limited research is available to support the learning outcomes of microworlds:

- It has been shown that children as young as 2 years of age have mastered sorting tasks in computer microworlds (Brinkley, 1988).
- In corporate applications, research revealed that microworlds can create meaningful, lifelike roles, and reward intelligent, rational, and well-planned, executive-type decisions (Keys, Fulmer, & Stumpf, 1996).

The following examples demonstrate the capabilities of microworld learning environments.

Interactive Physics

Interactive Physics is a research environment for exploring topics in Newtonian mechanics, such as momentum, force, acceleration, etc. It consists of a number of demonstrations, such as Car Crash (students' favorite, see Figure 8.2), Falling Object, and Projectile Motion, and many experiments, such as Particle Dynamics, Rotational Dynamics (see Figure 8.3), Equilibrium, Motion in a Plane, Collisions, and others.

More importantly, Interactive Physics provides objects and tools that enable the learners to design their own experiments to model Newtonian phenomena. Each

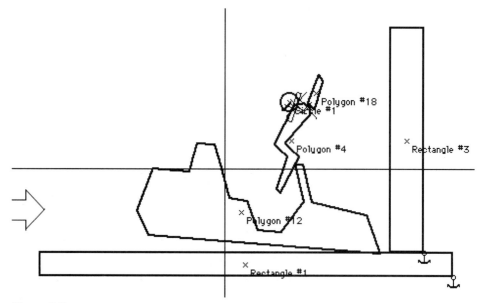

Figure 8.2
Car Crash Demonstration in Interactive Physics

Figure 8.3
Rotational Dynamics Experiment
in Interactive Physics

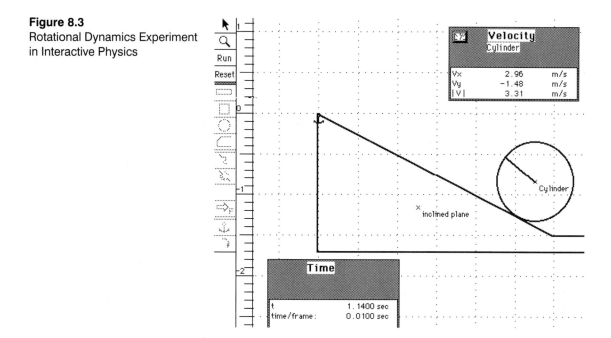

experiment and demonstration is a physics microworld that simulates a physical phenomenon that allows the learner to easily manipulate several attributes of the world, such as gravity, air resistance, elasticity of bodies, and various surface parameters. They can also choose the aspects of the microworld that they want to attend to by showing grids, rulers, vectors, axes, center of mass, and mass names. Students can turn on a tracker, which shows the motion of objects. They can also select meters, such as velocity, acceleration, momentum, various forces (friction, gravity, air), and rotation in order to measure the effects of changes in the variables that they designate. Interactive Physics is an excellent example of what I refer to as a microworld, because the experiments are simple to use, and they are syntonic. They are also very helpful to the teacher, because it would require thousands of dollars of equipment and many hours of work to set up the actual physics experiments that are contained in this environment.

SimCalc

The SimCalc project teaches middle and high school students calculus concepts through MathWorld, which is a microworld consisting of animated worlds and dynamic graphs in which actors move according to graphs. By exploring the movement of the actors in the simulations and seeing the graphs of their activity, students begin to understand important calculus ideas. In the MathWorld activity illustrated in Figure 8.4, students match two motions. By matching two motions they learn how velocity and position graphs relate. Students must match the motion of the

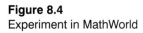

Figure 8.4
Experiment in MathWorld

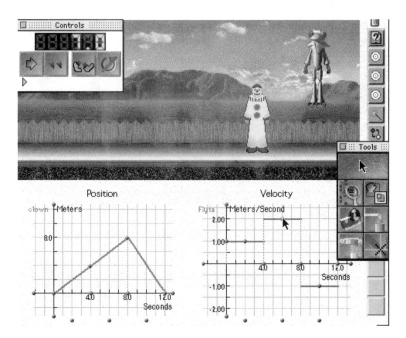

green and red graphs. To do this, they can change either graph. They iteratively run the simulation to see if they got it right! Students may also use MathWorld's link to enter their own bodily motion. For example, a student can walk across the classroom, and their motions would be entered into MathWorld by means of sensing equipment. MathWorld would plot their motion, enabling the students to explore the properties of their own motion.

Geometric Supposer

One of the best known microworlds is Geometric Supposer, a tool for making and testing conjectures in geometry through constructing and manipulating geometric objects and exploring the relationships within and between these objects (Schwartz & Yerushalmy, 1987). Geometric Supposer allows students to choose a primitive shape, such as a triangle, and construct it by defining points, segments, parallels or perpendiculars, bisectors, or angles (see Figure 8.5) (Yerushalmy & Houde, 1986). The program plots and remembers each manipulation and can apply it to similar figures. For example, if the students conjecture that "a median drawn from the vertex of any triangle to the opposite side bisects the angle" (p. 419), they can test it easily by asking Geometric Supposer to measure the angles or by applying the relationship to several other triangles. The student will learn immediately that the conjecture is not true. Constructing these test examples manually would require more effort than students are likely to generate, but the computational power of the computer makes this testing very easy.

Figure 8.5
Investigating Triangles with Geometric Supposer

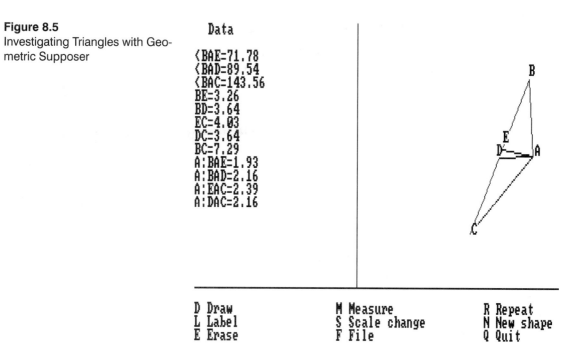

```
Data

<BAE=71.78
<BAD=89.54
<BAC=143.56
BE=3.26
BD=3.64
EC=4.03
DC=3.64
BC=7.29
A:BAE=1.93
A:BAD=2.16
A:EAC=2.39
A:DAC=2.16
```

```
D Draw        M Measure        R Repeat
L Label       S Scale change   N New shape
E Erase       F File           Q Quit
```

Geometry instruction is traditionally based on the application of theorems to prove that certain relationships exist among objects. This top-down approach requires analytic reasoning, which a majority of students find difficult. Geometric Supposer supports the learning of geometry by enabling the student to prove these relationships inductively by manipulating the components of geometric objects and observing the results. Rather than having the student apply someone else's logic, Geometric Supposer makes explicit the relationships between visual properties and the numerical properties of the objects (Yerushalmy, 1990). Rather than using the computer to provide conclusive results, the computer calculates the results of students' experiments. The research results with Geometric Supposer have been consistently positive.

Related Mindtools

In that microworlds are not all used to produce student representations, they are not like most other Mindtools. However, because they do engage learners in constructing mental models that identify the dynamic relationships among variables, they most resemble systems modeling tools (Chapter 7). They can be used effectively in combination with systems modeling tools, where learners build a systems model of the microworld in order to better understand the phenomena being tested. Students could also use expert systems to model the hypothesis testing that they do in the microworld. These rich combinations of Mindtools provide complimentary representations of ideas.

Coaching the Use of Microworlds in the Classroom

Because microworlds vary so much in both the content they represent and the skills they facilitate, it is difficult to provide prescriptions for how to support their use. The following are a few general principles for using microworlds to foster self-regulated learning:

1. **Computer-based microworlds support self-regulated learning.** This means that the teacher cannot always set specific goals or objectives for instruction but should encourage the learners to set goals for themselves. Requiring students to articulate these goals is very important to their intellectual development. So, before beginning to use the microworlds, students need to make a plan. What are the principles that they are investigating? What points do they want to make? What kinds of exploration or experimental results are required to make those points? What learning goals will they work toward?

2. **Microworlds best serve any curriculum as self-directed problem-solving practice.** Most microworlds are problem-solving spaces, permitting learners to generate their own hypotheses about ideas within the content domain being studied. This form of problem-solving practice is more likely to produce transfer of learning than more traditional problem sets.

3. **In a related concern, incidental learning should be accepted and encouraged when using microworld learning environments.** Incidental learning consists of the unintended, serendipitous learning that occurs when learners find something interesting. Schools normally impose strict agendas on learning and therefore deemphasize incidental learning in order to "cover the curriculum." Incidental learning is not rewarded. Because learners set their own goals in microworlds rather than the teacher or the curriculum, much learning from microworlds may be perceived as incidental. Allow learners to diverge from their own goals in order to explore new, interesting ideas.

4. **Encourage students to compare the objects in the microworld with objects and actions they are already familiar with.** Regularly ask them if they can think of things in the real world that behave as those in the microworld do. This is what Papert means by syntonic learning, and it is very important to the learning outcomes in microworlds, since microworlds are designed to model events in the real world.

5. **When learners get bogged down and are unable to generate problems, goals, and hypotheses, you should first model how to generate hypotheses and later coach them by prompting hypothesis-generating behaviors.** "What do you think will happen if . . . ?" This may be especially important in encouraging students to observe carefully the results of their actions in the environment and to modify their thinking in order to generate alternative hypotheses about the objects in the environment.

6. **Encourage students to collaborate in mixed groups of two or three.** Which collaborative arrangements work best will depend on the nature of the learning environment and the skills it requires.

7. **Ask students to report and reflect on their findings in each microworld to the class.** Reflection should not wait until they have concluded their investigations with the microworld. Rather, students should continuously review their progress on the project. Are we achieving our goals? What changes are necessary? How do we compare with other groups? Are we answering questions and making the points that we set out in our plan? After the project is completed, the students should reflect on the project. What have we learned about the content? What have we learned about working with each other?

You may choose to provide students with some or all of the criteria for evaluating microworld use (presented in the next section) to use for self-evaluation. Exploring microworlds engages meaningful thinking. Reflection cements the knowledge that learners construct.

EVALUATING MICROWORLDS AS MINDTOOLS

The critical, creative, and complex thinking skills that are engaged by microworlds vary with the simulation. They very probably engage more critical and creative thinking skills such as recognizing patterns, inferring inductively, hypothesizing, predicting, speculating, and visualizing than many other Mindtools (Jonassen, 1996). Using microworlds is seldom a constructionist activity, so they do not enable learners to represent their knowledge as overtly as other Mindtools. Yet they are unquestionably one of the best tools for engaging learners in constructing and testing internal mental models. If those internal models were manifested in systems models using systems modeling tools, the combination of microworlds and systems modeling tools would represent the most complete reification of mental models that exists.

Critical, Creative, and Complex Thinking in Microworld Use

The purpose of microworlds is to engage learners in hypothesis generation and testing, skills that naturally entail a large number of critical, creative, and complex thinking skills. However, the critical thinking skills engaged by microworlds are somewhat specific to the microworld. Tables 8.1, 8.2, and 8.3 identify the critical, creative, and complex skills involved in using Interactive Physics, SimCalc, and Geometric Supposer. Other microworlds would probably engage similar though different sets of skills. The skills in each table that are marked by an "X" are those that are employed by each process, based on an information-processing analysis of the tasks.

Table 8.1
Critical Thinking Skills Engaged by Microworlds

	Interactive Physics	SimCalc	Geometric Supposer
Evaluating			
Assessing information	X	X	X
Determining criteria	X	X	X
Prioritizing			
Recognizing fallacies	X	X	X
Verifying	X		X
Analyzing			
Recognizing patterns	X	X	X
Classifying	X		X
Identifying assumptions	X	X	X
Identifying main ideas			
Finding sequences		X	X
Connecting			
Comparing/contrasting			X
Logical thinking	X	X	X
Inferring deductively	X	X	X
Inferring inductively	X	X	X
Identifying causal relationships	X	X	X

Experimenting with phenomena requires many critical thinking skills (see Table 8.1), such as assessing what is known, recognizing problems, identifying causal relationships, and generating hypotheses (inferring deductively). All of the microworlds engage combinations of evaluating, analyzing, and connecting skills. The most important evaluating skills that Interactive Physics and SimCalc engage are assessing information and determining criteria. Their major requirements are connecting skills, such as logical thinking and inferring, as well as identifying causal relationships. Geometric Supposer potentially engages almost every critical thinking skill in order to evaluate figures, analyze them for their attributes, and reason logically in order to generate and test hypotheses.

Fewer creative thinking skills are engaged by microworlds because they are predefined (see Table 8.2). Imagining and synthesizing knowledge are the major creative skills engaged in order to generate and test hypotheses.

Complex thinking skills are those necessary for planning and carrying out experiments, so Interactive Physics, SimCalc, and Geometric Supposer are rich in these skills (see Table 8.3). Interactive Physics and Geometric Supposer are the two environments that engage any design skills. In these environments, students create their own demonstrations and experiments, which requires some of the design skills. Most microworlds, however, are more likely to engage problem-solving and decision-making skills.

Table 8.2
Creative Thinking Skills Engaged by Microworlds

	Interactive Physics	SimCalc	Geometric Supposer
Elaborating			
Expanding			
Modifying			
Extending	X	X	X
Shifting categories		X	X
Concretizing	X	X	X
Synthesizing			
Analogical thinking			X
Summarizing		X	
Hypothesizing	X	X	X
Planning	X	X	X
Imagining			
Fluency			
Predicting	X	X	X
Speculating	X	X	X
Visualizing	X	X	X
Intuition	X	X	X

Table 8.3
Complex Thinking Skills Engaged by Microworlds

	Interactive Physics	SimCalc	Geometric Supposer
Designing			
Imagining a goal	X	X	X
Formulating a goal	X	X	X
Inventing a product	X		X
Assessing a product	X		X
Revising the product			
Problem Solving			
Sensing the problem	X	X	X
Researching the problem	X	X	X
Formulating the problem	X	X	X
Finding alternatives	X	X	X
Choosing the solution	X		X
Building acceptance			
Decision Making			
Identifying an issue	X	X	X
Generating alternatives	X	X	X
Assessing the consequences	X	X	X
Making a choice	X		X
Evaluating the choice	X		X

Evaluating Students' Uses of Microworlds

How do you know when students make the most effective use of microworlds? That depends on the kind of microworld the students are using and the age and abilities of the learners who are using it. Figure 8.6 presents a number of rubrics that you can use to evaluate how your students use the microworld as their skills move from emergent to mastery. You will probably want to adapt these or add your own criteria as you evaluate your students' projects.

Advantages of Microworlds as Mindtools

The arguments for the use of microworlds as learning environments are diverse and extensive:

■ Microworlds provide an environment that encourages active participation and exploration (Papert, 1980).

Plausible hypotheses generated

◄───►

| Learner hypotheses not related to issues; inappropriate variables related; relationships not causally correct | Learner hypotheses correctly relate variables to issues; causal direction and scope are appropriate |

Appropriate manipulations to test hypotheses

◄───►

| Incorrect variables selected; not correctly operationalized in environment | Correct variables selected; correctly operationalized in environment |

Appropriate conclusions drawn from feedback

◄───►

| Feedback misinterpreted; incorrect conclusions drawn; learners' knowledge not transferable | Feedback interpreted correctly; appropriate conclusions drawn; learners' knowledge transferable to new situation |

Constructed experiments exemplify principles
(if microworld enables learners to design an experiment or demonstration)

◄───►

| Experiment chooses wrong variables or exemplifies them incorrectly; identifies wrong relationships | Experiment exemplifies variable correctly; identifies accurate relationships |

Figure 8.6
Rubrics for Evaluating Students' Uses of Microworlds

- The dynamic nature of microworlds encourages the production of sensory pluralities, which is a fundamental operation of intelligence on which the construction of numerical concepts, composite units, number sequences, and more general quantitative reasoning is based (Steffe, 1994).
- Microworlds contain understandable examples of complex natural phenomena and provide environments for representing those phenomena.
- Microworlds support exploration of phenomena through activities and provide the tools for facilitating that exploration.
- Microworlds allow the underlying concepts for exploring natural phenomena to be defined by the learner using characteristics of the microworld; they provide the tools for defining their world (e.g., speech and thought balloons in Bubble Dialogue).
- Microworlds support learning, from simple to complex skills.
- Microworlds integrate knowledge, skills, and attitudes through problem-solving activities.
- Microworlds provide instruction that is situated in rich, meaningful settings and they are thus more motivating than traditional learning activities.
- Microworlds support self-regulated learning, where learners identify their own goals and use the microworld to satisfy those goals.
- Microworlds are based on powerful ideas, which are major building blocks in students' mental models.
- Microworlds provide for experiential learning, so learners learn by doing, instead of just watching or listening to a description of how something works.

Limitations of Microworlds as Mindtools

There are few real limitations or disadvantages of microworlds:

- Microworlds are single purpose; that is, organized to explore a single content domain, and not adaptable to other purposes.
- Microworlds call on skills that students likely do not possess and must acquire, so their openness can be frustrating at first. To elucidate the relationships between objects in a microworld, other complex interactions and random factors present in the real environment are often sequestered. Consequently, some microworlds oversimplify relations to the extent that they often produce false representations of reality.

SUMMARY

Microworlds are a type of Mindtool that engages learners in hypothesis testing and mental model building. This chapter diverges most from the others in the book in that it describes constrained, predefined, exploratory learning environments for engaging learners in problem solving rather than tools for constructing knowledge representations. Microworlds are predefined discovery spaces that present constrained simulations of real-world phenomena, but they do not necessarily limit the learner to prescribed problems. Most microworlds, such as those described in this chapter, enable learners to construct and define their own problems to solve. The underlying notions of microworlds are representations of complex, real-world phenomena that facilitate exploration of those "micro" worlds and hypothesis testing about the components of that world. Allowing the learner to redefine the phenomena and the tools for exploring natural phenomena makes microworlds even more powerful Mindtools. Though many learners will not readily accept the responsibility for defining their own learning, the rewards of doing so will justify the effort required to coax, coach, and cajole learners into becoming explorers and knowledge constructors.

References

Brinkley, V. M. (1988). Effects of microworld training experience on sorting tasks by young children. *Journal of Educational Technology Systems, 16*(4), 349–364.

Burton, R. R., Brown, J. S., & Fischer, G. (1984). Skiing as a model of instruction. In B. Rogoff & J. Lave (Eds.), *Everyday cognition: Its development in social context.* Cambridge, MA: Harvard University Press.

Colle, H. A. G., & Randall, F. (1996). Introductory psychology laboratories using graphic simulations of virtual subjects. *Behavior Research Methods, Instruments, & Computers, 28*(2), 331–335.

diSessa, A., & Abelson, H. (1986). BOXER: A reconstructible computational medium. *Communications of the ACM, 29*(9), 859–868.

Draper, S. W., & Norman, D. (1986). Introduction. In D. A. Norman & S. W. Draper (Eds.), *User-centered system design.* Hillsdale, NJ: Lawrence Erlbaum Associates.

Hanna, J. (1986). Learning environment criteria. In R. Ennals, R. Gwyn, & L. Zdravchev (Eds.), *Information technology and education: The changing school.* Chichester, UK: Ellis Horwood.

Jonassen, D. H. (1996). *Computers in the classroom: Mindtools for Critical thinking.* Upper Saddle River, NJ: Prentice Hall.

Keys, J. B., Fulmer, R. M., & Stumpf, S. A. (1996). Microworlds and simuworlds: Practice fields for the learning organization. *Organizational Dynamics, 24*(4), 36–49.

Lawler, B. (1984). Designing computer-based microworlds. In M. Yazdani (Ed.), *New horizons in educational computing.* Chichester, UK: Ellis Horwood.

McMahon, H., & O'Neill, W. (1993). Computer-mediated zones of engagement in learning. In T. M. Duffy, J. Lowyck, & D. H. Jonassen (Eds.), *Designing environments for constructive learning.* Heidelberg, Germany: Springer-Verlag.

Papert, S. (1980). *Mindstorms: Children, computers, and powerful ideas.* New York: Basic Books.

Salomon, G. (1993). On the nature of pedagogic computer tools: The case of the writing partner. In S. P. LaJoie & S. J. Derry (Eds.), *Computers as cognitive tools.* Hillsdale, NJ: Lawrence Erlbaum Associates.

Schwartz, J. L., & Yerushalmy, M. (1987). The Geometric Supposer: Using microcomputers to restore invention to the learning of mathematics. In D. N. Perkins, J. Lockhead, & J. C. Bishop (Eds.), *Thinking: The second international conference.* Hillsdale, NJ: Lawrence Erlbaum Associates.

Steffe, L. J. (1994). Cognitive play and mathematical learning in computer microworlds. *Educational Studies in Mathematics, 26*(2–3), 111–134.

Thompson, A. D., & Wang, H. M. (1988). Effects of a Logo microworld on student ability to transfer a concept. *Journal of Educational Computing Research, 4*(3), 335–347.

White, B. Y. (1993). ThinkerTools: Causal models, conceptual change, and science education. *Cognition and Instruction, 10*(1), 1–100.

Yerushalmy, M. (1990). Using empirical information in geometry: Students' and designers' expectations. *Journal of Computers in Mathematics and Science Teaching, 9*(3), 23–33.

Yerushalmy, M., & Houde, R. A. (1986). The Geometric Supposer: Promoting thinking and learning. *Mathematics Teacher, 79*, 418–422.

PART FOUR

Interpretation Tools

P art 4 of this book describes a new class of Mindtool that I refer to as interpretation tools. Interpretation tools are discussed in these chapters:

Chapter 9 Intentional Information Search Tools as Mindtools
Chapter 10 Visualization Tools as Mindtools

Unlike most of the other Mindtools described in this book, which enable learners to construct knowledge bases, the tools described in these two chapters help learners to interpret information that they encounter while constructing knowledge bases. That is, these are meaning-making tools. They help learners to understand the ideas that they encounter.

Consider this short review of the learning process (from a constructivist perspective): Knowledge construction is a four-part process. The first and most important part is to articulate an intention to build knowledge. That may be stimulated by a question or problem, a failure to achieve something, a general curiosity, an argument, or anything that perturbs a person's understanding enough to want to make sense out of it. Having declared a desire to know, learners must collect and interpret information that relates to the declared intention. The tools in Chapter 9 and 10 support this part of the knowledge construction process. The third process is to build a new understanding and to represent it. Knowledge construction tools in Part 5 best support this part of the learning process. Finally, knowledge construction should result in some reflection about what was learned, how it was learned, and what it means. Most of the Mindtools in this book support the reflection process.

The Mindtools described in Part 4 support the finding and interpreting of information culled from libraries and the Internet. Some people may think this book should have a chapter devoted solely to the Internet for learning, which is the latest solution to most educational problems. Let me reiterate that this book is not about technology; it is about thinking and how technologies can support it. The Internet is an enormous repository of information that can either enhance or impede learning, depending on how it is used, but the Internet is not a Mindtool. As I point out in Chapter 9, surfing, cruising, or staggering through the Internet will probably not result in meaningful learning until and unless learners articulate an intention to use that information to do something meaningful. Once they do, they will need help in finding useful sources of information. That task is the subject of Chapter 9. Once learners find useful sources of information, which on the Internet is likely to include visualizations, they will need help interpreting them. The Mindtools described in Chapter 10 can support that. For those looking for the Internet chapter, it's Chapter 9. Sorry, but it's not *about* the Internet. There are already way too many books *about* the Internet. Rather, Chapter 9 briefly describes how to use the Internet and other information sources. I hope that's enough.

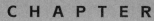

9

Intentional Information Search Tools as Mindtools

WITH SUSAN COLARIC

WHAT MAKES A SEARCH MEANINGFUL?

Most contemporary books about computers in education focus extensively—if not exclusively—on how to use the Internet and particularly the World Wide Web (WWW) for learning. In the early 21st century, the Web is the answer; what is the question? Many educators at all levels see the WWW as the solution to whatever educational problems they face. Every educational institution is struggling to enhance its web presence. Too many educators believe that embedding links to other web sites in text is good instruction. So much hype has been associated with the WWW that many educators seem to have lost sight of the most important issue—learning. In this chapter, I attempt to refocus attention on that issue by claiming that the WWW supports learning only to the extent that learners articulate an information need and intentionally search the web to fulfill that need. When learners search for information to fulfill a need, their purpose drives the learning. When that happens, we need to support or scaffold their search for information. Tools and methods for scaffolding that search are the subject of this chapter (see Figure 9.1).

The WWW is a worldwide hypertext system that presents text and multimedia resources with embedded links that support nonlinear reading. Ted Nelson, who coined the term *hypertext,* dreamed of a hypertext that would include all of the world's knowledge. He wanted to build such a hypertext and call it Xanadu. What he didn't realize was that no individual or group could ever do that. To collect that much information, responsibility for collecting, storing, and maintaining it must be

Figure 9.1
Intentional Searching as a Mind-tool

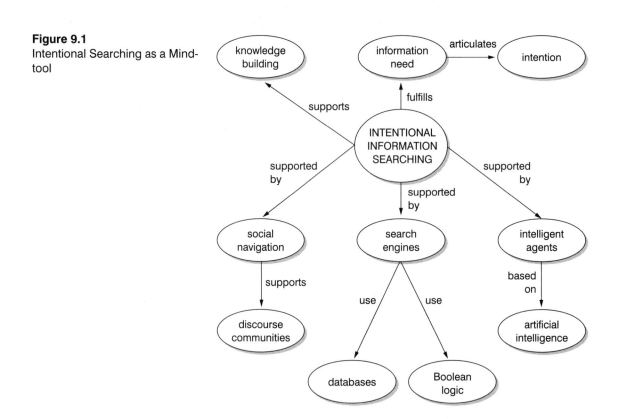

distributed. However, Xanadu is beginning to happen in the form of the World Wide Web. It is a worldwide distributed hypertext that emerged in the mid-1990s as a distributed computing option to the stand-alone multimedia computer. In the early stages, the WWW was used to store largely text-based documents on computers all over the world and allow users anywhere to access those documents. With the evolution of more powerful servers and desktop computers, the WWW is rapidly becoming a giant, distributed hypermedia knowledge base (see Chapter 11). Most Internet browsers, such as Netscape or Internet Explorer, can be enhanced with plug-in extensions, such as Shockwave, QuickTime, and QuickTime VR, to allow multimedia programs to be accessed, recorded, and replayed on any powerful desktop computer.

Among the concerns about the WWW as a learning tool is that there are so many interesting topics to explore and it is so easy to explore that students are often off-task, following links that take them away from, rather than toward, their learning goal. Getting lost in hyperspace has been a consistent problem for learners using hypertext. When users follow a number of links through a variety of information sources, they get lost (lose awareness of where they are in hyperspace) and forget how they got there. For learning purposes, an even greater problem is integration of information that learners find with their existing knowledge (Jonassen, 1988) and synthesis of that information into a meaningful communication. (See Chapter 11 for solutions to the latter problem.) That is, learners do not stop to relate new information to existing knowledge and so they do not adequately comprehend what they find. Understanding requires thinking. Browsing does not necessarily result in thinking and learning.

A self-regulated learner who keeps his or her information-seeking goals in mind and makes good decisions can find the WWW an essential information resource during intentional learning. That is the educational secret to the Internet—*intentionality.* When students say, "I am looking for information to help me answer a question/build my own knowledge base/evaluate someone else's ideas/etc.," then they are likely to learn from the experience. None of our research or wisdom claims that unfocused browsing engenders learning. Learners are easily distracted. Losing search focus only reinforces shallow learning and impedes meaning making. So, learners should have a clear purpose in mind when they are searching the WWW. They should be trying to fulfill an information need. When they articulate that need, they express an intention. That intentionality and focus are enhanced when a group of learners is committed to the same goals. They regulate each others' performance. So, when learners have an information need and they articulate that need in some coherent way, there is a high likelihood that they will benefit from searching the World Wide Web.

This chapter describes a number of tools for helping learners to articulate their intentions and to focus them into effective information searches on the WWW. Other tools and methods will no doubt emerge. In this chapter, however, we will focus on three methods: social navigation, search engines, and intelligent agents.

SOCIAL NAVIGATION

Thousands of individuals and groups are beginning to publish their ideas on the WWW (see Chapter 11), so thousands of new web sites are being added to the WWW every month. The sheer volume of information available makes navigating the WWW a difficult process. Add to that the wide range of structures, styles, and links used to design web sites, and navigation begins to appear nightmarish. Users have begun to help each other conquer the complexities of the web by collaborating directly or indirectly in the navigation task. When users e-mail URLs to others or create a web site with pointers to other favorite web sites, and other users start to use such pages as navigational tools, they are engaging in social navigation (Dieberger, 1997). Social navigation occurs when information users collaborate directly or indirectly in the navigational task. Direct social navigation, according to Dieberger, requires a form of discourse community, a group of individuals with common interests who agree to share ideas and resources. Indirect social navigation is supported by hit counters, usage paths of a group of users, or other indirect sources of information about the activities of others that provide evidence about how often information sources are being accessed. Directly supporting navigation within a discourse community will be more productive of learning than indirect.

Discourse communities assume different forms. Thousands of bulletin boards, Usenet, and NetNews services (see Chapter 13) support special interest discussion groups about a wide range of topics, from computer games to sexual deviancies. Thousands of chat rooms, multi-user domains (MUDs), object-oriented MUDs (MOOs) (see Chapter 12) connect millions of users who converse daily about every aspect of their lives. Often, these media provide URLs to other members to suggest web sites that they should visit. Likewise, thousands of web users are building web pages that are full of links to topics of interest to some community or people searching the WWW. They are reviewed, hand-selected lists of pointers to other web sites (Dieberger, 1997). For example, Figure 9.2 shows a web page that has been developed and maintained by a former student of mine, Martin Ryder. The page provides a number of links to WWW resources about the field of instructional technology. Clicking on those links takes the user to multiple sets of links to specific sites. Not only did Martin have to search out and evaluate the utility of these resources, but he also had to organize and present them in a manner that would make them usable by others. A great deal of intellectual work goes into social navigation web pages. These types of pages are not only a powerful form of communication but also a clear measure of understanding. That is, they can be assessed and evaluated as a measure of learning. How comprehensive are the resources? How well organized are they? How relevant are the sites; that is, how well have they been selected?

Dieberger (1997) has focused his research on designing social navigation places, which define the types of social interactions that take place within them. Why is a place important? Because, Dieberger argues, all human social activities are

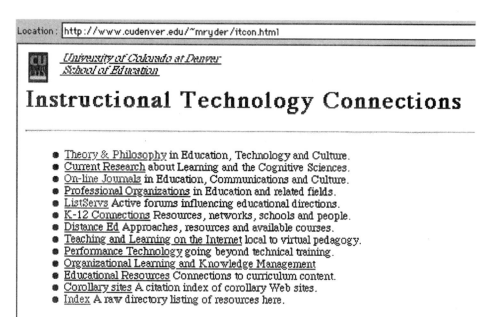

Figure 9.2
Social Navigation Web Page

influenced by the environment in which they take place. Different forms of interaction are acceptable in different places. So he seeks to build social negotiation spaces that support navigation on different issues. To that end, he has built Juggler, a HyperCard-based client that connects learners to a MOO (see Chapter 12). Learners navigate the MOO and find information and resources in different rooms. Whenever Juggler encounters a URL, it automatically accesses the URL's page from the WWW and loads it into the Netscape browser. In Figure 9.3, the front window shows the Juggler-based conversation, where users have embedded URLs, one of which is for a reading on Coleridge, which appears in Netscape on the background window. Juggler is a client that engages and supports social navigation. You can define rooms in the MOO that are associated with different issues or in the case of the MOO in Figure 9.3, different poems, poets, or interpretations. Creating discussion spaces that invoke web pages that represent different interpretations reinforces a more advanced state of intellectual development. Juggler also allows users to define or assume different characters by embedding home page URLs in each character, so that whenever anyone encounters that character in the MOO, they are automatically taken to his or her home page. Imagine students assuming the identity of a literary personality, creating a web page for that person, and then, in a Juggler-supported MOO, discussing literary issues of the day, just as the American expatriates did in Paris in the early part of the century.

Chapter 9

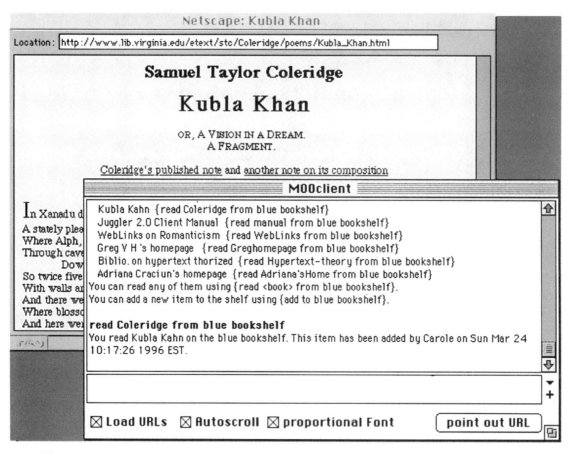

Figure 9.3
Juggler: A Client That Provides a Place for Social Navigation

SEARCH ENGINES

What Are Search Engines?

As described earlier, the WWW is a vast database of information that is unfortunately lacking in structure and organization. Anyone can develop a web site and include information, some of which may be valuable and some not. The key to doing research on the web is to find information relevant to what you need, at the time you need it, *and* to find information that is reliable and accurate. The first step in this process involves locating information; the second pertains to evaluating the source. In addition to social navigation (discussed in the previous section), most people turn to a search engine to help them identify appropriate web sites.

A search engine is a database on the WWW as well as the tools for generating the database and accessing it. People often group together under the term "search engine" two separate tools: directories and actual search engines.

Directories, such as Yahoo, are databases that use a hierarchical structure. This structure is familiar to most people because the groupings are by category, much like the subject sections in a bookstore. So if you are interested in finding information on the aurora borealis you could follow the path through the subject categories: science, astronomy, and northern lights. From here you can connect to a number of web sites that will show you what auroras look like from space and on Earth, explain how they are created, and show you where they can be found. Directories are an easy place to find information when you are looking on the web because the sites on them are reviewed by people and grouped by these people into appropriate categories.

To list a web page in a directory, the page developer submits a request to the directory along with suggestions as to which category it should be located in. The people working at the directory then examine the page and decide whether to include the page as a link from their directory and where it belongs. This takes quite a bit of time and effort, so only a small fraction of the available sites on the web are listed with each directory. To find obscure information or all the possible sites covering a subject, you need a more in-depth search. For this you need a search engine.

Search engines are also databases but they are compiled by computer programs—there is no human review of the pages and no hierarchical structure. Popular search engines are AltaVista, HotBot, and Lycos. Each of the engines works in conjunction with programs called *robots* (also referred to as *spiders* or *crawlers*) that travel across the Internet accessing web pages and storing links and information about each page. This information is arranged in the database so it can be accessed when someone requests information that matches.

Each robot operates differently. Some search all of the text in a web page, some just the heading and first few paragraphs; others include the hidden code of the page in the information they collect. Each one also searches at different speeds. Although web page authors can submit their page to the search engines, most pages are added to the database by the robot following links from other pages that it already knows about; therefore, the web sites listed with each search engine may be different.

Users access the information in search engine databases by typing in a word or phrase and the engine matches sites in the database that contain those words or phrases. When a result to a search is returned, relevancy scores are assigned that are usually expressed as a percentage. How high the percentage is depends on the location of the matched words on the web site and the frequency with which it appears; if the same relevancy rank is assigned to more than one site returned from a search, then the sites are simply alphabetized within the listing.

Each search engine operates differently in terms of how a search term can be entered, whether boolean logic or other advanced search capabilities are supported, and the different truncation symbols that may be used. Methods of ranking relevancy can also vary. In addition, search engines change their structure and capabili-

Figure 9.4
Search Cycle

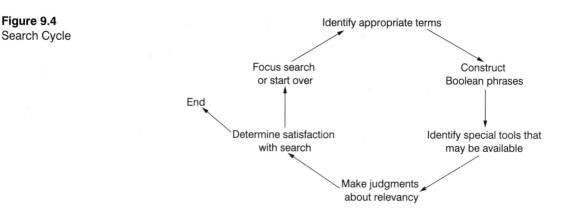

ties, often without notice, so it is difficult to know whether the search you performed one day will still be supported the next.

If you type the term "aurora" into a search engine, you might find information on the aurora borealis returned, but you are also likely to get advertisements for the Aurora automobile or the Hotel Aurora in Italy. Robots work by matching strings of letters together—there is no human review of the web sites to separate cars from constellations.

Search engines function as a Mindtool primarily because of their ability to promote reflective thinking. The learner must constantly reflect on and assess what he or she is looking for when using the search engine and how the information can be evaluated. The steps a learner goes through to accomplish a successful search may actually involve several circuits through a search cycle (see Figure 9.4).

During each step in the cycle, the learner is processing and developing information in meaningful ways in order to make the application fulfill his or her information need. The Internet is used as a storehouse of information, and the learner's job is to construct ways to retrieve only the information important to him or her at that particular place and time.

How to Use a Search Engine

Imagine your students are interested in finding out about King Tut. They can use an Internet search engine to find information about the excavation of his tomb, other tombs in the Valley of the Kings, and the King Tutankhamun exhibits at the Cairo Museum. Links from the previous sites might lead to an interest in the languages of Ancient Egypt and the differences between hieroglyphic, hieratic, and demotic writings or to an interest in the lesser known Valley of the Workers where tombs exist.

To start the search on King Tut, learners should identify all of the terms that they associate with King Tut (see Figure 9.5). The next step would be to go to the search engine that will be used and examine the Help section to learn the particular commands that are used. Then the learner would construct the search string (in this case using AltaVista commands):

((king (tut OR tutankhamun) AND (egypt* OR (valley NEAR kings) OR cairo) AND (ancient or histor* OR old) AND (tomb OR burial OR grave OR crypt)

The search string can be constructed on paper or typed into a word-processing program so that it can be copied and pasted into the search engine. The next step would be to go to the AltaVista search engine, choose the Advanced Search option, and enter the string into the box for a boolean expression (Figure 9.6). Clicking on the "Search" button would activate the search engine and the results would be returned (Figure 9.7). The learner could then click on the sites listed to judge whether the information was what he or she was looking for.

Submission of a search can take a variety of formats. The learners could construct web pages summarizing the information they found and include links to the sites they identified. Or they could use the sites as references in a written report.

Who	Where	When	What
King Tut	Egypt	ancient	tomb
King	Egyptian	historical	burial
Tutankhamen	Valley of the	old	grave
Tutankhamen	Kings	history	crypt
	Cairo		

Figure 9.5
Concept Block Diagram

Figure 9.6
Entering an Advanced Search in
a Search Engine

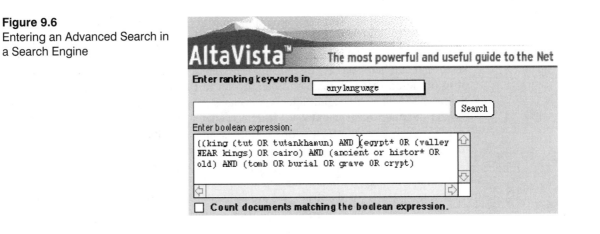

Netscape: AltaVista: Advanced Query ((king (tut OR tutankhamun) AND (egypt* OR (val

▶ **AltaVista found about 916 Web pages for you.** <u>Refine your search</u>

1. **Field Trip to Ancient Egypt**
   FIELD TRIP TO ANCIENT EGYPT. ORGANIZED BY MRS. DESLER'S 6TH GRADE HISTORY
   CLASSES. With a little research and imagination, it is possible to step into the.
   URL: www.edcoe.k12.ca.us/egypt.html
   Last modified 12-Aug-97 - page size 13K - in English [<u>Translate</u>]

   Amazon.com sugges
   <u>Books about ((king (tut ...</u>
   <u>Amazon.com Bestsellers</u>

2. **ART 263/MAN 263 The Business of Art - Sinclair Community College**
   Historic Perspective of how art has been used as a business venture college credit course offered by the Business
   Technologies Division and the Fine and
   URL: www.sinclair.edu/sec/artman263/ma263rp.htm
   Last modified 10-Mar-98 - page size 6K - in English [<u>Translate</u>]

3. **World Tours Website**
   Net News Number 3 - September 1997. 30 September, 1997. Welcome to Fisheye Netnews, our latest way to keep you up
   date with the happenings at Fisheye...
   URL: www.fisheye.com/news3.htm
   Last modified 8-Aug-98 - page size 11K - in English [<u>Translate</u>]

4. **Film and Video Resources for African Studies: Catalogue**
   The Institute of African Studies Emory University. Film and Video Resources for African Studies: Film and Video Catalogue.
   This section of the catalogue...
   URL: www.cc.emory.edu/COLLEGE/IAS/filmcat.htm
   Last modified 24-Oct-97 - page size 72K - in English [<u>Translate</u>]

5. **BJ Answers Her Mail**
   Home | News Flash | Dig This | FYI | Up Close | Daily Grind | SOS. BJ Answers Her Mail. Dear boy who asked me if they have
   SPAM in Egypt, YES!!! They sure.
   URL: website1.lanminds.com/odyssey/week4/BJResponses.html
   Last modified 14-Feb-98 - page size 3K - in English [<u>Translate</u>]

Figure 9.7
Results of Advanced Search Using a Search Engine

INTELLIGENT AGENTS

Intelligent agents are software programs that act on the behalf of people, that is, they act like *agents*. We have already discussed the complex and unorganized nature of information on the Internet. A number of intelligent agents are now being marketed that can help learners by filtering this web of information, evaluating the utility of information that is found, and passing on to the learner only those items which the learner needs. Intelligent agents automate the retrieval and processing of information obtained from the WWW. In effect, they act as personal research assistants who regularly check information resources and identify and summarize relevant information for you.

There are many types of intelligent agents. *Autonomous agents* are personal assistants that may initiate communication with other networks or users, perform monotonous tasks for the user, and even monitor the activities of the user. This latter type of agent can even modify the user's interface based on how she or he performs different tasks. Other agents read and sort users' mail, forwarding certain kinds of messages to people who may find it relevant. Other agents regularly read news sources (online newspapers or magazines), identifying articles that may be of interest to the user and downloading them to the user's computer. One of the most commonly used agents is the meeting scheduler, which automatically checks the calendars of people who need to meet and schedules the meeting for them. There are numerous cases when meeting agents compete, so the smartest agent controls the group.

The agents that we are most interested in for supporting information searches are the information retrieval agents that search numerous sources for relevant information. These agents use search engines (described earlier), but rather than using a single search strategy (as most users do), these agents select several methods to find the most relevant information for the user.

What makes these agents a Mindtool? They have intelligence. The user delegates responsibility to the agents to use that intelligence to perform on his or her behalf. It is the user who determines how the agent functions. While the agent may learn about the user's habits and adapt its performance to those habits, the user controls the goals and actions of the agent so the user can rely on it.

Agents often appear to function independently because of the intelligence that is programmed into them. That intelligence is often based on neural networks, which are adept at examining materials and discerning patterns in the data. Some are programmed to perform only simple actions (e.g., filter e-mail messages into mailboxes) while other agents interact with other agents in complex ways. Agents may even negotiate with other agents. More often, however, they are assigned the task of going out onto the network to search for materials, saving the user enormous amounts of time surfing the web.

Examples of Intelligent Agents

A number of information retrieval agents exist. The *Web Browser Intelligence Agent* ("Webby") adds agent intelligence to a web browser, allowing users to remember wherever they have been on the web and what they found there, and Webby can help them recall any word in any page that they've visited. It can alert a user, before they go to a page, whether the site is not available or the access time will be slow, via red/yellow/green web "traffic lights." It also helps them navigate more productively through the web by learning their preferences and patterns for searching for information (http://www.networking.ibm.com/wbi/wbisoft.htm).

Knowledge Utility (KnU) is a general-purpose hypermedia system offering intelligent information retrieval and management. KnU allows groups of users to weave together all forms of data, connecting knowledge into meaningful patterns that aid users in retrieving appropriate information. KnU allows an individual to identify interconnections among pieces of knowledge from different disciplines, and leaves a tangible and persistent record of that process of research and exploration. To accomplish this, KnU keeps user-specified relationships between data objects, allowing the users to receive information that is tailored to their interest patterns.

Data returned to each user is automatically prioritized based on the preferences learned from that user, using Bayesian networks (http://www.software.ibm.com/data/knu/).

E-mail is one of the biggest sources of information. How do you identify the really important messages in the flood of messages? IBM has a research prototype called the Information Overload Assistant that is designed to automatically categorize and act on e-mail messages based on user preferences. It uses rule-based intelligence (see Chapter 6) to figure out how the user handles e-mail and then automates the process.

Why use intelligent agents? They alleviate the learner's workload, and they function independently, usually notifying the user when they have completed the work. Perhaps the biggest intellectual benefit accrues from training the agent, because that forces the learner to reflect on and clearly articulate information needs in a way that is understandable to the agent. So the user and the technology form an intellectual partnership. Neither can function without the other.

Related Mindtools

Social navigation uses synchronous (Chapter 12) and asynchronous (Chapter 13) means of communication to support navigation through the Internet as well as the Internet itself. Search engines and intelligent agents make use of the Internet and WWW as information sources.

Search engines, as described earlier, are databases (Chapter 3) of URLs and WWW information. As such they are really metadatabases, that is, databases of databases of information.

Finally, intelligent agents employ artificial intelligence techniques to search through the WWW for particularly relevant information. They share some commonality with expert systems (Chapter 6), which also emerged from artificial intelligence research. Agents can function as expert systems that search the web and evaluate the relevance of information sources in terms of the needs of the learner.

Coaching the Use of Intentional Searches in the Classroom

The following steps are useful when teaching learners how to conduct a search.

1. *Make* a plan. Before beginning, students need to make a plan for the search. What do they want to find? That would depend on what they plan on doing with the results of their search. Are they producing a hypermedia knowledge base? Writing a report? Filling in a database? What points do they want to make? What learning goals will they work toward? Students need to articulate their needs in terms of their purpose. When working with students, I insist that they tell me two things before accessing the Internet. First, they have to articulate clearly the kind of information they are seeking and why they want it. Second, they have to write a search strategy (see Search Engines section earlier) for finding it.

2. *Use* tools or strategies to search the WWW. To introduce students to the structure and functions of search engines, you may want to demonstrate the steps in a search cycle. Given a question such as "How do coral and sponges on the floor of the ocean keep predators from attacking them?," the first step would be to identify appropriate terms. A concept block diagram (see Figure 9.8) can help to identify key terms and alternate terms; guiding questions go across the top with concepts and alternate concepts listed in the column underneath.

The concept block diagram can then be used to construct the boolean expression (see Figure 9.9): (reef or coral or sponge) and (ocean or sea or marine or salt water) and (defense or protection or repel or toxin or poison).

The learner will need to construct the boolean expression only after reviewing the Help section for the search engine he or she will be using since each engine varies its structure. The Help section can also assist in identifying appropriate special tools that may be used, such as typing in "feature:image" when using HotBot to make sure the search returns only those pages containing photographs or illustrations.

3. *Evaluate* the usability of the information. As your students visit web sites that have been identified, they need to evaluate the information that they find there. Does the information in each web site support the students' purpose? That is, does

What they are	Where they are	Fighting predators
Reef	Ocean	Defense
Coral	Sea	Protection
Sponge	Marine	Repel
	Salt water	Toxin
		Poison

Figure 9.8
Concept Block Diagram

	AND	
What they are	**Where they are**	**Fighting predators**
Reef	Ocean	Defense
Coral	Sea	Protection
Sponge	Marine	Repel
	Salt water	Toxin
		Poison

Figure 9.9
Concept Block Diagram with Boolean Operators

the site contain the information that they need to fulfill their intention? Are there any ideas at the site that can be used in their reports to answer the questions that they have stated? This type of reflective thinking allows the learner to reevaluate what he or she really needs and what is missing. If the learner thinks the original search worked, then satisfaction is attained and the searching stops. Otherwise, the learner can narrow the search by adding additional terms, expand the search by removing some of the terms, or simply scratch the original search and start over.

4. *Use* secondary sources. The search that students completed in the previous step would identify numerous web sites. After refining their search, if necessary, students would then look for web pages that have been developed by other students or people with similar interests that provided links to other sites. Each of those links could be searched and evaluated as well. This would allow them to socially navigate the web. If your school has access to intelligent agents, then you might want to program the agent and send it searching as well.

5. Critically *evaluate* the information. During the 1970s, many educational and children's advocacy groups promoted critical viewing curricula to ensure that elementary and junior high school students did not just watch television, but instead monitored it. While watching TV, children should be aware that TV programs and their messages are created to achieve specific results, that each person interprets programs and messages differently, and that TV programs have an underlying economic purpose.

"Neophytes in the high-tech world often *mistake downloading for thinking*" (Healey, 1998, p. 251). Students, often with teachers' and parents' blessings, construct their own representations by appropriating information and graphics from other web sites without evaluating the viability of the ideas. There are no Internet police. Anyone can put anything on an Internet server (propaganda, pornography, and perjury), and they often do. Commercial sites are the fastest growing type of site on the Internet. Organizations committed to hatred are finding a new voice on the Internet. Students are the most likely victims. It is vital that students learn how to discriminate fact from fiction, information from opinion, and reality from fantasy. Before your students download anything, they should become Info-Tectives (Healy, 1998, pp. 252–3) by asking these questions:

- Who provided this information? Why?
- Is someone trying to sell us a product or point of view?
- What kind of site did it come from (com = commercial, gov = government, edu = educational institution, org = nonprofit organization). How might the source affect the accuracy? Can we believe everything that comes from the government or an educational institution?
- What biases are likely held by the providers?
- If quotes or data are provided, are they properly referenced?
- How can we validate the information provided? Can we check the sources?
- Does the information represent theory or evidence, fact or fiction, etc.? How do we distinguish between these?

■ How do the visuals, sound, or animation influence how we interpret the information? Do visuals and text convey the same meaning?

Learning these critical viewing skills should be mandatory for any students using the Internet to collect information.

6. *Collect* the information, *use* it for the purpose intended, and *attribute* its authorship. Collect the information from the Internet by copying and pasting, paraphrasing, or interpreting (preferably) in order to meet the students' needs. My third requirement for students is triangulation. Before using any idea, they must find three separate sources that say the same thing.

Like critical viewing skills, students must learn about the sanctity of intellectual property. The ideas belong to the producer. You cannot steal them. If students use information from a site, they need to learn to properly attribute authorship. A good deal of case law will be required to clarify copyright issues on the web. However, copyright should not be a legal issue for your students; it should be a decency issue. A good option is to copy the web site URL in your students' web site, rather than copying the information. Students can produce their own social navigation pages as part of their web sites.

7. Students *reflect* on the activity. Reflection should not wait until the project is completed. Rather, students should continuously review the information they find as well as any progress toward fulfilling their goals. Are we achieving our goals? What changes in search strategy are necessary? Are we answering questions and making the points that we set out in our plan? After the project is completed, the students should reflect on the project. What have we learned about the content that we collected? What have we learned about working with each other? You may choose to provide students with some or all of the criteria for evaluating student searches (presented in the next section) to use for self-evaluation.

EVALUATING INTENTIONAL SEARCHING AS MINDTOOLS

Critical, Creative, and Complex Thinking Skills Engaged in Intentional Searches

Intentional searching is very likely to engage critical, creative, and complex thinking skills, largely because the activity is intentional. However, it is difficult to predict precisely which skills will be engaged without knowing the nature of the intentions and the search.

The primary skills engaged by intentional search are critical skills, especially those focused on evaluating information (Table 9.1). A few analyzing skills are also used, though not nearly as many as with other Mindtools. Notice that the use of intelligent agents offloads nearly every critical thinking skill to the computer. That is, the computer performs most of the cognitive operations for the learner. Intelli-

Table 9.1
Critical Thinking Skills Engaged by Intentional Searching

	Social navigation	Using search engines	Using intelligent agents
Evaluating			
Assessing information	X	X	
Determining criteria	X	X	
Prioritizing	X	X	
Recognizing fallacies	X	X	
Verifying	X	X	X
Analyzing			
Recognizing patterns			
Classifying			
Identifying assumptions	X		
Identifying main ideas	X	X	
Finding sequences			
Connecting			
Comparing/contrasting		X	
Logical thinking			
Inferring deductively		X	
Inferring inductively			
Identifying causal relationships			

gent agents are powerful examples of distributing cognitive activities to the computer.

Even fewer creative thinking skills are engaged by intentional searching (Table 9.2). Social navigation extends information by linking alternative representations. Both social navigation and the use of search engines use a couple of synthesizing skills in formulating a search. The most consistent use of creative thinking skills occurs when formulating search strategies for use with search engines. Searching for information does not consistently engage creative thinking.

Almost no complex thinking skills are required for intentional searching. Creating social navigation sites involves creating a product, though it is not usually as complex as that developed with other Mindtools. Intentional searching can be considered a form of rule-based problem solving. Formulating a search strategy involves higher order rules but does not regularly engage the kinds of problem-solving and decision-making skills that are used with other Mindtools. Because of the limited use of complex thinking skills in information searching, the table of complex thinking skills was omitted from this chapter.

Intentional searching is a means to an end. It is not the same as most of the other Mindtools, which are intended to help learners construct a knowledge base reflecting their understanding. Intentional searching is an important process that

Table 9.2
Creative Thinking Skills
Engaged by Intentional Search-
ing

	Social navigation	Using search engines	Using intelligent agents
Elaborating			
Expanding			
Modifying			
Extending	X		
Shifting categories			
Concretizing		X	
Synthesizing			
Analogical thinking			
Summarizing	X		
Hypothesizing			
Planning	X	X	
Imagining			
Fluency			
Predicting		X	
Speculating			
Visualizing		X	
Intuition		X	

learners use to help them construct their knowledge bases, so it is supportive of other Mindtools. However, because searching and finding relevant information play such essential roles in the knowledge construction process, I felt that it was worth considering how computer tools could facilitate that process. Intentional information searching tools are intended to help learners find information that they need to better represent their ideas. The tools described in this chapter help them to do that.

Evaluating the Quality of Intentional Searches

What makes an effective search? That will depend somewhat on the age and ability of your learners. Younger learners may not be expected to use as many concepts in their search strings or may not understand the concept of truncation or boolean logic. The rubrics shown in Figure 9.10 offer some guidelines for evaluating your students' searches:

Advantages of Intentional Searches

Intentional searches have these advantages:

■ Provide access to enormous collection of information.
■ Support meaning making by addressing learners' information needs.

Accuracy of concepts identified

←——————————————————————————————→

No important concepts   All important concepts
identified; unrelated   identified; no unrelated
concepts included   concepts included

Inclusion of variable concepts

←——————————————————————————————→

No variables to main con-   Significant number of concepts
cepts identified; variables   identified; variables identified
identified but not grouped   and grouped appropriately;
appropriately; variables   variables identified are related
identified not related to   to main concept
main concept

Accurate construction of Boolean expression

←——————————————————————————————→

No or inappropriate use   Appropriate use of AND/OR/
of parentheses; no or   NOT/NEAR; appropriate use of
inappropriate use of AND/OR/   parentheses; appropriate use
NOT/NEAR   of imbedded phrases

Selection of relevant sites

←——————————————————————————————→

Sites chosen not related   Sites chosen related to the
to the original search   original search question;
question   small number of highly relevant
                                         sites chosen

Figure 9.10
Possible Rubrics for Evaluating Intentional Searching Skills

Limitations of Intentional Searches

Intentional searches do, however, have limitations:

- Learning the differences between the search engines can be time consuming and they change fairly frequently—not easily learnable.
- Most search engines are trying to make the search easier, so unless an engine such as AltaVista is used in the advanced search mode the thinking on the part of the learner becomes less complex; AltaVista recently changed their simple search page to a question format where you type in a question as to what you are looking for.
- Does not "represent" knowledge in the way the other Mindtools do.
- Cannot be cumulative. A search done one day will return different results the next day—at this point there isn't any way to save and return to a search.

SUMMARY

What makes social navigation, search engines, and intelligent agents Mindtools? First, they address an intentional goal to fulfill an information need. Second, there is some intelligence in the tool. That is, the tool represents a way of thinking.

In this chapter, we have described three ways to support intentional searches of the Internet. In the coming years, increasingly sophisticated tools will become available to support Internet searching.

References

Dieberger, A. (1997). Supporting social navigation on the world-wide web. *International Journal of Human-Computer Studies, 46,* 805–825.

Healey, J. M. (1998). *Failure to connect: How computers affect children's minds—for better or worse.* New York: Simon & Schuster.

Jonassen, D. H. (1988). Designing structured hypertext and structuring access to hypertext. *Educational Technology, 28*(11), 13–16.

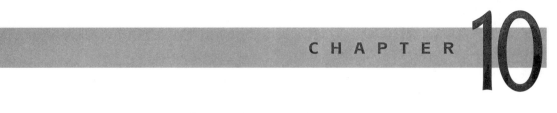

Visualization Tools as Mindtools

WHAT ARE VISUALIZATION TOOLS?

Humans are complex organisms who possess well-balanced sensorimotor systems with counterbalanced receptor and motor effector systems, which enable them to sense perceptual data and act on it using complex motor systems. Likewise, humans have reasonably keen aural perception, allowing them to hear a large range of sounds. Those sounds can be replicated or at least responded to orally by forcing air through the diaphragm, palette, and lips to create an infinite variety of sounds. However, our most sophisticated sensory system, vision, where the largest amount and variety of data are received by humans, has no counterpoising effector system. We can receive visual input, but we have no output mechanism for visually representing ideas, except in mental images and dreams, which cannot be easily shared with others. These mental images are powerful mediators of meaning making. We humans often have to visualize something before we can make sense of it, but sharing those visions is problematic. Therefore, according to Hermann Maurer, humans need visual prostheses for helping them to visualize ideas and to share those images with other.

To some extent, draw and paint packages provide those visual prostheses, enabling us to visually represent what we know. They provide sophisticated tools which enable us to draw and paint objects electronically. However, in order to represent our mental images using paint/draw programs, we have to translate those images into a series of motor operations, because it is not yet possible to dump our mental images directly from our brains into a computer. Skilled artists commonly use these tools to visualize ideas, which can help others to interpret ideas. But what is needed are tools that help most of us, who are unskilled artists, to visualize ideas.

This chapter describes a new but rapidly growing class of tools that allow us to reason and represent ideas visually without the artistic skills required to produce original illustrations. These tools help us to interpret and represent visual ideas and to automate some of the manual processes for creating images. Most of these tools are being used for visualizing scientific ideas in geography, meteorology, chemistry, and physics. Researchers in geography are especially interested in visualization tools to enhance map reading and interpretation of ideas in physical geography. Unlike the generalized representational capabilities of most Mindtools, visualization tools tend to be very task and domain specific. That is, there are no general-purpose tools for visualizing ideas across domains, except for draw and paint programs. Rather, visualization tools closely mimic the ways in which different images must be interpreted or created in order to make sense of the ideas (see Figure 10.1).

Visualization tools can have two major uses, interpretive and expressive (Gordin, Edelson, & Gomez, 1996). Interpretive tools help learners view and manipulate visuals, extracting meaning from the information being visualized. Interpretive illustrations help to clarify difficult-to-understand text and abstract concepts, making them more comprehensible (Levin, Anglin, & Carney, 1987). Expressive visualization helps learners to visually convey meaning in order to communicate a set of beliefs. Crayons and paper or paint and draw programs are powerful expressive tools that learners use to express themselves visually. However, they rely on graphical talent. Visualization tools go beyond paint and draw programs by scaffolding or supporting some of the expression. They help learners to visualize ideas in ways that make them more easily interpretable by other viewers.

HOW ARE VISUALIZATION TOOLS USED AS MINDTOOLS?

Snir (1995) argues that computers can make a unique contribution to the clarification and correction of commonly held misconceptions of phenomena by visualizing

Figure 10.1
Visualization Tools as Mindtools

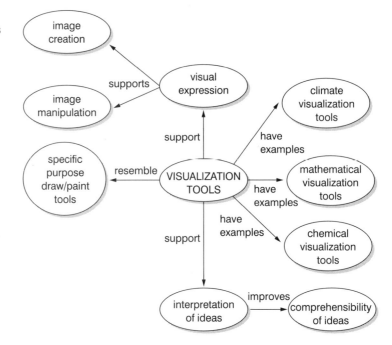

those ideas. For example, the computer can be used to form a representation for the phenomenon in which all the relational and mathematical wave equations are embedded within the program code and reflected on the screen by the use of graphics and visuals. This makes the computer an efficient tool to clarify scientific understanding of waves. By using computer graphics, one can shift attention back and forth from the local to the global properties of the phenomenon and train the mind to integrate the two aspects into one coherent picture (Snir, 1995).

Numerous visualization tools provide reasoning-congruent representations that enable learners to reason about objects that behave and interact (Merrill, Reiser, Bekkelaar, & Hamid, 1992). The graphical proof tree representation in the Geometry Tutor (Anderson, Boyle, & Yost, 1986) visualizes problem solution sequences.

Mathematical Visualization

Mathematics is an abstract field of study. Understanding equations in algebra, trigonometry, calculus, and virtually all other fields of math is aided by seeing their plots. Understanding the dynamics of mathematics is aided by being able to manipulate formulas and equations and observe the effects of that manipulation. Programs such as Mathematica, Maple, and MathLab are often used to visually represent mathematical relationships in problems so that learners can *see* the effects of any problem manipulation, such as manipulation of the values of a sin function in Figures 10.2 and 10.3. Porzio (1995) found that calculus students who used Mathematica were better able to make connections between numerical, graphical, and symbolic representations than students who used calculators or students learning via traditional methods. Engineering mechanics students who used Mathematica solved problems requiring calculus more conceptually when compared to traditional students who focused only on the procedures (Roddick, 1995). Being able to interrelate numeric and symbolic representations with their graphical output helps learners to understand mathematics more conceptually. Students in math classes and in science classes that use different forms of math can learn mathematical functions more effectively by seeing them.

Figure 10.2
Mathematica Visualization

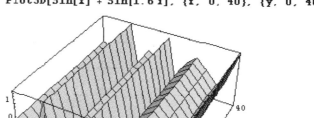

Plot3D[Sin[x] + Sin[1.6 x], {x, 0, 40}, {y, 0, 40}]

Out[6]= · SurfaceGraphics ·

Figure 10.3
Visualization of a Manipulated
Formula

In[1]:= Plot3D[Sin[x] + Sin[2.1 x], {x, 1, 20}, {y, 1, 20}]

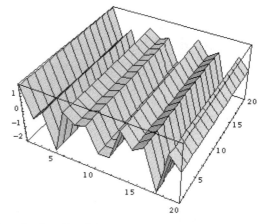

Out[1]= · SurfaceGraphics ·

Figure 10.4
Descent Path of Space Shuttle in
Mathematica

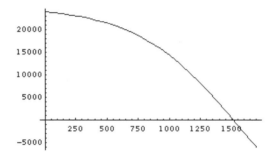

```
Clear[v,t]

NDSolve[ {v'[t] == g ( v[t]^2 / 25000.0^2 - 1.0},
           v[0]==24000.0}, v[t], {t,0.0,1700.0}]


{{v[t] ->
    InterpolatingFunction[{0., 1700.},
        <>][t]}}


Plot[ Evaluate[v[t] /. %], {t,0,1700}]
```

Mathematica is also useful for visualizing experiments. Figure 10.4 shows the plot of the descent of the space shuttle. Being able to visualize its descent makes it more understandable.

I do not mean to imply that Mathematica, Maple, and MathLab are merely visualization tools. They are much more powerful than that. They are powerful calculators, computers, storehouses of mathematical algorithms and handbooks, analyzers of data input, and systems modeling tools as well. They support students in every aspect of mathematics and statistics learning. However, for purposes of this chapter, they are powerful visualization tools.

Scientific Visualization

The Learning Through Collaborative Visualization (CoVis) Project supports collaboration among students, teachers, scientists, and educators in the design and use of a scientific collaboratory (Edelson, Pea, & Gomez, 1996). CoVis provides project-based problems to science students studying atmospheric and environmental sciences. They learn how science applies to the real world and how it raises social and political issues. Questions that have been addressed by students include the effects of global warming on the climate, immediate and long-term weather forecasting, the role of ocean temperatures on continental climate, and many others.

To help students understand climatic data, CoVis has developed a suite of tools for visualizing weather phenomena, including the Weather Visualizer, the Climate Visualizer, and the Greenhouse Effect Visualizer. These tools incorporate massive amounts of data and represent those data by colorizing portions of weather maps to convey different aspects of the weather and climate. Different colors represent, for instance, different temperatures or radiant energy, making it easier to understand the interrelationships between variables.

The Greenhouse Effect Visualizer provides atmospheric data relating the earth's energy cycle to its climate (Gordin et al., 1996). Students explore climatic processes by interpreting visuals. It enables students to call up maps from the World Wide Web that visualize the levels of incoming solar radiation, reflectivity of the earth's atmosphere, reflected sunlight, absorbed sunlight, surface temperature, earth's emissions, greenhouse effect energy, and radiation for different seasons or different months of the year. Comparing the output of these enables students to make conjectures about the greenhouse effect (Gordin, Edelson, & Pea, 1996) while investigating global warming. Comparing these data through different visualizations enables students to hypothesize cause-and-effect relationships about greenhouse effect variables. Students call up weather data sets from the WWW and plot the effects using the visualizer (see Figure 10.5), allowing them to better conceptualize the relationships embedded in the data.

The Supportive Scientific Visualization Environments for Education (SSciVEE) Project has extended the visual interpretation function of the Greenhouse Effect Visualizer and other tools to support visual expression by learners. They developed expression tools by asking learners to express themselves through drawings with crayons and paper. Students were interested not only in climatic issues but also physical geography variables such as population density, economic factors, disease, and so on. Based on their investigations, Edelson, Pea, Clark, Gordin, and Brown (1998) describe WorldWatcher software (http://www.worldwatcher.nwu.edu/), which visualizes data sets generated by the scientific community, including climatic data such as solar energy, surface temperature, greenhouse effects, energy balance, precipitation, humidity; physical geography, such as elevation, vegetation, plant energy absorption, and soil type; and human geography, such as population density,

Figure 10.5
Greenhouse Effect Visualizer

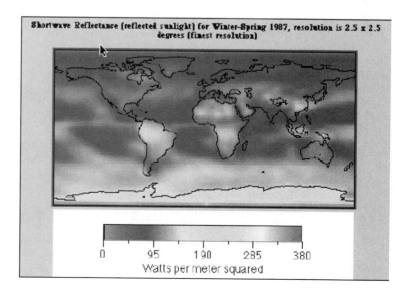

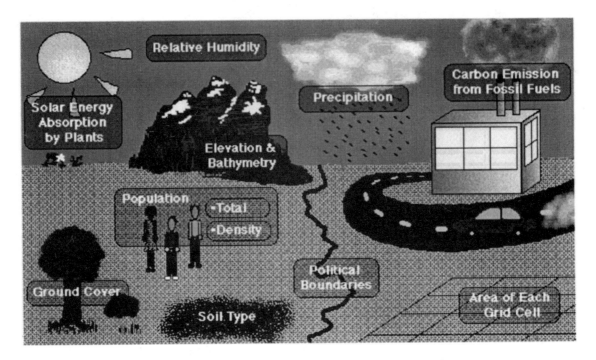

Figure 10.6
Information Visualized in WorldWatcher

carbon emissions, and political boundaries (see Figure 10.6). WorldWatcher also enables learners to build their own climatic and geographic visuals using the same data from various scientific databases.

It is important to note that these visualization tools help learners to conduct scientific inquiry. They visualize data and ideas for a purpose, not just for clarification. They allow students to better understand concepts so that they can generate hypotheses and conduct various investigations.

Chemical Visualization Tools

An excellent example of expressive visualization tools is provided by the growing number of tools available for visualizing chemical compounds. Understanding chemical bonding is difficult for most people, because the complex atomic interactions are not visible and are therefore abstractions that students usually only read about. Static graphics of these bonds found in textbooks may help learners to form mental images, but those mental images cannot be manipulated or conveyed to others. Tools such as MacSpartan enable students to view, rotate, and measure molecules using different views (see Figure 10.7) and also to modify or construct new molecules. These visualization tools make the abstract real for students, helping them to understand chemical concepts that are difficult to convey with static displays earlier in the chemistry curriculum (Crouch, Holden, & Samet, 1996).

Figure 10.7
MacSpartan Software Tool for
Visualizing Chemical Com-
pounds

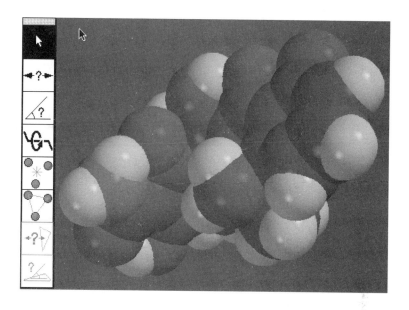

Figure 10.7
MacSpartan Software Tool for
Visualizing Chemical Com-
pounds

These chemical visualization tools provide different views of the same compounds (compare Figures 10.7 and 10.8), but also enable learners to use the objects
to the side of each screen to build and test various compounds. The programs let
students know when they try to make bonds that are not chemically possible.

Figure 10.8
MacSpartan Molecular Con-
struction Tool

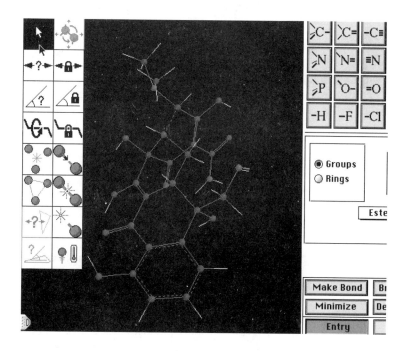

Related Mindtools

Visualization tools are distinct from most Mindtools, largely because their major use is for interpretation of information rather than for construction of knowledge bases. Most Mindtools support construction of knowledge, but not of products. Essentially, visualization tools are special-purpose draw and paint programs, so to the degree that you believe that draw and paint programs can function as Mindtools, so can visualization tools.

Coaching the Use of Visualization Tools in the Classroom

Visualization tools are normally used to support some kind of investigation or larger learning activity. They are not used, as are many Mindtools, to produce a final product, that is, a knowledge base. Rather, they are used to help learners to interpret ideas or to represent ideas while conducting and investigating a topic. For instance, the CoVis visualization tools enable students to see long-term trends in weather to help them make forecasts or suggest environmental solutions. The students use the tools to answer sophisticated questions about the effects of volcanoes on weather or predictions about temperatures far into the future (Edelson et al., 1996). These are the kinds of questions that geoscientists ask, so the investigations are authentic.

Because visualization tools are not used in a consistent manner, it is impossible to suggest how to generally use them. Coaching learning must be done in the context of the larger, investigative project.

EVALUATING VISUALIZATION TOOLS AS MINDTOOLS

It is also difficult to evaluate the effectiveness of visualization tools outside the context of the project in which they are being used. The project requirements may require that the same tools be used in different ways. Visualization tools are intended to support other activities. In reality, visualization tools are a good example of computer-supported scaffolding of learning—helping learners comprehend ideas and perform tasks that they otherwise would be unable to.

Evaluating Students' Use of Visualization Tools

The most direct way to evaluate students' use of visualization tools is to ask a group of students to perform the same project activities without the use of the visualization tools and compare their performance with students who use the visualization tools. You can then attribute any performance advantages to the visualization tools.

Advantages of Visualization Tools

Visualization tools offer these advantages:

- Clarify and correct commonly held misconceptions of phenomena by visualizing those ideas (Snir, 1995).
- Support specific kinds of reasoning.
- Enable learners to manifest visual ideas more easily and accurately.

Limitations of Visualization Tools

As with other tools, visualization tools have some limitations:

- Can become an intellectual crutch if used too consistently.
- Often requires high-resolution computers, which may not be readily available.

SUMMARY

Visualization tools can help learners to understand and express ideas that they otherwise might not be able to. They are tools that represent abstract ideas visually, enabling learners to use their most highly developed sensory system. Visualization tools are normally used to support performance in investigative projects, so they are scaffolds that enable learners to complete projects that otherwise would be difficult to complete. In this chapter, I have described only a small sample of the visualization tools that are available. Whenever your learners are having difficulty comprehending an idea, think about whether visualizations of those ideas might help. You can look for visualization tools in that domain, or you can use draw and paint programs to create your own supportive visualizations and test them on your learners to see whether a picture really is worth a thousand words.

References

Anderson, J. R., Boyle, C. F., & Yost, G. (1986). The geometry tutor. *Journal of Mathematical Behavior, 5,* 5–19.

Crouch, R. D., Holden, M. S., & Samet, C. (1996). CAChe Moleular modeling: A visualization tool early in the undergraduate chemistry curriculum. *Journal of Chemical Education, 73*(10), 916–917.

Edelson, D., Pea, R., Clark, M., Gordin, D., & Brown, M. (1998). *The SSciVEE Project: Supportive scientific visualization environments for education.* http://www.covis.nwu.edu/sciviz/sciviz.html.

Edelson, D., Pea, R., & Gomez, L. (1996). Constructivism in the collaboratory. In B. G. Wilson (Ed.), *Constructivist learning environments: Case studies in instructional design.* Englewood Cliffs, NJ: Educational Technology Publications.

Gordin, D. N., Edelson, D. C., & Gomez, L. (1996, July). Scientific visualization as an interpretive and expressive medium. In D. Edelson & E. Domeshek (Eds.), *Proceedings of the second international conference on the learning sciences* (pp. 409–414). Charlottesville, VA: Association for the Advancement of Computers in Education.

Gordin, D. N., Edelson, D. C., & Pea, R. D. (1996, April). *Supporting students' science inquiry through scientific visualization.* Paper presented at the annual meeting of the American Education Research Association, New York.

Levin, J. R., Anglin, G. J., & Carney, R. N. (1987). On empirically validating functions of pictures in prose. In D. M. Willows & H. A. Houghton (Eds.), *The psychology of illustration, Vol. 1, Basic research.* New York: Springer-Verlag.

Merrill, D. C., Reiser, B. J., Bekkelaar, R., & Hamid, A. (1992). Making processes visible: Scaffolding learning with reasoning-congruent representations. In C. Frasson, C. Gauthier, & G. I. McCall (Eds.), *Intelligent tutoring systems: Proceedings of the second international conference, ITS'92* (pp. 103–110). (Lecture Notes in Computer Science, No. 608). Berlin: Springer-Verlag.

Porzio, D. T. (1995). *Effects of differing technological approaches on students' use of numerical, graphic, and symbolic representations and their understanding of calculus.* ERIC Document Reproduction Service No. ED 391 665.

Roddick, C. S. (1995). *How students use their knowledge of calculus in an engineering mechanics course.* ERIC Document Reproduction Service No. ED 389 546.

Snir, J. (1995). Making waves: A simulation and modeling computer tool for studying wave phenomena. *Journal of Computers in Mathematics and Science Teaching, 8*(4), 48–53.]]

PART FIVE

Knowledge Construction Tools

Part 5 of this book describes a new class of Mindtools that I refer to as knowledge construction tools. Knowledge construction tools include multimedia, desktop publishing, hypertext, web site construction, CD-ROMs, and a host of related technologies. In Chapter 11, I have included all of these under the term *hypermedia*. Hypermedia are structured, interconnected multimedia knowledge bases that use all of these technologies. So, the knowledge construction tools described in this part are all included in:

Chapter 11   Hypermedia as Mindtools

The most important concept in this section is *constructionism*. Papert (1990) coined the term to describe "the theory that knowledge is built by the learner, not supplied by the teacher" and "that this happens especially felicitously when the learner is engaged in the construction of something external or at least sharable . . . a sand castle, a machine, a computer program, a book" (p. 3). Constructionism claims that learners construct knowledge most naturally and completely while they are constructing some artifact.

While all Mindtools support knowledge construction, hypermedia is an especially constructionist tool.

The rationale for constructionism is *knowledge as design* (Perkins, 1986), which argues that knowledge acquisition is a process of design, that it is facilitated when learners are actively engaged designing knowledge rather than interpreting and encoding it. Learners become designers when they focus on the purpose for acquiring information, its underlying structure, generating model cases, and using the arguments entailed by the subject matter to justify the design. Hypermedia is a powerful tool for engaging and supporting these activities. The people who learn the most from instructional materials are the designers, not the learners for whom they are designed. So let students become designers rather than learners and knowledge constructors rather than knowledge users. They will learn more in the process.

References

Papert, S. (1990). Introduction by Seymour Papert. In I. Harel (Ed.), *Constructionist learning*. Boston: MIT Laboratory.

Perkins, D. N. (1986). *Knowledge as design*. Hillsdale, NJ: Lawrence Erlbaum Associates.

Hypermedia as Mindtools

WHAT ARE MULTIMEDIA AND HYPERMEDIA?

Multimedia

Multimedia involves the integration of more than one medium into some form of communication. Multimedia such as slide/tape presentations, interactive video, and video productions have been used in education for years. Most commonly, though, this term now refers to the integration of media such as text, sound, graphics, animation, video, imaging, and spatial modeling into a computer system (von Wodtke,

1993) (see Figure 11.1). Modern multimedia workstations include high-resolution monitors, sound and video compression cards, high-capacity fixed and removable storage devices (multigigabyte hard drives, tape, Zip, and Jazz drives), and very high speed processors (approaching gigahertz speeds). Multimedia computers are able to capture sound and video, manipulate those sounds and images to achieve special effects, synthesize and produce sound and video, generate all sorts of graphics, including animation, and integrate them all into a single, seamless presentation. The software required to produce these effects is increasingly easy to use, requiring students only a few hours to master. With a little experience, individuals can become their own artists, publishers, or video producers.

Multimedia presentations get and hold students' interest because they are usually multimodal, that is, they stimulate more than one sense at a time. Many educators believe this is essential when working with today's video generation. Little current research exists on learning effects from multimedia; however, multiple-channel research from the past implies that when the channels provide complementary information, learning may increase. When the information in different channels is redundant, no improvement occurs. And when the information in different channels is inconsistent or distracting, learning decreases. These findings need to be verified with current multimedia products.

Hypermedia

Hypermedia is simply the marriage of multimedia and hypertext. Hypertext is based on the term *hyper,* meaning above, beyond, super, excessive—more than normal. Hypertext is beyond normal text. Normal text is linear, and is constructed to be read from beginning to end. The author uses a structure and a sequence to influence the reader's understanding of the topic. Hypertext refers to a nonsequential, nonlinear method for organizing and displaying text (Jonassen, 1989) that was designed to enable readers to access information from a text in ways that are most meaningful to them (Nelson, 1981). Hypertext is supertext because the reader has much greater control of what is read and the sequence in which it is read. It is based on the assumption that the organization the reader imposes on a text is more personally meaningful than that imposed by the author. Hypermedia is hypertext with multiple representation forms (text, graphics, sounds, video, etc.).

The most pervasive characteristic of hypermedia is the *node,* which consists of chunks of text, pictures, video clips, and so on. The most common metaphor for a node is a card, so a node contains information on a card. Nodes are the basic unit of information storage in hypermedia. While reading hypermedia, you can access any node (card or screen) in the hypermedia knowledge base, depending on what you are interested in looking at. Imagine a large hypermedia knowledge base on the history of the United States. Each node might consist of different documents, video clips of battles, speeches from important people, charts or graphs of economic indicators, and so on. While researching a particular theme, you could access whatever information you thought was relevant. In some hypermedia systems, the user can add to or change the information in a node or create his or her own nodes of information, so the hypertext can be a dynamic, growing knowledge base, representing

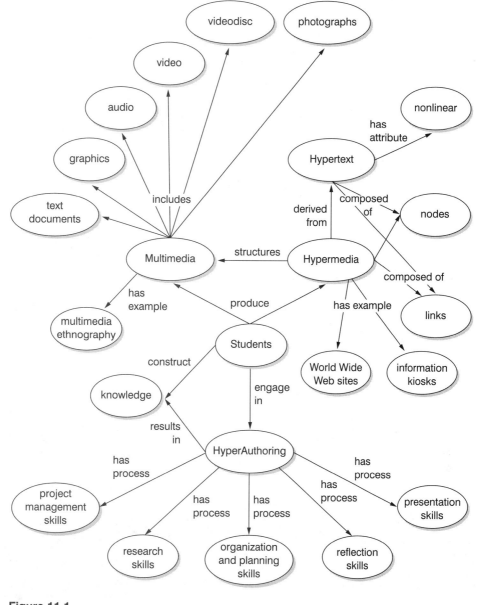

Figure 11.1
Hypermedia as Mindtools

new and different points of view. Hypermedia makes information more accessible and interesting (i.e., anchored to rich, sensory data).

In a hypermedia system, the nodes are accessed by following *links* that connect them. Links in hypermedia systems typically describe associations between the nodes that they connect. That is, while reading one node, you have links (usually identified as hot buttons or hot spots) that will take you to another node of information. At any node, you may have access to hundreds of other nodes, or only one or two. Links are usually indicated by highlighted words, which you point at and click in order to learn more about the topic. However, buttons that activate links may be part of a picture. Having arrived at the new node describing that term, you may want to return to the node from which you came or go on to another node. The structure of nodes and links forms a network of ideas in the knowledge base.

Hypermedia systems permit users to determine the sequence in which to access information (browsing), to add to the information to make it more personally meaningful, or to build and structure their own knowledge base. Like most information systems, interaction is the most important attribute. Hypermedia information systems provide interactivity by permitting dynamic user control of the information in the knowledge base.

The organization or architecture of hypermedia systems is open. The same set of nodes can be organized in many different ways to reflect many different conceptual orientations or perspectives. The hypermedia author may create a very tight structure, restricting access to information in ways that make it most easily understood, or the structure may be completely open, with immediate access to any node in the knowledge base. Large hypermedia knowledge bases, such as the knowledge base on British literature developed by the Intermedia project, may consist of 5,000 or more nodes. Learners can access any of those nodes at any time or follow theme-oriented links to related information.

Although hypermedia affords users many options, some significant problems have plagued hypertext users while browsing through existing hypermedia. The most commonly acknowledged problem when using hypermedia is that of navigation. Hypermedia documents can contain thousands of nodes, each with multiple links to other nodes, so it is easy for users to get lost in hyperspace, becoming disoriented, losing track of the route they took, unable to find their way out of the hypermedia document or to the topic they were exploring earlier. Although most hypermedia documents provide an array of options to the user, they typically do not provide suggestions for where the user should begin or proceed after beginning. This lack of direction can result in disorientation of the user.

Perhaps the greatest problem related to using hypermedia to facilitate learning is how learners will integrate the information they acquire in the hypertext into their own knowledge structures (Jonassen, 1989). Once information has been found in a hypermedia document, it needs to be related to what the learner already knows. Then learners must reorganize what they know in order to accommodate the new information. However, when learners are busily browsing hypermedia, they are often trying to take in more than they can accommodate. How can this be facilitated?

A solution to these problems is to think of hypermedia not as a source of knowledge to learn *from*, but rather as a Mindtool to construct and learn *with*. Learners can create their own hypermedia that reflect their own perspectives or understanding of ideas as they collaborate with other learners. The primary belief of this book is that students learn more by constructing instructional materials than by studying them. Ultimately, we could think about eliminating textbooks in the classroom and enabling learners to research ideas and develop their own interpretations in hypermedia. A quick caveat, though. It is important to realize that novice hypermedia producers will not be able to begin producing sophisticated programs immediately. However, like all Mindtools, it is the process of engaging in knowledge representation that is of most value, not the product.

HOW ARE HYPERMEDIA USED AS A MINDTOOL?

Hypermedia construction is an example of "knowledge as design," which refocuses the educational process away from one of knowledge as information and the teacher as transmitter of that knowledge (Perkins, 1986) to one of teachers and students as collaborators in the knowledge construction process. Hypermedia composition places students in the authors' seat so that they may construct their own understandings, rather than interpreting the teacher's understanding of the world. When constructing hypermedia, learners are actively engaged in perceiving different perspectives and organizing their own representations that reflect their sense of the communities to which they belong. Learners participate and interact with the hypermedia environment in order to invent and negotiate their own view of the subject (Jonassen, Myers, & McKillop, 1996).

- Hays, Weingard, Guzdial, Jackson, Boyle, and Soloway (1993) found that as students' experiences with hypermedia construction increase, their documents become more integrated rather than merely annotated text. Students were very enthusiastic about hypermedia production, believing that they were learning more because they understood the ideas better.
- Spoehr (1995) showed that students who build hypermedia apparently develop a proficiency to organize knowledge about a subject in a more expert-like fashion; they represent multiple linkages between related ideas and organize concepts into meaningful clusters. Superior knowledge representations support more complex arguments in written essays. Most importantly, the conceptual organization skills acquired through building hypermedia are robust enough to generalize to material students acquire from many other sources.
- Learning Spanish is facilitated by building hypermedia presentations in Spanish because they are personal representations of student knowledge (Toro, 1995).
- Fifth graders who built hypermedia that compared the lifestyles of American colonists to their own supported their inference-making skills (Lehrer & Romberg, 1996).

There are many wonderful examples of learners as hypermedia authors that have been reported in the literature. Space limitations permit me to share only a few.

Designing Information Kiosks

Beichner (1994) described a project where junior high school students worked cooperatively to assemble content materials from a wide variety of sources in order to create a touch-sensitive kiosk to be installed in the local zoo. Using HyperCard and an interface board to permit video display directly on the computer screen, students created a simple information hypermedia program for the kiosk. They worked with an on-screen audio recorder, a video tool to operate the videodisc player (see Figure 11.2), color painting and text tools, and a data-linking tool for connecting pieces of information. They used these tools to make hot spots on the kiosk screen. By touching these areas, zoo visitors could see and hear animals, look for more information, or even print an information sheet, complete with a map of the zoo and student-generated questions and comments about the animal on the screen.

The multimedia production tools enabled students to grab a "snapshot," a video sequence, or an audio sequence from the videodisc and place it onto the screen being created; create text or colorful drawings; or capture images from a scanner or electronic camera. Anything placed on the information screen could be moved, resized, and deleted through the use of a single set of keystrokes.

To prepare the multimedia kiosk, students began by talking to zoo visitors and staff. Students became interested in the people who would be viewing their multimedia information screens. They quickly gained independence, and within a few weeks

Figure 11.2
Multimedia Editing Tools Used by Students to Create an Information Kiosk

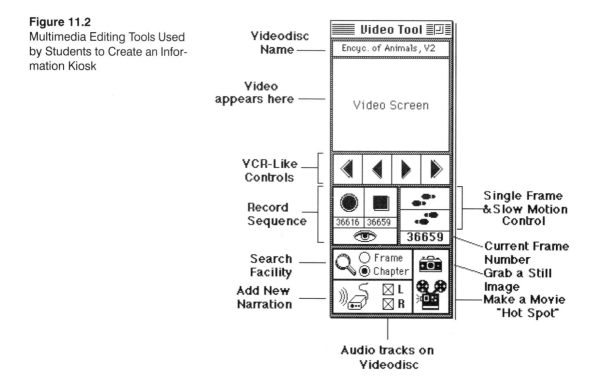

they demonstrated a strong desire to work on their own. Once they had mastered the software, roles changed rapidly. Students not only picked out what information and layout designs they would use, they also began showing other students and even their teachers how to best use the equipment and software. They began skipping study halls and lunch periods in order to work on their screens. Often the computer coordinator would arrive in the morning to find students who had come in early and were waiting for her to open the door.

The reason for this enthusiasm was that students saw that the work they were doing had importance—it was a real-world problem. It was worthwhile for them to learn new material and uncover additional resources. By establishing an environment where creative thinking about the content material is combined with real-world assignments, students will learn content, enjoy the learning process, and recognize that they have created something worthwhile that serves their community.

Hypermedia Publishing: Learners as Hypermedia Authors

Lehrer (1993) developed a tool, HyperAuthor, to engage eighth graders in designing history lessons. Knowledge, he believes, evolves from a process of design. It is not something to be transmitted from teacher to student, so students should design their own hypermedia compositions, a process he calls HyperComposition. The process requires learners to transform information into dimensional representations, determine what is and is not important, segment information into nodes, link the information segments by semantic relationships, and decide how to represent ideas. This is a highly motivating process because the ideas in the presentation are owned by the students. Ownership is the key to constructivism.

Students in the research group were high- and low-ability eighth graders developing hypermedia programs on the Civil War. They conducted library research and found pictures and video clips to exemplify many of the points they wanted to make. Students enjoyed assuming control of their learning and began to see history more as a process of interpretation than of memorization. In the process, they acquired knowledge "that was richer, better connected, and more applicable to subsequent learning and events" (Lehrer, 1993, p. 221). Research conducted by Carver, Lehrer, Connell, and Erickson (1992) showed that students worked harder, were more interested and involved, and collaborated and planned more than learners who only studied hypermedia.

Lehrer, Erickson, and Connell (1995) conducted another study on ninth-grade students developing hypermedia on World War I lifestyles between 1870 and 1920, immigration, and imperialism. They found similar results: on-task behavior increased over time, and students perceived the benefits of the planning and transforming stages of development, such as taking notes, finding information, coordinating with other team members, writing interpretations, and designing the presentation.

Figure 11.3 presents a montage of graphics that the learners created to illustrate ideas in their presentations, including charts to show the probability of soldiers returning home safely, the balance of power among the competing countries, corsets

Figure 11.3
Icons Used to Illustrate Ideas in
HyperAuthor Presentations

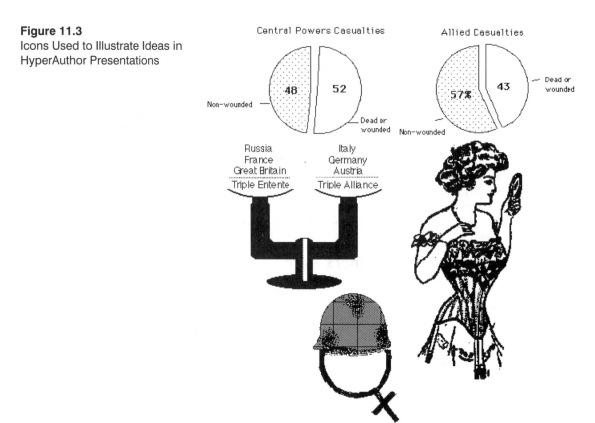

illustrating contemporary versus past lifestyles of women, and a helmet to illustrate the fight for women's rights. The results of research on hypermedia design are clear. When learners become designers, they engage readily and willingly in higher order thinking. What teacher would not favor these results?

Multiple Voices.   We recently participated in a study with seventh-grade English and social studies students to discover what rhetorical constructions, cognitive strategies, and social negotiations students engage in when constructing their own hypermedia documents (McKillop, 1996). We used ethnography, grounded theory, and phenomenology (including questionnaires, student learning logs, interviews, document analysis, videotaping, and observation as data sources) to study the process of composing hypermedia, including the composing process, construction of hyperpathways, use of media, utilization of potentials and constraints of the tech-nology, and the social construction of the knowledge presented. We asked these questions: How will students compose? How will they collaborate? How will they approach and deal with the new environment? How will they work through links and spaces? How will they employ media? and How will they utilize the constraints and potentials of the technology?

During the course of the study, seventh-grade students worked on a poetry unit and a biography unit. They collected multimedia artifacts—sounds, images, videos, and texts—which they digitized for use in constructing a StorySpace (Eastgate Systems) multimedia document. In addition to this hypermedia tool, each student developed skills in using SoundEdit Pro for digitizing voiceovers and music; Adobe Premiere for digitizing video and creating original QuickTime movies; Adobe Photoshop linked to Desk Scan for digitizing images; and ClarisWorks for word processing.

I have described the constructions of the poetry groups elsewhere (Jonassen, Peck, & Wilson, 1999), so here I will briefly describe the activities of the biography groups from the social studies classes. The biography groups were given the task of researching a famous person's life. They chose personally relevant individuals, including John Kennedy, Colin Powell, Sadam Hussein, Paul Revere, Martin Luther, and Mother Seton. They brainstormed ways to present the projects such as dressing up as Martin Luther (homemade monk suit and all), sitting Paul Revere atop a horse and filming part of the famous ride, capturing part of the Kennedy assassination video from the movie *J.F.K.* One group decided to focus on a family tree to introduce their subjects. The students chose to tell their biographies from the first-person perspective. All introduced their individuals in movies with first-person monologues. They all maintained some sort of first-person narrative throughout their hypermedia knowledge bases. One group chose to recount Paul Revere's life through a series of diary entries (see Figure 11.4).

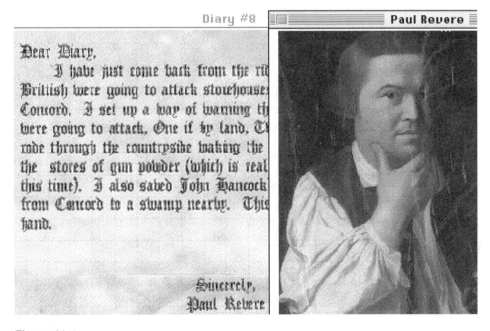

Figure 11.4
Picture and Diary Excerpt from Students' Biography of Paul Revere

Figure 11.5
Web View of StorySpace Document

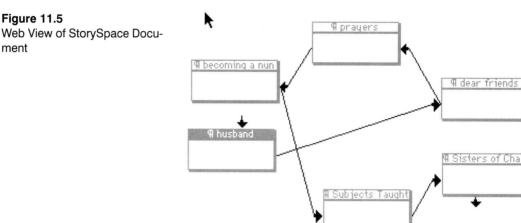

The students spent the rest of the time writing scripts and narratives, scanning images, recording and digitizing sound, creating movies, and planning and executing story spaces. Most of the linking that these students did was implicit in the narrative structures in which their projects were presented. StorySpace also provides a "web view" that graphically presents links between spaces. Figure 11.5 shows the topical organization of another group's project on Mother Seton. Each space in this web view has two features: (1) the title of the space, which when clicked on, reveals a window for writing text and media called the *writing space* (Figure 11.5); and (2) the organizational space, in which subordinate spaces are represented by identical miniature boxes. The strings between boxes indicate author-generated hyperlinks between text/media contained in each of the writing spaces. Not all of the links in a document are visible at one time because each space can contain more spaces inside spaces inside spaces and so on. When the reader double clicks in the organizational space, a new web view of the next hierarchical level of spaces and links is displayed. A single click on the title of the space *becoming a nun* in Figure 11.5 reveals the writing space in which words, graphics, music, or video clips can be placed.

Hypermedia Ethnography.   Conversational learners naturally seek opinions and ideas from others in order to become part of the knowledge building and discourse communities. Reflective learners articulate what they are doing, the decisions they are making, the strategies they are using, and the answers they are finding, while reflecting on the meaningfulness of it all. Multimedia environments may be used to engage both conversational and reflective learning, in this case, through multimedia ethnography.

Ethnographers are persons who investigate the customs, habits, and social behaviors of races and peoples. Ethnography has traditionally been used to research native, indigenous populations. Ricki Goldman-Segall (1992, 1995), at the University of British Columbia, has developed a multimedia platform, called *Learning Constellations,* for supporting ethnographic investigations and interpretations by students. *Learning Constellations* allows students to construct multimedia programs, including videos, pictures, and narratives written by them, about the topic of investigation. Her students have used *Learning Constellations,* for instance, to investigate the effects of clear-cutting in the British Columbia rain forests and examining the lives and histories of the First Nations of the northwest.

Learning Constellations also allows readers to contribute their own interpretations of original stories or create their own stories. These stories come from multiple authors (what Goldman-Segall calls *multiloguing,* rather than dialoguing) and are linked together in clusters or constellations of perspectives. These multilogues produce what Clifford Geertz (1973) calls "thick descriptions" of phenomena. The constellations of videos and stories that students produce represent larger and different patterns of meaning about the topics being studied (see Figure 11.6). "Layers build; stories change; patterns emerge; and inquiry becomes reflexive practice" (Goldman-Segall, 1995, p. 6). It is that kind of reflection that makes *Learning Constellations* a powerful multimedia experience.

The student storytelling afforded by *Learning Constellations* leads to the social construction of knowledge. Students work together to investigate issues in multiple levels of conversation (see Figure 11.7). Students go out into the real world and investigate socially relevant problems. They collect evidence about those problems, usually in the form of video interviews and documentaries. They analyze, digitize, and assemble those videos into multiple-voice story chunks, called "stars," which include the videos and the student annotations of them. These stars, produced and told by different people to represent their unique points of view, are assembled into larger groupings called "constellations." As other students or the public examine the students' multimedia database, they add their own views and annotations. Why? Because "the process of making discoveries and the process of recursive reaction, within the data and among the users, that meaning of an event, action, or situation

Figure 11.6

Perspectives Available from *Learning Constellations* Knowledge Base

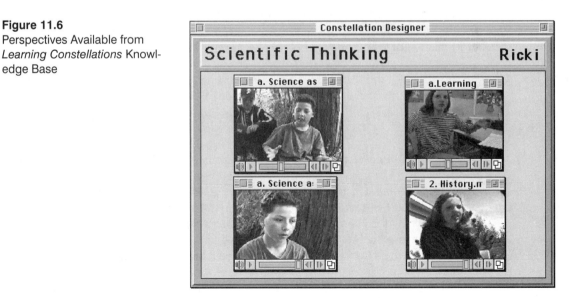

Figure 11.7
Available Perspectives

can be negotiated" (Goldman-Segall, 1992, p. 258). Having students design and film their own video narratives creates a video culture in the classroom—not a passive culture of viewing video, but rather a culture of constructing videos to tell a complex and important story. In becoming video ethnographers, students become friends with the camera; become a participant recorder by training fellow researchers, teachers, and students on how to use video for observation; become a storyteller by selecting video chunks and writing narratives; and become a navigator by exploring the use of video in new situations (Goldman-Segall, 1992).

Designing Multimedia Web Sites

Designing and developing web sites has become the preferred mode of hypermedia construction these days. Students everywhere are developing sophisticated web sites that provide important information to users around the world. One of my favorites is the Virtual Schoolhouse (Jonassen et al., 1999). Students at the Andrew Robinson Elementary School in Jacksonville, Florida, have created a *virtual schoolhouse* (http://www.rockets.org/). Students created and maintain their web site in collaboration with their teachers, principal, and local businesses. The site provides a very interesting, easy-to-use tour of their school, providing lots of information about what students are learning. It features student artwork.

Drawings of the building are used as clickable maps, so users of the web site click on pictures to virtually tour the school. Figure 11.8 shows, for example, the lobby. By clicking on a door, you move through it. When you click on the door to the administrative offices, you see a counter, plants, and labeled doors for the principal, assistant principal, counselor. When you click on the principal's door, you see the image shown in Figure 11.9.

Each image has many links to other places and information. In the principal's office, for example, clicking on the file drawer labeled "Teachers" brings up a list of links to the classrooms and information about the teachers. Follow the link to the computer teacher's lab, and you'll see artwork of a row of computers, the monitors of which show the names of software the students use (HyperStudio, Digital Chisel, etc.). If you click on one of the monitors, you get information about that software, how the students use it, and more.

Where will the students take the project in the future? They want to develop a *virtual reality* tour, of course. Using a new software product called RealVR, the students decided that they should add virtual reality capability to their site. Figure 11.10 provides a small sample of what their virtual reality site looks like. The picture you see moves in any direction. If you hold the mouse button down and drag in any direction, the image scrolls. You can turn all the way around (360 degrees), and keep going. You can look up and down, and by using the shift and command keys you can zoom in and out.

Although virtual reality adds a new dimension to their site, I hope that it does not completely replace their artwork, which adds personal meaning. The students are now faced with a series of new decisions to make about how to integrate this new technology with their existing artwork. It is obvious from their web site that

Figure 11.8
Introduction to Virtual Schoolhouse

Sketch by Nereus Manning, 5th Grade Student
Please explore our school by clicking on the colored areas.

Figure 11.9
Principal's Office in the Virtual
Schoolhouse

Figure 11.10
Virtual Lobby

these students are growing intellectually through their use of state-of-the-art tools. This is a great example of how web site development gives new meaning to their reading, writing, artwork, communication skills, and computer skills.

Related Mindtools

In a sense, multimedia is the amalgam of all other media, so it could be composed of any other communication form. In that case, any other information sources, including databases, spreadsheets, semantic nets, and expert systems, could be included. In reality, however, multimedia makes scant use of most of these resources. Probably the most related Mindtool is the semantic network, which can be used as a structure for hypermedia knowledge bases. Jonassen (1990, 1991) described how semantic nets can be modeled in the interface of multimedia and hypermedia systems, so that the experts' organization of ideas can be mapped onto the materials. Research has cast some doubt on the effectiveness of this approach, however (Jonassen & Wang, 1993).

Coaching the Construction of Hypermedia in the Classroom

Lehrer (1993) has developed a very good framework for HyperComposition, which consists of four major processes:

1. **Students *make* a plan.** Planning requires that students make decisions about the major goals of the knowledge base (who is the audience, what they should learn), what topics and content will be included in the knowledge base, the relationships among the topics (how they will be linked), and how the interface will look (what functions should be provided to the learner). We have modeled certain processes, such as using notecards to represent nodes and connecting them with pieces of string. You, the teacher, must guide but not control this process. Probably the most important thing that you can do is to give the students a meaningful task, usually to design and develop some instruction for their peers. In the kiosk example described earlier, students were compelled by the real-world nature of the task; they were producing a multimedia program that would be used to guide visitors through a zoo. The task was meaningful because it was real world. Ask questions; don't give directions. Lehrer (1993) suggests questions such as the following:

- How are you going to organize your presentation, and why?
- How are you going to decide on what to include and what to leave out?
- Can you draw a map of the flow of your program? Does it seem logical?
- Which stories do you want to include, and what do they represent?
- Which are the most important themes in describing your content? How did you determine that they were the most important?

If students are missing a crucial part of the plan, then make sure they know about it. The students also need to decide how they will collaborate to complete all of the tasks required to construct the program.

2. *Access,* *transform,* and *translate* **information into knowledge.** This is the heart of the learning process. This is where students construct their own understanding of the content. Be sure not to transmit your own. Students must search and collect relevant information to fulfill their planned presentation, select the most important information and interpret it for whatever media they are using, develop and represent new perspectives, and allocate their interpretations to nodes. This interpretive process requires that students decide how information will be represented (text, graphics, pictures, video, audio) and then decide how the information will be linked to provide access to the readers. Our research has shown that students are usually very considerate of the viewers of their programs; they want their products to be desirable.

3. *Evaluate* **the knowledge base.** Students must evaluate the effectiveness of their productions. Has it met its goals? Will the readers like it? Student producers must assess how they represented and organized the information. They then need to try out the program with users and solicit their feedback.

4. *Revising* **the knowledge base.** Based on the feedback they get during tryouts, students should correct any content errors that may have been reported and reorganize the program to make it more accessible or meaningful for the users.

5. *Reflect* **on the activity.** After the project is completed, the students should reflect on the project. What have we learned about the content they were representing? What have we learned about hypermedia production for representing what they know? What have we learned about working with each other? You may choose to provide students with some or all of the criteria for evaluating student hypermedia presentations (presented in the next section) to use for self-evaluation. The activity of constructing hypermedia engages a range of meaningful learning. Reflection cements the knowledge that learners construct.

EVALUATING HYPERMEDIA CONSTRUCTION AS MINDTOOLS

Designing hypermedia presentations is a complex process that requires many skills of learners. Carver et al. (1992) listed some of the major thinking skills that learners need to use as designers, including the following:

1. *Project management skills:* Creating a time line for the completion of the project; allocating resources and time to various segments of the project; assigning roles to team members

2. *Research skills:* determining the nature of the problem and how the research should be organized; posing thoughtful questions about the structure; searching for information using textual, electronic, and pictorial sources of information; developing new information with surveys, interviews, questionnaires, and other sources; analyzing and interpreting all of the information collected to find and interpret patterns

3. *Organization and representation skills:* deciding how to segment and sequence information to make it understandable; deciding how information will be represented (text, pictures, video); deciding how the information will be organized (hierarchy, sequence) and linked

4. *Presentation skills:* mapping the design onto the presentation, implementing the ideas in multimedia; attracting and maintaining the interest of the audience

5. *Reflection skills:* evaluating the program and the process used to create it; revising the design of the program using feedback.

You can create a checklist and ask or observe students about their use of these skills. These skills call on a variety of critical, creative, and complex thinking skills. In the next section, I analyze those skills that are needed to research information, design the hypermedia presentation, and manage the project, the three major classes of activity identified by Carver et al. (1992).

Critical, Creative, and Complex Thinking in Hypermedia Construction and Use

The most difficult and engaging part of the multimedia design and development process, as evidenced in Tables 11.1, 11.2, and 11.3, is organizing and designing the

Table 11.1
Critical Thinking Skills Engaged by Hypermedia Development

	Researching information	Organizing and designing presentation	Managing project
Evaluating			
Assessing information	X		
Determining criteria	X	X	
Prioritizing	X	X	X
Recognizing fallacies	X	X	
Verifying	X		
Analyzing			
Recognizing patterns		X	
Classifying	X		
Identifying assumptions	X	X	
Identifying main ideas	X	X	
Finding sequences	X	X	
Connecting			
Comparing/contrasting	X		
Logical thinking			
Inferring deductively		X	
Inferring inductively	X		
Identifying causal relationships			X

presentation. However, responsibilities do vary some. Researching the information that will go into the presentation involves critical thinking skills more than creative or complex thinking skills (Table 11.1). Organizing that information involves evaluating and analyzing skills, as the learners determine what information is useful and relevant to the presentation. Similarly, designing and organizing the presentation involves many critical thinking skills, especially analyzing. Learners must determine the purpose of the presentation and evaluate different approaches to organizing it. In addition to good negotiating skills, this step requires critical thinking. Note that managing the multimedia development project does not require many critical thinking skills.

Creative thinking is primarily involved in organizing and designing the presentation (Table 11.2). Selecting or designing multimedia resources such as graphics, animation, sound, and video involves elaborating on the plan and imagining and synthesizing how it should look. If this part of the process is not done well, the audience's attention will not be maintained. This is the part that learners usually enjoy the most. However, retrieving information to go in the multimedia program also involves creative thinking skills for designing questionnaires and other data-gathering instruments. If students botch this part of the process, there will be little of meaning or importance to present.

Organizing and designing the presentation requires the most complex thinking skills (Table 11.3). However, project management also uses a number of problem-

Table 11.2
Creative Thinking Skills Engaged by Hypermedia Development

	Researching information	Organizing and designing presentation	Managing project
Elaborating			
Expanding	X	X	
Modifying	X	X	
Extending		X	
Shifting categories	X	X	
Concretizing		X	
Synthesizing			
Analogical thinking			
Summarizing	X	X	
Hypothesizing			
Planning			X
Imagining			
Fluency		X	
Predicting		X	X
Speculating		X	
Visualizing		X	
Intuition		X	

Table 11.3
Complex Thinking Skills Engaged by Hypermedia Development

	Researching information	Organizing and designing presentation	Managing project
Designing			
Imagining a goal		X	
Formulating a goal		X	X
Inventing a product		X	
Assessing a product		X	
Revising the product		X	X
Problem Solving			
Sensing the problem		X	
Researching the problem	X		
Formulating the problem		X	X
Finding alternatives		X	
Choosing the solution		X	
Building acceptance			X
Decision Making			
Identifying an issue		X	X
Generating alternatives		X	X
Assessing the consequences			X
Making a choice		X	
Evaluating the choice		X	X

solving and decision-making skills. Ensuring that team members know what to do and that all the activities are scheduled and completed on time so that the presentation can come together is a complex thinking process that requires a lot of simultaneous thinking. Producers often have to be able to do several things at the same time. While simultaneous thinking is not as important in organizing and designing the presentation, a great many problems need to be solved. Deciding how to capture video, creating pictures and animations, and programming them into the presentation are examples of complex thinking activities.

Evaluating Student Hypermedia Productions

In addition to assessing the students' use of project management skills, research skills, organization and representation skills, presentation skills, and reflection skills or their use of critical, creative, and complex thinking skills, Figure 11.11 presents a number of rubrics that you may use to evaluate the hypermedia programs and web sites that your students construct as their knowledge and skills move from emergent to mastery. You will probably want to adapt these or add your own criteria as you evaluate your students' projects.

Accuracy of information in nodes

← ── →

Information is out of date,
inaccurate, unclear, plagiarized

Information is timely, accurate,
well documented, properly
attributed

Representation of information in nodes

← ── →

Overuse of one or more media;
representations convey no
meaning—used for their own sake

Text, graphics, sound, video are
balanced; each used to convey
ideas uniquely and clearly; media
enhance understanding of ideas

Quality of media representations

← ── →

Sounds is warbling, fuzzy,
distorted, too loud, or too quiet;
graphics are fuzzy, unbalanced,
unclear; video is jiggly, jerky,
unfocused, or not concentrated
on topic

Sound is clear, undistorted,
sufficient loudness; graphics are
focused, undistorted, well labeled,
well balanced; video shots are
smooth, stable, with smooth
transitions

Links are meaningful and descriptive

← ── →

Links are random; don't afford
navigation to locations; unlabeled
and unclear as to purpose

Links support smooth navigation;
explicate ideas; clearly labeled as
to type; support navigation by users

Screen design

← ── →

Objects move around screen;
unbalanced composition; effects
are distracting; overuse of color,
objects, or effects

Consistent placement of objects;
balanced objects; effects are
helpful and not distracting

Nodes organized in meaningful, informative structures

← ── →

Content too large or too small
to be accessible or useful;
inconsistent use of nodes

Content broken into digestible
nodes with clear purpose; labeled

Purpose of hypermedia knowledge base clear to user

← ── →

Purpose unclear; knowledge
base not interesting or useful
to users

Purpose communicated to users;
meets their needs, interests or
purposes

Figure 11.11
Rubrics for Evaluating Student Hypermedia Productions

Evaluating Multimedia and Hypermedia Software

There are different kinds of tools to support multimedia and hypermedia products. I will briefly review some of these.

Multimedia Production Packages. A number of powerful, expensive commercial software packages are available for producing multimedia programs. The first group is designed to produce one-way multimedia presentations. Programs such as Microsoft Powerpoint, Adobe Premiere, Astound, and Cinemation for the Macintosh are powerful multimedia presentation development systems. They import graphics and play QuickTime movies but usually have limited animation capabilities. A number of packages are designed to produce interactive multimedia presentations. Advanced systems, such as Macromedia Director for the Macintosh and Authorware Professional for the Macintosh and Windows machines, add full animation capabilities and higher levels of interactivity, all at a cost of up to $5,000. These systems are designed to produce glitzy programs and are not used as often in schools as they are by commercial producers.

Hypermedia Development Packages. The most commonly used packages for producing hypermedia in schools are a midrange class of tools, such as SuperCard for the Macintosh and Toolbook for Windows machines. Producer versions cost up to $500 but afford a great deal of flexibility in programming more complicated instructional hypermedia programs. In most cases, the price of this flexibility is having to learn an object-oriented scripting language in order to produce advanced interactivity. These programs import graphics and movies but have limited production capabilities. They produce card-oriented presentations. A number of school-based projects rely on Toolbook and SuperCard because of their flexibility, but they are not as easy to learn to use as the next class of multimedia and hypermedia tools.

Some school-based multimedia production projects that were described in this chapter have resulted in the development of multimedia authoring systems. Products such as Mediatext and HyperAuthor have limited capabilities for importing multimedia resources, but they are designed to provide a friendly, easy-to-use authoring environment for students, and they are very inexpensive. They have to be obtained from the authors. Commercial hypermedia authoring tools for schools, such as HyperStudio and Digital Chisel, are easy-to-use packages with a student-oriented interface. Although these are easy to use, they offer limited kinds of interactivity and flexibility. My personal favorite is StorySpace from Eastgate Systems. Available for Macintoshes and Windows machines, it emphasizes the hyperlinking and organization of ideas in a semantic network-type interface, yet affords the inclusion of sounds, graphics, and video.

Web Development Packages. The World Wide Web is rapidly becoming the primary publishing medium for student-produced hypermedia projects. Publishing on the Web requires that HTML (hypertext mark-up language) be added to text and other materials. Most application software, like word processors, is able to save files with HTML coding in it automatically. Most of the multimedia and hypermedia products listed before also produce HTML versions of their programs. Additionally, a large number of web development packages are now available to support hypermedia development for the web. Programs such as PageMill, Front Page, Home Page, and many others provide user-friendly tools for designing and producing World Wide Web pages. These are very popular in schools.

Advantages of Hypermedia as Mindtools

Hypermedia constructions present these advantages:

- Learners are much more mentally engaged by developing materials than by studying materials. The search for information supports more meaningful learning when students plan to publish their products.
- Multimedia permits concrete representations of abstract ideas and enables multiple representations of ideas (Hays et al., 1993).
- Students constructing multimedia and hypermedia are actively engaged in creating representations of their own understanding by using their own modes of expression. Multimedia affords more creative expression than text-only presentations.
- Students are highly motivated by the activity because they have ownership of the product. They are normally very proud of their productions.
- Building multimedia and hypermedia orients teachers and students away from the notion that knowledge is information and the teacher's role as transmitter of it (Lehrer, 1993).
- Designing knowledge in the form of multimedia presentations promotes the development of critical theories of knowledge (not every design is successful) and critical thinking, such as defining the nature of the problem and executing a program to solve it (Lehrer, 1993).

Limitations of Hypermedia as Mindtools

Hypermedia constructions have these limitations:

- Construction of multimedia and hypermedia is a time-consuming process.
- There are more significant hardware and software requirements for multimedia construction than for other Mindtools. To integrate audio, graphics, and video into presentations, a scanner, an audio/video capture card, a larger-than-normal color monitor, speakers, a video camera, and more sophisticated multimedia software are needed. The software tools are not terribly expensive, but the hardware can be. Usually only one or two multimedia production machines are needed per school, so this will limit the cost somewhat.

SUMMARY

The recent, phenomenal growth of multimedia and the World Wide Web has changed the face of computing. Most personal computers today are multimedia workstations, replete with large screens, stereo speakers, and high-density storage devices to accommodate memory-hungry multimedia programs. In educational computing circles in the early 1990s, multimedia was the answer; what was the question? Commercial software producers focused nearly all of their products for multimedia publication on the Web. It is very unlikely that this web-multimedia mania will substantively affect learning in schools unless and until students become the drivers. Most students today have grown up with multimedia, so delivering the same kind of instruction in multiple channels may attract but will not sustain their attention. However, allowing students to become designers of multimedia and hypermedia engages those students who become involved in new ways. Hypermedia provides a useful conceptual framework for designing multimedia materials. The combination of creativity and complexity required to author hypermedia in a form that is intrinsically motivating to students (multimedia) makes it probably the most compelling and potentially effective of all Mindtools. The richness of representational forms available in multimedia knowledge bases is greater than that in all other Mindtools. More future research will very probably document the effects of designing *with* hypermedia rather than learning *from* it.

References

Beichner, R. J. (1994). Multimedia editing to promote science learning. *Journal of Educational Multimedia and Hypermedia, 3*(1), 55–70.

Carver, S. M., Lehrer, R., Connell, T., & Erickson, J. (1992). Learning by hypermedia design: Issues of assessment and implementation. *Educational Psychologist, 27*(3), 385–404.

Geertz, C. (1973). *The interpretation of cultures.* New York: Basic Books.

Goldman-Segall, R. (1992). Collaborative virtual communities: Using Learning Constellations, a multimedia ethnographic research tool. In E. Barrett (Ed.), *Sociomedia: Multimedia, hypermedia, and the social construction of knowledge.* Cambridge, MA: The MIT Press.

Goldman-Segall, R. (1995). Configurational validity: A proposal for analyzing ethnographic multimedia narratives. *Journal of Educational Multimedia and Hypermedia, 4*(2), 163–182.

Hays, K. E., Weingard, P., Guzdial, M., Jackson, S., Boyle, R. A., & Soloway, E. (1993, June). *Students as multimedia authors.* Paper presented at the Ed Media conference, Orlando, FL.

Jonassen, D. H. (1989). *Hypertext/hypermedia.* Englewood Cliffs, NJ: Educational Technology Publications.

Jonassen, D. H. (1990). Semantic network elicitation: Tools for structuring of hypertext. In R. McAleese & C. Green (Eds.), *Hypertext: The state of the art.* London: Intellect.

Jonassen, D. H. (1991). Representing the expert's knowledge in hypertext. *Impact Assessment Bulletin, 9*(1), 93–105.

Jonassen, D. H., Myers, J. M., & McKillop, A. M. (1996). From constructivism to construc-tionism: Learning *with* hypermedia/multimedia rather than *from* it. In B. G. Wilson (Ed.), *Constructivist learning environments: Case studies in instructional design* (pp. 9–106). Englewood Cliffs, NJ: Educational Technology Publications.

Jonassen, D. H., Peck, K., & Wilson, B. G. (1999). *Learning with technology: A constructivist perspective*. Upper Saddle River, NJ: Merrill/Prentice Hall.

Jonassen, D. H., & Wang, S. (1993). Acquiring structural knowledge from semantically structured hypertext. *Journal of Computer-Based Instruction, 20*(1), 1–8.

Lehrer, R. (1993). Authors of knowledge: Patterns of hypermedia design. In S. P. LaJoie & S. J. Derry (Eds.), *Computers as cognitive tools*. Hillsdale, NJ: Lawrence Erlbaum Associ-ates.

Lehrer, R., Erickson, J., & Connell, T. (1995). Learning by designing hypermedia docu-ments. *Computers in Schools, 10*.

Lehrer, R., & Romberg, T. (1996). Exploring children's data modeling. *Cognition & Instruc-tion, 14*(1), 69–108.

McKillop, A. M. (1996). Unpublished doctoral dissertation, Pennsylvania State University.

Nelson, T. (1981). *Literary machines*. Swarthmore, PA: Author.

Perkins, D. N. (1986). *Knowledge as design*. Hillsdale, NJ: Lawrence Erlbaum Associates.

Spoehr, K. T. (1995). Enhancing the acquisition of conceptual structures through hyperme-dia. In K. McGilly (Ed.), *Classroom lessons: Integrating cognitive theory and classroom practice*. Cambridge, MA: Bradford Books.

Toro, M. A. (1995). The effects of HyperCard authoring on computer-related attitudes and Spanish language acquisition. *Computers and Human Behavior, 11*(3/4), 633–647.

von Wodtke, M. (1993). *Mind over media: Creative thinking skills for electronic media*. New York: McGraw-Hill.

PART SIX

Conversation Tools

P art 6 of this book describes another new class of Mindtool that I refer to as conversation tools. The chapters in this part cover conversation tools:

When most people think about learning, they assume that it occurs only in individuals; it results in changes in the mind; and that it can be measured and described quantitatively. And whatever it is, learning occurs in the head. Without dealing with the philosophical assumptions of such beliefs, let me suggest that there are new theories of learning (at least new to our field) that conceive of learning as a social process, not just an individual one. Social constructivists believe that learning is the dynamic interplay between the activities that people engage in and the sense of that activity that they socially negotiate. Knowledge in this view is not an object that is acquired and possessed by individuals. Rather, it is embedded in the social relations and identities of the learners as well as in the conversations and social discourse they use to make meaning of the activities and events they are part of.

Learning, at least to some degree, results from social negotiation of meaning. When learners share ideas, question each others' beliefs, argue about the meaning of something, they are building community knowledge as well as establishing their identity. When people socially co-construct meaning, the primary medium of discourse is a story. Listen to most conversations, and you will hear people telling stories that relate to the stories that the previous speaker just told. They provide a natural flow of conversation.

The point is simple: students don't always have to learn *from* the teacher. They can also learn by discussing problems, beliefs, and expectations with each other. Technology can support social learning through computer conferencing. Most people engage in social discourse every day as a way of solving problems, articulating their identity, and co-constructing meaning. Millions of people spend many hours per week doing the same with strangers in chat rooms, user groups, and multi-user dungeons all over the Internet. The next two chapters focus on how these synchronous and asynchronous conferencing methods can be used to engage your students in social learning. Supporting meaningful conversations among your students and between your students and others around the world shows them new perspectives and helps them to collaboratively construct knowledge in new learning communities.

Synchronous Conferencing as Mindtools

WITH CHAD CARR

WHAT IS SYNCHRONOUS COMMUNICATION?

Synchronous communication (also known as *real-time* communication) usually occurs face to face, with two or more people communicating with each other at the same time and typically, though not necessarily, in the same place, thanks to telephones, video conferences, etc.

Synchronous conferences occur when two or more computers are connected to each other over a network to share data (e.g., text, audio, video, files, etc.), enabling people to communicate with each other at the same time. Synchronous connections are open to each other. They are real time.

Synchronous conferences can support networked learning communities consisting of students and teachers communicating with other students, teachers, mentors, experts or others that may enhance teaching or learning. Even before the development of the World Wide Web (WWW) in the early 1990s, many of us were meeting and chatting via the Internet. There were hundreds of servers that provided such capabilities such as Internet Relay Chat and multi-user domains such as MUDs, MOOs, MUSEs, and MUSHs, each of which served hundreds or even thousands of users (Bartle, 1990) (see Figure 12.1). The benefits of communicating synchronously using these applications include low cost, cross-platform compatibility, and distance compatibility.

Internet Relay Chat (IRC) is the oldest form of synchronous conferencing. It provides for basic interactions through typed messages between a group of users (see Figure 12.2). Members who join the group discussion appear in the right column; the discussion then unfolds line by line in the left column. This form of discussion is still popular, but can be confusing to young students or IRC novices because lines tend to be added very quickly as the number of participants increases (Schiano, 1997).

Figure 12.1
Synchronous Conferencing as a Mindtool

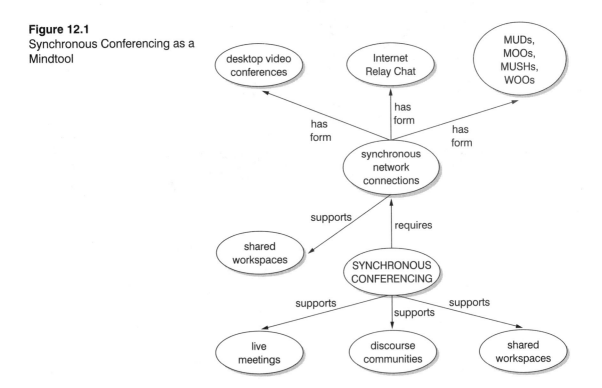

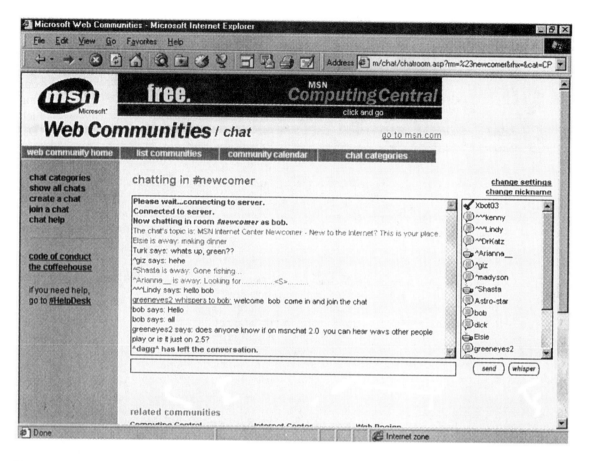

Figure 12.2
Internet Relay Chat Using the Microsoft Network

Extensions of IRC have incorporated more explicit and elaborate online environments. These shared, online environments have become known as multi-user
domains (MUDs), MUDs object-oriented (MOOs), multi-user, web-based, object-
oriented (WOOs), multi-user, shared-hallucinations (MUSH), etc. A benefit of
these synchronous conferencing applications is the ability to save or print an entire
conversation. The simplest of these are the text-based MUD and MOO formats (see
Figure 12.3). As you can see near the bottom of Figure 12.3, participants can use
commands to find out more about the environment including what objects are present (e.g., books, statues, pool tables, paintings, etc.), who is present (e.g., who,
how long, where from, how old, etc.), and where else they can visit in the virtual
environment (e.g., the gym, the parlor, etc.)

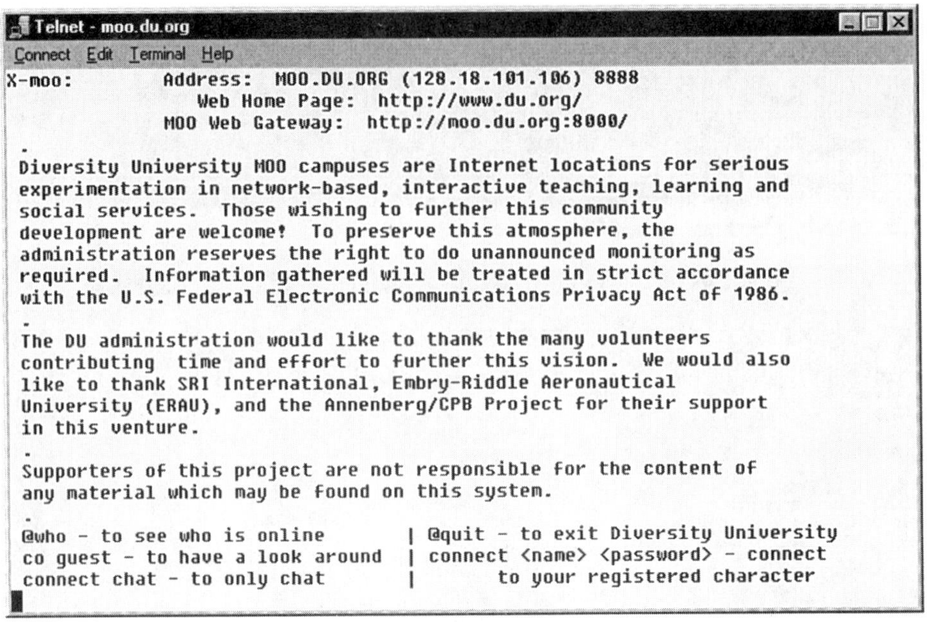

Figure 12.3
Diversity University's MOO

Out of these primitive, text-based conferencing environments have come more sophisticated virtual environments that include visual objects, environments, and characters that can communicate via pop-up text bubbles or audio (see Figure 12.4). The participants can dress themselves as different avatars (e.g., singer, young person, police officer, smiley-face, etc.) travel to different locations in the environment, and participate in online games (e.g., pinball, backgammon, etc.) while conversing.

A newer and even more sophisticated mode of synchronous communication through networked computers is *desktop videoconferencing*. Desktop conferencing may include the transmission of "live" data between computers over a network, including audio, video, text, files, screens, pictures, and shared applications (see Figure 12.5).

Microsoft's Netmeeting software supports the following kinds of interactions:

■ Live text chat (can be saved or printed)
■ Shared whiteboard space (can be saved or printed)
■ Video images, live pictures of participants or prerecorded video
■ Audio

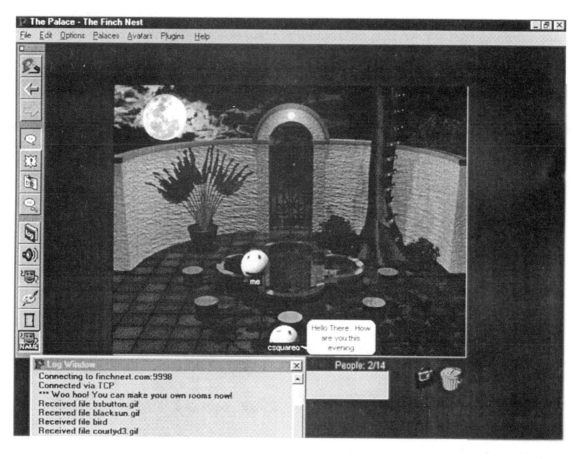

Figure 12.4
The Palace—A Virtual Environment

■ File transfer (instantly send files back and forth)
■ Application sharing (can share entire control of an application with distant users).

Such conferencing capabilities used to be reserved for large corporations. Now, an average computer and a modem-based Internet connection will allow such communications. Microsoft Netmeeting (http://www.microsoft.com/netmeeting/) is a free software application that works only on Windows computers. CU-SeeMe (http://www.cuseeme.com) is a free software application originally developed at Cornell University that works on both Macintosh and Windows PCs, but it does not support file transfer or application sharing.

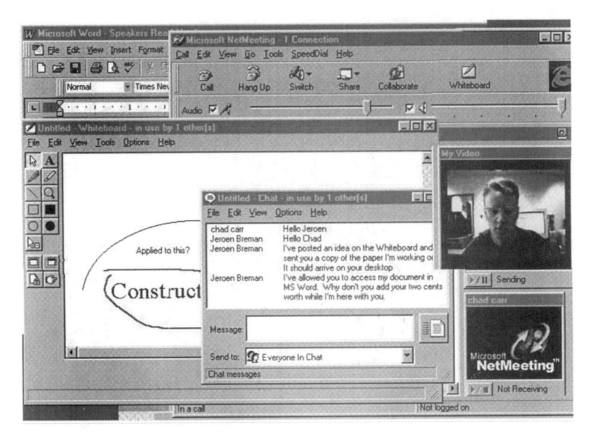

Figure 12.5
Videoconferencing Using Microsoft Netmeeting

HOW IS SYNCHRONOUS CONFERENCING USED AS A MINDTOOL?

The use of computers as learning tools has traditionally focused on individualized methods of instruction (Saettler, 1990). However, social interaction is becoming increasingly recognized as being critical to the learning process (Bruffee, 1993; Lave, 1988). Meaningful learning is less focused on transmission and more committed to negotiation and discourse (Schegloff, 1991). Global network technology can provide students with the ability to develop their social, reading, writing, communication, and collaboration skills through participating in online discussions. Through opportunities to participate in global discourse, students are exposed to a greater diversity of perspectives, so their outlooks may become less parochial. Learning becomes a process of enculturation into a community of learners or practitioners. Usually, practitioners exist outside of the classroom community.

Synchronous conferencing enables learners to become discursive members of those communities.

Two kinds of computer-based tools can be used to foster socially shared cognition through conversations: live (synchronous) conversations and reflective (asynchronous) conversations in computer conferences (see Chapter 13). The focus of this chapter is on the former. Synchronous conversation environments, such as Internet Relay Chat, PC conferences, MUDs, MOOs, WOOs, and MUSHs, function as networked, text- and graphics-based virtual environments for immersing learners in conversation. Early fears about addiction and loss of personal identity have been replaced by the importance of sociality and a preference for strong interpersonal interactions over large social gatherings in MUDs (Schiano, 1997). Synchronous communication allows students to test and refine what they are learning in a community that offers immediate feedback for their thinking and writing processes.

Interpersonal exchanges may include keypals, global classrooms, electronic appearances, electronic mentoring, and impersonations (Harris, 1995). They may also focus on collaborative construction of databases, electronic publishing, electronic field trips, and pooled data analysis. Environments that foster learning communities that share common goals and collaborate to accomplish them exemplify socio-cognitive tools.

The truth is that we do not really understand the best applications nor the limitations of synchronous communication as Mindtools. Most of us believe that student socializing in chat rooms has limited educational benefit. So what conditions are necessary for live discussions to be productive? A purpose or focus of conversation. Students must be planning a project, debating an issue, resolving a problem—some intellectual focus of discussion. Another important characteristic of synchronous communication, we believe, is an object or artifact in a shared workspace. When students are collaborating to create or construct a presentation, report, or problem solution, then they are more intellectually focused. There needs to be some electronic artifact in a shared workspace that represents, in itself, the fruits of intellectual labor. By supplying a context for learning, these virtual environments form communities of learners and facilitate more meaningful learning (Farquhar, 1996).

Examples of Synchronous Conferencing as a Mindtool

Internet Relay Chat.   Matusevich (1995) describes how she, in the context of an instructional unit on Wales with her fourth-grade students, arranged for a conversation with a teacher in Wales. This real-time communication session allowed learners to "ask-the-expert," thereby focusing the communication. It is important to ensure that a remote communication partner will be present during the conference and to put a finite time frame around an "ask-an-expert" activity.

Desktop Conferencing.   Consult Andres (1995a, 1995b) and Vacca (1995) for examples of how this technology is being used in the Global Schoolhouse and Scientist on Tap projects. In the Scientist on Tap example, a team of expert volunteers has gradually emerged that is willing to interact with students both via e-mail and via CU-SeeMe conferencing.

According to a teacher who participated in a Scientists on Tap activity, "[the activity] . . . opened our students' cognitive window by creating a new 'virtual schoolhouse' only made possible through worldwide electronic networking" (Andres, 1995b). Andres goes on to claim that "As budgets shrink and resources within the school building diminish, the Internet can connect students to the expanding resources of a "global schoolhouse" limited only by bandwidth and populated with fellow students, teachers, scientists, astronauts, and other experts around the world.

Role Playing/Debating.   Synchronous conferences can support some very interesting role-playing exercises. Jonassen, Peck, and Wilson (1999) described a video role-playing activity that would also work well for synchronous conferences. Years ago, the comedian Steve Allen produced a television show called "A Meeting of Minds." Each episode featured very improbable combinations of four guests (e.g., Ghengis Khan, Marie Antoinette, Socrates, and Charles Manson) from different historical eras in a talk-show setting moderated by Steve Allen. He would provide initial questions, and off they would go, usually culminating in passionate exchanges of ideas and beliefs. This is a rich idea for getting groups of students reasoning beyond surface-level meaning about ideas. Your students could portray the roles of famous figures from history, literature, local politics, or whatever topic you are discussing. The important point is that they represent different beliefs, perspectives, or attitudes about the topic. These online debates would certainly test any student's understanding of issues and the characters they were portraying. Issues are everywhere. Again, peruse any copy of *Time* or *Newsweek*, and issues will pour off the page. These make great topics for synchronous debates or role plays.

Shared Workspaces.   Shared workspaces (see Chapter 13) are not commonly available for synchronous collaboration. In shared workspaces, users can collaboratively work on (share) the same document. The systems that enable this synchronously are too expensive for most schools, and they require very high speed computer networks to support them. Within a few years, these may become available to schools. When they do, they should greatly enhance synchronous conferencing as a Mindtool. Why? We believe that synchronous conferences are most effective when they are focused on some specific goal or object. When students are intentionally working on some object, they are less likely to devolve into distracting social discussions. That is, the object helps them to stay on task.

Related Mindtools

Obviously, the most related Mindtool is asynchronous conferencing technologies, such as e-mail, LISTSERVs, newsgroups, and so on (see Chapter 13). They are both communications technologies. However, asynchronous conferences are often more structured and reflective than synchronous conferences.

Coaching the Use of Synchronous Conferencing in the Classroom

Gay and Lentini (1994) identified a process for engaging learners in online collaborative work. We have adapted it slightly (to expand beyond collaborative instructional design) and we recommend it as a good guideline to help students stay focused:

1. *Orientation:* Become familiar with the communication and information resources and the building materials; establish contact with the other groups; and become familiar with the environment and the problem that needs to be solved.
2. *Define the problem:* Articulate the problem; discuss the emergent characteristics that define it as a problem.
3. *Subdivide the problem:* Define the task, set goals, establish requirements and set boundaries.
4. *Establish roles:* Identify the individuals and groups responsible for solving each aspect of the problem.
5. *Seek information:* Ask specific technical questions and look for information in the databases or from other members of the teams.
6. *Share information:* Answer questions, share drawings, hold materials up to video cameras so that other groups can see designs, gesture over the video channel, refer others to relevant information, and report on progress.
7. *Monitor:* Watch communication channels to monitor other groups' progress and understand what they are doing.
8. *Negotiate understanding:* Make sure all parties understand the content of the lesson or topic.

EVALUATING SYNCHRONOUS COMMUNICATION AS MINDTOOLS

Critical, Creative, and Complex Thinking in Synchronous Conferencing

As with asynchronous conferences (Chapter 13), synchronous conferencing may or may not engage critical, creative, or complex thinking. The nature of the thinking engaged by the correspondence depends on what students are conversing about. If the topic of discussion engages higher order thinking, synchronous conferencing may well support critical, creative, and complex thinking. The nature of the problem, issue, or task posed by the teacher or the object that students are working with in a shared workspace will determine the level of thinking. As discussed in Chapter 13, asynchronous conferencing more predictably engages reflective thinking than synchronous. So it is important for the success of synchronous conferences to pose interesting, engaging questions, problems, or projects for your students to resolve in synchronous discussions. Assessing the specific critical, creative, and complex thinking skills engaged by synchronous conferences will depend on the topic being discussed and the level of participation by the learners.

The primary critical thinking skills likely to be engaged by synchronous conferencing are evaluating skills. Assessing messages that other participants contribute and identifying themes and assumptions are the primary critical thinking activities. Evaluating the ideas being discussed and connecting those ideas with others is the most difficult part of synchronous conferences, since they are not threaded. When a large number of conferees enters the conference, sorting out the threads of conversation becomes even more difficult. Participants must determine criteria for what makes a useful message and apply those criteria to evaluating others' messages. Students must prioritize the messages that they will respond to, recognize fallacies in those messages, and verify the accuracy of the information provided. With synchronous conferences, these activities must be accomplished "on the fly" while more messages are constantly being added. This is what makes synchronous conferences harder than asynchronous.

Creative thinking is used in asynchronous conferencing when participants elaborate on ideas provided by others and then synthesize new positions or solutions to the problems posed. Conferees elaborate messages by expanding (personalizing), modifying, or concretizing others' contributions, as well as by shifting topics.

The complex thinking skills engaged by asynchronous conferencing, as stated before, really depend on the complexity of the task that was posed by the teacher. Complex thinking is most likely to occur in shared workspaces, where students are collaboratively planning and designing a product, in which case students must imagine and formulate a goal and invent, assess, and revise the product in real time. This is a compelling activity. That product development often involves various elements of problem solving and quite a bit of decision making. However, as stated before, it is difficult to anticipate which of these skills will be engaged without knowing the nature of the product or object on which students are collaborating.

Evaluating Student Synchronous Conferencing

When students communicate synchronously about an issue or a problem, you may be able only to evaluate the quality of their outcome. Criteria for evaluating that outcome would, of course, depend on the nature of the outcome. Without knowing that, you can only evaluate the quality of student contributions to the conversation. With asynchronous conferences, you can measure the quantity (number and length) of student messages that are sent to the conference. That is not enough information however to evaluate the quality of student messages. Figure 12.6 presents a number of rubrics that you can use to evaluate the quality of student contributions to synchronous computer conferences as their knowledge and skills move from emergent to mastery. You will probably want to adapt these or add your own criteria as you evaluate your students' projects.

Student messages on–task and relevant

← ── →

Student messages are random, unrelated to task or issue; focus on personal concerns; off-task

Student messages related closely to discussion; elaborate, modify, or comment on issue or task of conference

Originality of student ideas

← ── →

Student messages mimic or recapitulate other messages; do not add meaningful information

Student messages contribute new perspective to conversation

Conversation is threaded/organized

← ── →

Student messages random; do not address specific issues; threads of conversation lost or disorganized

Student messages directly address other messages; relate to specific issues; threads of conversation identified and maintained

---

Figure 12.6
Rubrics for Evaluating Student Contributions to Synchronous Conferences

Advantages of Synchronous Conferencing as Mindtools

Synchronous conferencing has this advantage:

- Sense of immediacy is compelling. Live interactions produce more motivation to contribute.

Limitations of Synchronous Conferencing as Mindtools

Consider these limitations of synchronous conferencing:

- Easy to lose focus or purpose; distractions are probable.
- Easy to lose track of which thread of conversation you are discussing.
- Difficult to avoid having the conferences devolve into a social discussion, because synchronous conferences are often social in nature.

SUMMARY

Synchronous computer conferences are a relatively new phenomenon, so very little research into educational applications has occurred. Most chats and MOOs are used for social gatherings where users may assume different identities. The implications for learning have not been thought through. Yet synchronous conferencing is a potentially powerful medium for supporting collaboration and social negotiation. In the coming years, many new applications of synchronous conferences will likely become evident.

References

Andres, Y. M. (1995a). The Global Schoolhouse project [WWW document]. URL http://www.gsn.org.

Andres, Y. M. (1995b). Scientist on tap: Video-conferencing over the Internet [WWW document]. URL http://gsn/article.sot.html.

Bartle, Richard. (1990). *Interactive multi-user computer games.* Colchester, Essex, UK: MUSE, Ltd.

Bruffee, K. (1993). *Collaborative learning: Higher education, interdependence, and the authority of knowledge.* Baltimore, MD: Johns Hopkins University Press.

Farquhar, J. D. (1996). *The Internet as a tool for the social construction of knowledge.* Paper presented at the annual meeting of the Association for Educational Communications and Technology, Indianapolis, IN. (ERIC Document Reproduction Service No. ED 397 793)

Gay, G., & Lentini, M. (1994). *Communication resource use in a networked collaborative design environment.* Paper presented at the American Educational Research Association Conference, San Francisco, CA. (ERIC Document Reproduction Service No. ED 385 226)

Harris, J. (1995, February). Organizing and facilitating telecollaborative projects. *The Computing Teacher, 22*(5), 66–69.

Jonassen, D. H., Peck, K. L., & Wilson, B. G. (1999). *Learning with technology: A constructivist perspective.* Upper Saddle River, NJ: Prentice Hall.

Lave, J. (1988). *Cognition in practice: Mind, mathematics and culture in everyday life.* New York: Cambridge University Press.

Matusevich, M. (1995). Montgomery Country Public Schools: Projects [WWW document]. URL http://pixel.cs.vt.edu/melissa/projects.html.

Saettler, P. (1990). The evolution of American educational technology. Englewood, CO: Libraries Unlimited.

Schegloff, E. A. (1991). Conversation analysis and socially shared cognition. In L. Resnick, J. Levine, & S. D. Bernard (Eds.), *Socially shared cognition* (pp. 150–172). Washington, DC: American Psychological Association.

Schiano, D. J. (1997). Convergent methodologies in cyber-space: A case study. *Behavior, Research Methods, Instruments, & Computers, 29*(2), 170–273.

Vacca, J. R. (1995, October). CU on the Net. *Internet World,* pp. 81–82.

Voss, J. F., & Means, M. L. (1991). Learning to reason via instruction in argumentation. *Learning and Instruction, 1*(4), 337–350.

Asynchronous Conferencing as Mindtools

WHAT IS ASYNCHRONOUS COMMUNICATION?

Asynchronous communication (not at the same time; also known as *delayed* communication) occurs when only one person can communicate at a time. Telephone answering machines and faxes are asynchronous. One person leaves a message, and the other returns the call in hopes of communicating synchronously with the original caller, but more often than not ends up leaving another asynchronous message. Most forms of computer-mediated communication (CMC) are asynchronous. Users leave notes, papers, pictures, or any other type of communication for each other

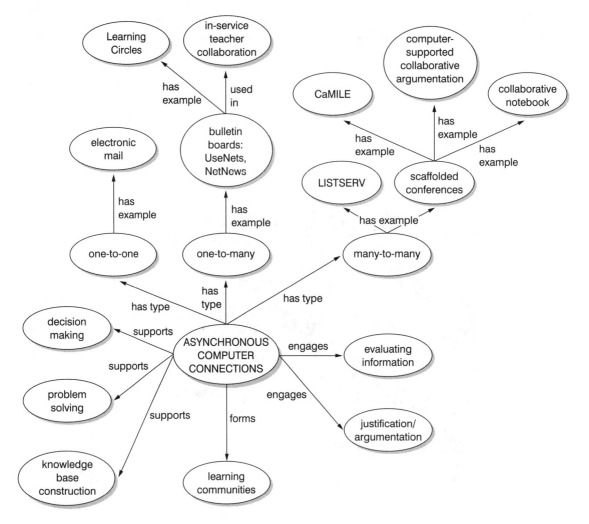

Figure 13.1
Asynchronous Computer Conferencing as Mindtools

that is encoded into digital form, transmitted, and later decoded. There are several common forms of asynchronous communication (see Figure 13.1).

E-Mail (One-to-One Communication)

The most common form of CMC is the electronic mail (e-mail) message. E-mail consists of messages that are sent through networks of computers from your host computer (school system, university, or commercial service, such as America Online or Prodigy) to another computer, anywhere in the world. You use an e-mail program (known as a client) on your computer to compose a message, and the computer sends it through network linkages to be stored temporarily on another computer. The user to whom you addressed your message uses his or her client to retrieve the message from the host computer. Metaphorically, you ask that your message be deposited in someone's mailbox, which is really dedicated file space on the host computer. Addresses can be complicated, but typically they observe the following pattern:

user@host_computer.institution.domain.network or country code

Sending a message to *user335@engr.psu.edu* would direct a message to the person identified as user335 through networks to the computer in the College of Engineering (engr) at Penn State University (psu), which is in the educational domain (edu). A message to *president@white_house.gov* would presumably direct your message to the president on the White House computer, which is in the government domain.

Messages can include any form of text characters and be about any subject. Most e-mail programs also allow you to attach formatted documents and files to be sent to the recipient's address. You can also send graphics or applications programs after they have been converted to binary files (encoded into ones and zeros).

E-mail can support a number of learning techniques, such as learning contracts, mentorship and apprenticeship, and correspondence study (Paulsen, 1994). Learning contracts are formal agreements between teacher and learner that set out learning goals, methods, and time lines. Each of these is facilitated by the direct correspondence between teacher and learner that e-mail affords. Likewise, teachers may continue to mentor or apprentice learners through e-mail. These tele-apprenticeships resemble face-to-face apprenticeships (Levin, Haesun, & Riel, 1990). Correspondence study and distance education are made possible by e-mail. Rather than playing telephone tag for weeks with a tutor, students in many courses at England's Open University receive fairly rapid and direct feedback from their tutors via e-mail. E-mail generally ensures that messages are received, and those messages are typically more directly related to students' questions than those tutors would receive in a classroom.

Bulletin Boards (One-to-Many Communication)

Bulletin board services (BBSs) are special-purpose computer programs that enable individuals to post messages to a metaphorical bulletin board (send messages to a host computer for storage) or to read messages contributed by others (retrieve files from the host computer) and copy them to their computer. BBSs are usually established to support a discourse community, individuals who share a common interest and want to communicate about it. BBSs provide access to newspapers, magazines, classified advertisements, announcements, and so on. Large BBSs are also available that support special-interest discussion groups oriented to a wide range of topics, from computers to sexual deviancies. Many of these BBSs contain computer application programs, such as games, that can be downloaded (copied) to your computer. In all of these applications, one person is communicating individually with a larger group of people.

BBSs have several functions, including conferencing, questionnaires or polling, file access, news, lectures, and access to databases. The most common application is news services.

More than 2,000 news networks—NetNews or UseNet services—provide news and announcements in a bulletin board fashion on many social, recreational, computer, or alternative topics. More than 500 UseNet groups provide information and discussion space on computer issues, such as data compression techniques, computer languages in common use, computer platforms and operating systems available, and software sources. UseNets also list jobs, items for sale, and services such as tax preparation and investment guidance. More than 3,000 groups provide information on topics as diverse as baseball, poetry, model railroading, and *Star Trek* memorabilia. Cultural information on more than 100 countries can also be accessed. Many nationally prominent newspapers offer their news online, and there are numerous "talk" groups focusing on current issues such as abortion and gun control. It is likely that any topic you have an interest in is serviced by one or more UseNet groups. These services enable you to post a question to be answered, give your opinion about a topic, or make friends with like-minded individuals. Unlike bulletin boards, news networks are updated continuously.

The cost and time delays of publishing and distributing print journals—especially academic ones with a limited number of subscribers—are forcing many to consider electronic publishing. Posting articles on a BBS and restricting access to them through subscriptions allows articles to be published much more quickly (often within hours as opposed to months or even years). Electronic journals also support more collaborative authorship between distant authors. Authors may send versions of the article back and forth, cowriting and coediting the article up until its publication.

Bulletin boards are also sources of lectures. Transcripts of speeches or lectures can be posted to bulletin boards, news networks, or computer conferences so they will be available for additional reflection and/or analysis. The full text of nearly every speech delivered by the president is immediately available through the Internet. If you missed a class lecture or a presentation by a prominent speaker, you may be able to obtain the lecture immediately on a network. Such a lecture may be more comprehensible to visually oriented learners than the live lecture, because it can be reviewed and scrutinized more easily and does not require note taking.

BBSs may be supported by large organizations, such as universities (on large, high-speed server computers), or by individuals on their personal computers. Large servers and high-speed communication lines are required when a large number of people access the service. However, individuals or small school groups can also host a bulletin board. You simply need to connect a dedicated microcomputer to a dedicated telephone line (usually) and load bulletin board software on it. This software manages access to the computer and receipt and distribution of files. These types of bulletin boards have grown rapidly to support teaching in remote parts of the country and world, where teachers can call up the bulletin board computer in order to get or send such ideas including innovative teaching ideas or lesson plans.

Computer Conferencing (Many-to-Many Communication)

As new technologies and issues confront education, individuals want to discuss them with each other. With travel costs soaring, physically assembling at, say, a conference venue to discuss them is becoming increasingly difficult, so professionals are beginning to connect to computer conferences instead to discuss their ideas. Computer conferences are asynchronous discussions, debates, and collaborative efforts among a group of people who share an interest in a topic. These virtual conferences connect people who may be continents away from each other as if they had come together for the discussion. This form of knowledge sharing is usually timely and informative and may be gratifying. Technically, there is little, if any, difference between bulletin boards and computer conferences. The differences are in the intention of the individuals and form of the communication.

Computer conferencing is commonly used to create virtual classrooms. Virtual classrooms are communications and learning spaces located within a computer system (Hiltz, 1986). At Penn State, we are now offering courses in technology integration, including a Mindtools course, via WWW conferencing technology. The World Campus delivers several other university degrees and certificate programs asynchronously.

Computer conferencing asks why it is necessary for students to share the same physical space with a teacher in order to listen to the teacher, ask questions, get assignments, and otherwise communicate with the teacher. Most of those forms of communication can easily and effectively be mediated by computers, enabling students at a distance to join classes they would otherwise be prevented from attending. Urban universities, for example, create virtual classrooms through computer conferencing, thereby reducing traffic, pollution, and parking costs.

Computer conferencing also supports long-distance collaboration among learners. Whether on different continents or at the school across town, learners can correspond and collaboratively construct newspapers, newsletters, or other documents, solve problems, conduct experiments, debate, or simply share ideas and perspectives. As discussed later, when learners have a wider audience for their writing or other scholarly activities, they tend to invest more effort in the process and learn more.

Computer conferencing has given rise to numerous online interest groups—people with a common interest who convene in electronic conferences about that interest. More than 2,000 such groups send hundreds of thousands of messages to each other daily (Howse, 1992). Many of these groups support teachers and education, such as the electronic Academic Village at the University of Virginia, which links public school teachers, teacher education students, and university faculty with teachers across the United States and in foreign countries (Bull, Harris, & Drucker, 1992).

Computer discussion groups provide a public forum or communication space in which anyone who is a subscriber or member of the conference can contribute ideas to the group. Groups may start with specific contributions in the form of a lecture or an article and then be opened up for discussion, interpretation, and argumentation by the members of the group or class. Discussion in most conferencing systems may be held at the whole-group level or be broken up into more specific or user-focused discussions of subtopics. Individuals may comment on the original ideas or on comments by other participants, thus creating an electronic discussion of ideas.

These groups are open to individuals who may be great distances apart, and ideas can be added at any time of day or night, both by the teacher and by the students. In fact, the teacher who monitors an electronic classroom discussion has much better access to how each of the students is thinking about the topics than in a face-to-face class. As Romiszowski and de Haas (1989) point out, these interactions are more democratic because all students have the same tools for communicating their ideas. These authors also mention that there is increased potential for deeper or more thoughtful classroom interaction because individuals can reflect on and think over ideas—or even look up information—before responding (typically not possible in real classrooms). Perhaps most important is that learners end up with a complete record of the discussion, reducing the anxiety that one will miss something important in note taking, which often disrupts the communication process.

In addition to discussion groups, computer conferencing also supports debates, simulations, role playing, and collaborative construction of knowledge bases (Paulsen, 1994). Debates are natural applications of computer conferences, with teams of learners assigned issues and positions to argue. The research skills engaged to develop arguments that will adequately present the group's position are considerable. Many business simulations are mediated by computer conferences in which individuals are assigned roles and interact with each other. Effective simulations require a well-structured set of activities and very careful monitoring of the contributions, but the experience can be very powerful.

Role plays are like simulations in that learners may assume a variety of roles and attempt to reason like the individuals they represent. For example, the University of Michigan involved schools all over the world in an Arab–Israeli conflict simulation in which students were assigned roles as either the combatants, the United States, or the former Soviet Union (Goodman, 1992). Other students represented the religious interests of the Muslims, Christians, and so on. These types of interactions are more engaging than hearing only the teacher's perspective, and they enhance multicultural awareness among the participants. Students can also conduct experiments or observe the environment and collaboratively contribute to a common knowledge base. Examples of this are described later in this chapter.

Computer conferencing is technologically accomplished in three ways: via bulletin boards, e-mail, and special conferencing software. BBSs can be used to support postings about ideas in special-interest folders, but they often lack some of the functions that are desirable in a conference. Computer conferencing is most commonly conducted via e-mail, which supports conferencing through LISTSERVs. Individuals can subscribe to a LISTSERV much as they might subscribe to a newspaper. Any message that is sent to the LISTSERV mailbox is automatically forwarded to every other subscriber to the service.

LISTSERV conferences are usually focused on a single topic or issue. They are effective because they do not require more sophisticated software and do not use much storage space on the host computer. Once like-minded individuals have located one another through the general conference, they can correspond individually or in small groups by sending personal messages to each other.

Computer conferencing is also supported by special conferencing software, such as FirstClass or Lotus Notes. This software requires users to log on to a remote computer in order to communicate with others. Multiple conferences can be established, with small groups discussing some ideas, while the larger conference discusses others. File sharing and shared workspaces enable conference participants to work collaboratively on documents and projects. Conferencing systems can also provide security and anonymity for conference participants. A number of special-purpose, scaffolded computer conferences (described later in this chapter) are emerging to engage and support specific kinds of thinking among conference participants.

HOW IS ASYNCHRONOUS CONFERENCING USED AS A MINDTOOL?

Asynchronous conferencing is different from synchronous conferencing (Chapter 12) primarily in the level of reflective and constructive thinking that it affords. Synchronous conferencing does not require nor does it support reflection before speaking. Learners are inclined to register their first thoughts in a chat room and these thoughts are not usually as coherent or cogent as ideas that have developed more slowly. In asynchronous conferences, learners read a response and decide whether or not to respond, how to respond, and the likely consequences of such a response. Harasim (1990) found that learners perceive themselves as reflecting more on their thoughts while computer conferencing than when engaged in face-to-face or telephone conversations. Carefully considering and constructing responses to issues involves more analytical thinking. The "need to verbalize all aspects of interaction within the text-based environment can enhance such metacognitive skills as self-reflection and revision in learning" (Harasim, 1990, p. 49). These are important thinking skills. Perhaps no Mindtool described in this book better facilitates constructive, social learning than asynchronous conferencing, because it supports reflection on what one knows and, through communication of that with others, may lead to conceptual change.

Asynchronous conferencing also focuses activity more than synchronous discussions. Kwon (1998) found that conferencing groups who were making decisions and solving problems made fewer social and off-task comments during several sessions when compared with face-to-face groups.

Computer conferencing supports the social negotiation of ideas about the content that is being studied, as well as the collaborative construction of new knowledge. As groups of individuals provide different perspectives and interpretations, debate, argue, and compromise on the meaning of ideas, they are deeply engaged in knowledge construction.

Numerous examples demonstrate the use of asynchronous conferencing to engage learners in critical, collaborative, and self-regulated thinking and learning.

Learning Circles

Developers of the Global Learning Circles Project, in which classrooms in the United States are connected to classrooms around the world via the AT&T Learning Network, believe that when students write for a larger, networked audience of peers, they are more motivated to perform than when they write only for their teacher's red pen. Cohen and Riel (1989) found that papers written to communicate with peers were more fluent, better organized, and clearer than those written merely for a grade. Collaboratively authoring newspapers and booklets by collecting articles from partner schools around the world also results in better use of grammar and syntax (Riel, 1990).

The Learning Circles project facilitates collaboration among small groups of classrooms (therefore learning *circles,* rather than large, amorphous groups of readers). Collaboration, of course, requires closer communication and is easier with a known audience than an imaginary audience. The project staff has worked with elementary, middle, and high school students by outlining group tasks and time lines, with each school managing one project around its curriculum for the group, which as a whole produces a publication. This is a good example of a global application of reciprocal teaching (Palinscar & Brown, 1984). Classes in each learning circle agree on a project, and the students become authors, reporters, poets, and researchers, responding to requests from the other classes in the circle regularly via e-mail. Joint publications are planned and carried out, and students reflect on the experiences they have had. Riel (1993) described a number of learning circles, such as the following:

- Elementary students in Saudi Arabia sponsored a project on solutions to the Gulf crisis. Together with their partners in different countries, they discussed world dependence on oil, kingdoms, democracies, and conflicts between political and religious beliefs.
- Intermediate students in West Virginia sponsored a project in which inmates answered the questions of students in the Learning Circle about a range of social problems from their personal life experiences. The inmates' reflections on their life decisions have had a very strong effect on students, who live in a range of social settings and conditions.
- Students in British Columbia sponsored the "Environmental Investigator" as their section of a collective newspaper, The Global Grapevine. They asked the eight schools in their Learning Circle for essays or poetry centered on local environmental issues.
- High school students designed studies of the homeless, illiteracy, or substance abuse, or explored differences in family patterns or causes of suicide across cultures.

■ Students in Belgium sponsored a research project on waste caused by excessive packaging of goods. Students collected and compared the packaging of many different types of products and assessed the best and worst examples in different countries.

Learning Circles are designed to expose students to different points of view, enhance multicultural awareness on a global scale, and develop cooperative skills for dealing with people in different cultures (Riel, 1993). These are powerful learning outcomes by anyone's standards.

In-Service Teacher Education

In Catalonia, Spain, the Department of Education has set up a network, XTEC, to provide databases of educational resources for teachers and a computer conferencing service that enables students to get to know students and teachers in other schools and to consult expert teachers and students in other schools (Simón, 1992). Courses on educational innovations such as spreadsheets and online retrieval (Mindtools are popular in Spain, too) are offered through conferences to teachers all over the region. Tutorial instruction is supplied by the conference, with teachers submitting their assignments to the tutor via a file transfer system. Teachers then engage in "tele-debates" on suggested teaching methods via the conferencing system. Both students and teachers think the technology is exciting and effective because of the individualization afforded by the system—especially the e-mail correspondence with distant tutors.

In the United States, the Beginning Teacher Computer Network was started at Harvard in 1987 to provide support and mentoring for graduates in their first year of teaching (Merseth, Beals, & Cutler, 1992). The network enables rookie teachers to ask questions, make comments, and request materials. Conversations on the net have included questions on teaching methods, such as collecting homework and fostering classroom discussion; values topics, such as how to counsel a sexually active teenager; content suggestions; case studies; and content discussions. The new teachers are spread all over the country but find it helpful to maintain an umbilical link to their teacher-preparation program during that crucial period.

Scaffolded Conferences

A number of problems regularly occur with asynchronous conferences. Students create responses to one thought while a string of others go by. Students have a tendency to change topics at will, or simply misinterpret the meaning of another student's entry. It is hard to follow the threads of conversation and to know how to respond to which message. Because effective communication requires some shared understanding, new types of asynchronous conferences have emerged to structure the communication. These structured conferences analyze the kind of thinking that learners should be doing and design conference software to require learners to communicate that way. The structuring of the conversation is a form of scaffold that helps learners to think and perform in ways that they are not able to independently.

Collaboratory Notebook.   Computer conferencing has been used effectively by the CoVis project to connect learners from around the country in dialogues about science. In addition to visualization tools (described in Chapter 10), the CoVis project has developed a scaffolded computer conference known as the Collaboratory Notebook (Edelson, Pea, & Gomez, 1996). The Collaboratory Notebook is a collaborative hypermedia composition system designed to support within- and cross-school science projects. What is unique about the Collaboratory Notebook is that it focuses on project investigations rather than curricular content. During a project, the teacher or any student can pose a question or a conjecture (Figure 13.2), which can be addressed by participants from around the country. Conversations may be public or private.

The Collaboratory Notebook provides a scaffolding structure for conversations by requiring specific kinds of responses to messages. For instance, to support the conjecture made in Figure 13.2, a student may add evidence, such as that shown in Figure 13.3. When responding to a conjecture, learners can only "provide evidence" or "develop a plan" to support that conjecture. This form of scaffolded conversation results in more coherent and cogent conversations. In addition to scaffolding con-

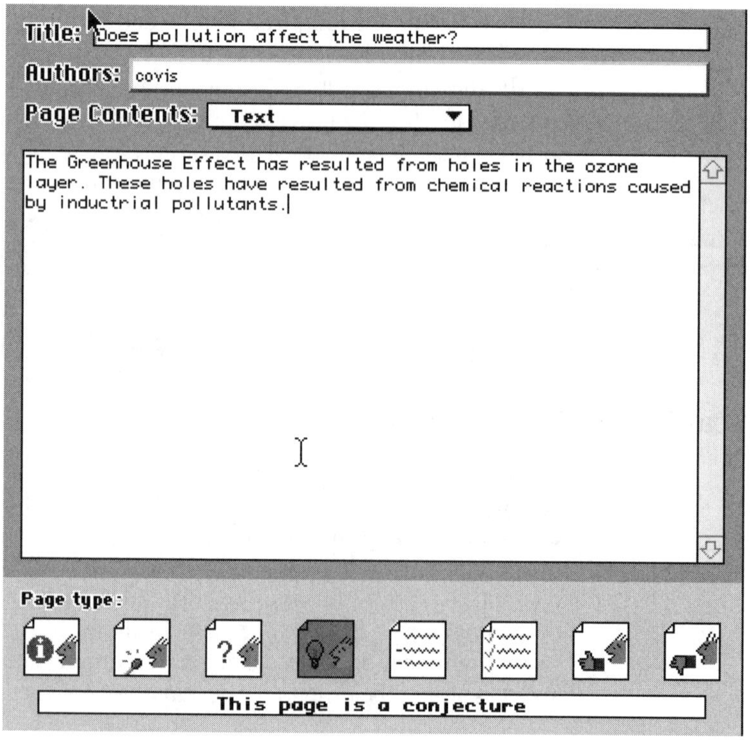

Figure 13.2
Conjecture Made in the Collaboratory Notebook

Title: Does pollution affect the weather?
Authors: covis
Page Contents: Text

The Greenhouse Effect has resulted from holes in the ozone layer. These holes have resulted from chemical reactions caused by inductrial pollutants.

Page type:

This page is a conjecture

Figure 13.3
Evidence to Support a Conjecture in the Collaboratory Notebook

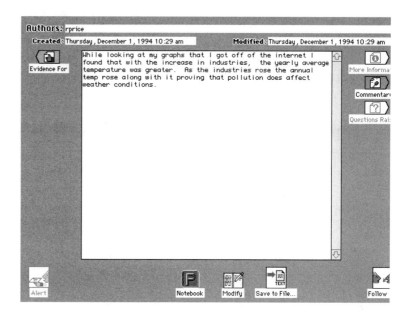

versation, the Collaboratory Notebook also produces a notebook record of the conversation for review and reconsideration by the learners.

Computer-Supported Collaborative Argumentation. Another method for structuring communication is through supporting collaborative argumentation (Jonassen & Carr, in press; Shum, 1997). Computer-supported collaborative argumentation (CSCA) is the process of using technology to support argumentation during problem solving. The problem-solving process takes place as follows:

1. Pose/define problem.
2. Generate proposals.
3. Create supporting arguments.
4. Evaluate proposals/arguments.
5. Make a decision (based on agreement or consensus).

To support this process, the CSCA tool we have developed provides a hierarchical framework to help structure our communications (see Figure 13.4). In our structure, we define a problem that is a statement of an unknown, something that is unsettled, such as a problem to be solved, a controversy, or an issue to be reconciled. A proposal is a recommendation for action in response to the problem. Proposals are directed at specific problem statements. An argument is comprised of evidence that supports a specific proposal. Thus, in order to *elaborate* on a *problem*, students submit *proposals* with *supporting arguments*.

The CSCA tool is meant to provide students with a means to help organize and represent their knowledge so they can make informed decisions toward resolving a

Figure 13.4
CSCA Is Hierarchically Arranged

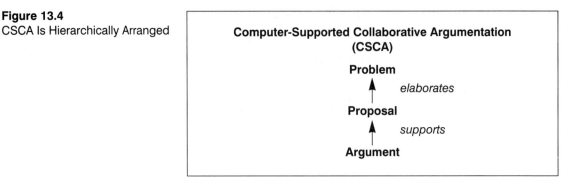

particular problem. For example, let's take a look at how a sample map could be formed around the problem stated as "Should we have grades in school?" (see Figure 13.5). In this example, the problem (Should we have grades?) is *elaborated* by three proposals set forth by different students. The type of proposal (i.e., *Postponement*) is written in italics. Below the type, the student states his or her proposal. Below this, the student *supports* his or her proposal with an argument. Again, the argument type is written in italics and is followed by the student's statement. Though this argument is small, neat, and balanced, we certainly do not imply that most arguments will turn out that way. They are likely to be much more detailed, natural, and elaborate.

In order to interact with others using CSCA, the tool employs a concept mapping interface that enables learners to create *nodes* (i.e., problems, proposals, or arguments) at each level—one at a time (see Figure 13.6) and view them all at once (see http://www.personal.psu.edu/csc126/CSCA).

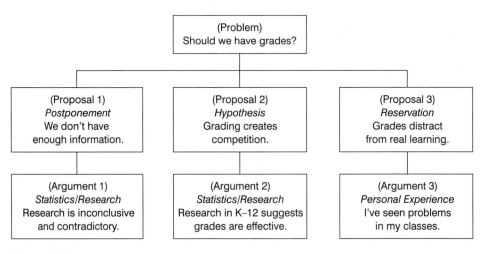

Figure 13.5
Create One or More Nodes at Each Level

Figure 13.6
Sample Results Compiled While
Using the CSCA Tool

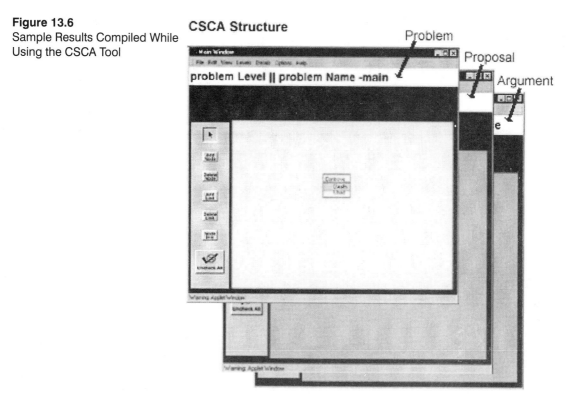

CSCA Structure

We believe that one of the best uses of conversation tools to support social negotiation is afforded by CSCA. Instructional practices such as CSCA can help promote the development of argumentative reasoning skills required to negotiate effectively. Voss (1991) characterizes informal argumentation as "reasoning performed in non-deductive situations that are essentially everyday situations of life and work, including the academic and professional disciplines." This implies that informal argumentation is not bound by rules of logic, but involves inference making, justification, and explanation. However, argumentation is the central intellectual ability involved in solving problems (Cerbin, 1988), especially in collaborative or group settings. So, CSCA may be used to scaffold formal argumentation in order to help students to reason more effectively.

CaMILE NoteBase.   A third example of scaffolded conversations is provided by a program called CaMILE. Developed at the EduTech Institute at Georgia Tech, the basis of CaMILE is a collaborative NoteBase where students post notes associated with group discussions. Each note that is added is a response to a note that someone else has contributed to the discussion. Students enter a Comment note (bottom window of Figure 13.7) into an ongoing discussion (top window of Figure 13.7). In addition to the text, the student has included a QuickTime movie, as evidenced by the multimedia margin, which shows links to pictures, sounds, spreadsheets, or any

Figure 13.7
A Comment Note Added to
CaMILE NoteBase

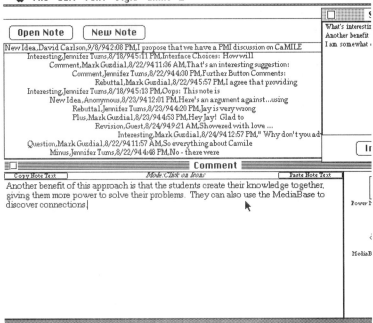

other kind of file. CaMILE also provides space for making suggestions (upper right) based on the Comment note. When a student reading through a discussion finds a note that she or he wishes to comment on, the student must specify the kind of response it is (a Question, a Comment, a Rebuttal, an Alternative; see Figure 13.8). Having to specify the response type scaffolds the development of discussion and argumentation skills. CaMILE has been replaced by WebCaMILE, a web-based version of the program with the same functionality but a different interface.

Shared Workspaces

For more than a decade, the computer science field has focused much research on computer-supported collaborative work (CSCW). CSCW projects provide users with a suite of tools that help them to perform work. Examples of CSCW systems include the following:

- *Answer Garden:* Allows field service (hot-line) organizations to develop databases of frequently asked questions (FAQs), which help users find answers they want.
- *Argument Noter:* Networks people around the world to share/see/change documents.
- *Collaboratory:* Multimedia tool provides for idea generation, project management, information sharing documents in conference.

Figure 13.8
Specifying the Response Type in CaMILE

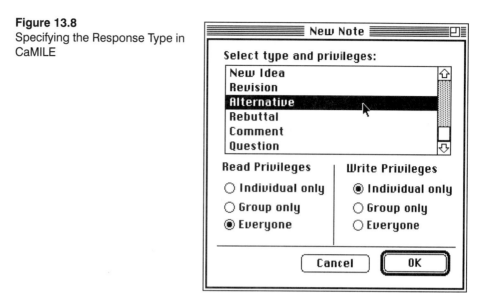

- *DOMINO:* Regulates division of labor procedures within an office.
- *InConcert:* Automatically tracks and distributes all tasks in a work-flow process.
- *OptionFinder:* Meeting system supports brainstorming and modeling of issues.
- *Quilt:* Tools used for collaborative document production by manipulating hypertext nodes.
- *CRUISER:* Connects offices for informal interaction; simulates going down hallways, holding impromptu conversations, including privacy blinds.

CSCW applications can be very constructivist. If you provide people better tools that scaffold their work, it may not be necessary to teach them. CSCW tools enable people to work collaboratively to socially co-construct some object. Typically, CSCW provides just-in-time training where the learning is integrated with work.

CSCW provides people with shared workspaces, places where they can collaboratively work on the same documents. These shared workspaces have traditionally required specific software applications that were too expensive for schools. However, a new project is making shared workspaces available to users through the World Wide Web. BSCW (Basic Support for Cooperative Work) enables asynchronous collaboration over the Web. BSCW is a shared workspace system that supports document upload, event notification, group management, versioning, threaded discussions, and more (Figure 13.9). Any workspace can be accessed using a standard web browser (Netscape, Internet Explorer). Using CGI (common gateway interface) and upload and download protocols, BSCW enables users to download documents to their computers, work on them with common application software (like PowerPoint, Excel, Word, or most other Mindtools described in this book), and upload their product back to the web server. BSCW notifies the work group of the changes and automatically assigns a new version number to the object. BSCW supports threaded

Figure 13.9
BSCW Shared Workspace

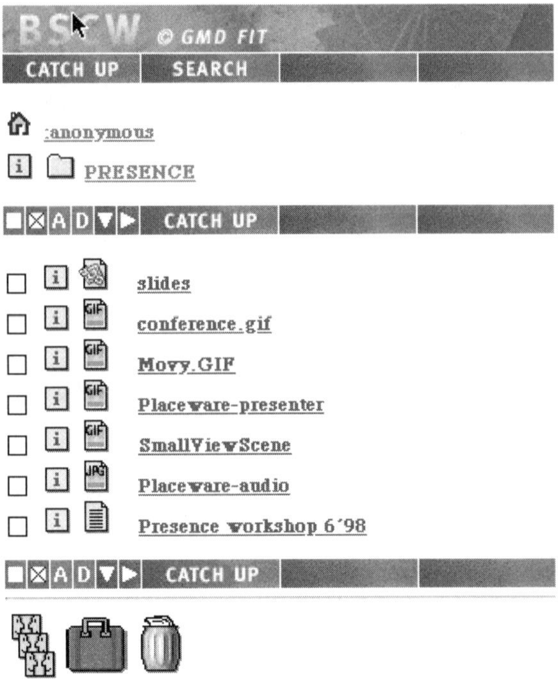

conferences about the processes used by the work group. Making shared work-spaces available to users anywhere in the world through the WWW will greatly enhance collaborative knowledge construction projects. Virtually every Mindtool application described in this book can be supported through the BSCW server.

BSCW is available on a public server for all interested users free of charge. The server software is also available for most Unix systems and Windows NT.

Related Mindtools

The most similar Mindtool to asynchronous conferences, of course, is the synchronous conference (Chapter 12). While synchronous and asynchronous conferencing use similar technologies, they can engage substantively different mental processes. In synchronous conferences, participants are more focused on establishing an identity, whereas asynchronous conferences enable learners to reflect more on the issues and problems being discussed.

Some conferencing tools use a concept mapping (see Chapter 4) interface to help users sort out the issues. Beyond their surface similarity, there is very little functional similarity between the concept maps and computer conferences.

Conferencing tools are frequently used to collaborate at a distance on the construction of other Mindtools, most commonly hypermedia and multimedia knowledge bases. Students discuss issues such as style, treatment, the inclusion or exclusion of certain material, and evaluation of their efforts. As stated before, having an artifact as the focus of a discussion generally enhances the level and meaningfulness of the discussion.

Coaching the Use of Asynchronous Conferencing in the Classroom

The facilitator or moderator of a computer conference plays a very important role in ensuring the meaningfulness of an electronic discussion, just as a teacher manages a classroom discussion. It is important that participants maintain a view of the structure of a discussion—that is, what are the issues and the positions on those issues—while avoiding definitive statements that may impede discussion. Teachers as conference moderators need to be coaches, not sources of knowledge. Several themes may emerge in a conference, with different aspects of the themes being discussed by different individuals. Several activities are important (Romiszowski & de Haas, 1989; Romiszowski & Jost, 1989):

1. Assure students that they can really communicate with the system. Motivating learners and overcoming phobias and anxieties may be the most important process. Welcome each new user to the conference.
2. Ensure that learners have access to the computer network through directly connected computers or computers with modems so they can log on frequently.
3. Provide active leadership. Start by playing host, welcoming participants to the conference, and establishing a nonthreatening climate.
4. Periodically summarize the discussion and make sure that it does not drift off the theme or become too fragmented. Ask participants for clarification of their ideas, and resolve disputes or differences in interpretation.
5. Periodically prompt nonparticipants to contribute ideas or reactions to the conference and reinforce at least the initial contributions. You may want to send students private mail that provides feedback or other interpretations. Periodically throw out engaging questions or issues that can clarify ideas or become a new focus for discussion.

Eastmond and Ziegahn (1994) have developed a design model to support CMC courses. To them, it is important to apprise learners of the role of CMC in the course activities and requirements. In addition to staffing up such a course, including designer/developer, system administrator, and moderator/instructor, they recommend apprising learners in the syllabus about their

■ required participation—in lieu of attendance
■ CMC learning strategies—becoming interactive, dealing with multiple threads and perspectives
■ effective online communications—recording notes in appropriate threads, keeping track of threads, and conveying messages in proper tone and length
■ conference structure—including course area, personal area, and course map
■ computer use, training, and support.

Eastmond and Ziegahn (1994) go on to recommend a number of CMC instructional activities, such as

- instructor-led discussions to introduce the group, the topic, and themes
- brainstorming lists of ideas related to the topic
- a guest lecturer to lead discussion on a special topic
- short small-group discussions moderated by students
- individual presentations of term projects
- off-line activities, preferably consisting of real-world experiences
- face-to-face sessions with members of the group
- textbooks and media to support topics under discussion.

We are only beginning to learn how to maximize the effectiveness of CMC learning experiences. In the next few years, these processes should become well researched and reliable.

EVALUATING ASYNCHRONOUS COMMUNICATION AS MINDTOOLS

Critical, Creative, and Complex Thinking in Asynchronous Conferencing

As with synchronous conferencing, asynchronous conferencing may or may not engage critical, creative, or complex thinking. The nature of the thinking engaged by the correspondence depends on what students are conversing about. If the topic of discussion engages higher order thinking, asynchronous conferencing will support critical, creative, and complex thinking. The nature of the problem, issue, or task posed by the teacher can either engender recall or it can engender complex problem-solving behavior. Although asynchronous conferencing more predictably engages reflective thinking, those reflections are not necessarily productive. So it is important for you to pose an interesting, engaging question or problem for your students to resolve. Assessing the specific critical, creative, and complex thinking skills engaged by asynchronous conferencing will depend on the topic being discussed and the level of participation by the learners. I will briefly consider the generic effects of asynchronous conferencing next.

The primary critical thinking skills that are normally engaged by asynchronous conferencing are evaluating skills. Assessing messages that other participants contribute and identifying their assumptions are the primary critical thinking activities. Evaluating the issues being discussed and connecting those ideas with others in the conference are necessary for meaningful participation. Participants must determine criteria for useful messages and apply those criteria to evaluating conference messages. They have to prioritize the messages that they will respond to, recognize fallacies in those messages, and verify the accuracy of the information provided. Asynchronous conferencing is largely an evaluative activity.

Creative thinking is used in asynchronous conferencing when participants elaborate on ideas provided by others and then synthesize new positions or solutions to the problems posed. Conferees elaborate messages by expanding (personalizing), modifying, or concretizing others' contributions, as well as shifting topics.

The complex thinking skills engaged by asynchronous conferencing, as stated before, really depend on the complexity of the task that was posed by the teacher. Meaningful issues and problem-solving tasks in which participants collaboratively develop answers to difficult issues are more likely to engage complex thinking skills. Conferencing may be more complex because of the multiple interactions and the differences of opinions and perspectives that are typically represented in most conferences.

Evaluating Student Asynchronous Conferences

When students communicate about an issue or a problem, you need to evaluate the quality of their contributions. In addition to the quantity (number and length) of student messages that are sent to the conference, Figure 13.10 presents a number of rubrics that you can use to evaluate the student contributions to asynchronous computer conferences as their knowledge and skills move from emergent to mastery. You will probably want to adapt these or add your own criteria as you evaluate your students' projects.

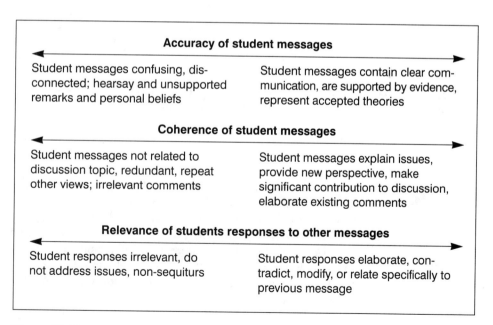

Figure 13.10
Rubrics for Evaluating Student Contributions to Asynchronous Conferencing

Advantages of Asynchronous Conferences as Mindtools

Asynchronous conferencing has these advantages:

- The primary goal of education, according to many theorists, is to socialize youth. Typically that process occurs only at a local level. Networked computers, however, are an even greater agent for the propagation and dissemination of social skills on a local, regional, national, and even international level (Margolies, 1991). In fact, those who perceive e-mail as important for their social life use it more.

- Hiltz (1986) found that classroom interchanges produced more interaction and involved more exchanges between students than did face-to-face interchanges. This is probably because individuals have the ability to remain anonymous, so they reduce personal fears while enhancing academic efficacy. (Note that not all forms of conferencing afford anonymity.) Hiltz also showed that undergraduates felt they had better access to the instructor through conferencing, and the courses were more interesting than traditional courses.

- Conferencing is likely to enhance the effectiveness of collaborative efforts among learners, because it improves access to other group participants, eliminates social distinctions and barriers between those participants, contributes to a sense of informality, and fosters a stronger group identity (Pfaffenberger, 1986).

- Berge and Collins (1993) discuss the independence of time afforded by asynchronous conferencing. Unlike face-to-face meetings, computer conferences are open and available 24 hours a day, 7 days a week. Time can also be allocated to reflecting on a message before responding, in order to develop one's arguments or position. Students may do their work when it is convenient or when they are most alert.

- Students may argue and disagree without involving excessive conflict (Phillips & Santoro, 1989). This is especially helpful for introverted, shy, and reflective people.

- Conferencing supports collaborative learning. When working in groups, students accomplished more task objectives and participated more uniformly (Scott, 1993).

- Planning documents collaboratively enhances the writing of apprehensive and nonapprehensive writers (Mabrito, 1992). Conferencing is an effective means for teaching collaborative problem solving and other tasks.

- When compared to a traditional classroom, where the teacher contributes up to 80% of the verbal exchange, computer conferencing shows instructor contributions of only 10% to 15% of the message volume (Harasim, 1987; Winkelmans, 1988). Allowing learners to generate questions, summarize content, clarify points, and predict upcoming events is applicable to other educational tasks. When performed online, these types of activities can facilitate the discussion of various structural relationships within the subject matter.

Limitations of Asynchronous Conferences as Mindtools

Asynchronous conferencing is subject to these limitations:

- The technical complexities of asynchronous conferencing and the resulting difficulties of connecting to the system and learning how to use new software are often very frustrating and anxiety inducing. High frontloading of technical skills may be necessary in order to become a user. Networking issues are complex, and the jargon is inscrutable to the novice. Seek software that optimally combines user-friendliness and resources. Be patient and keep asking questions.
- Users must be somewhat skilled as communicators; that is, they need facility with the language. Unfortunately, not all learners have this facility.
- The primary mode of input is text, which means that users must be moderately skilled as typists. That is problematic for many, particularly since the text editors for much conferencing software are comparatively primitive.
- The user interfaces in much of the software are unfriendly and difficult to use. The state of the art in software design is improving rapidly, however, so this should become less of a problem in the near future.
- Conferencing among individuals on different continents several time zones apart can appear to be delayed for hours or even days. The delays may reduce the impact of certain messages or feedback.
- Participation within groups of users varies. While full participation in asynchronous conferences is as desirable as full participation in classroom discussions, technophobia or communications anxieties can prevent a number of individuals from participating fully. People can become "lurkers" when they post an idea and nobody responds or even acknowledges it, or when they are harshly or rudely treated.
- In group decision-making situations, computer-mediated decision making produced more polarized decisions than did face-to-face situations (Lea & Spears, 1991). Decision making takes longer and may result in the use of stronger, more inflammatory, and more personalized expressions (Siegel, Dubrovsky, Kiesler, & McGuire, 1986). Moreover, anonymity may increase—rather than diffuse—anxiety.
- Conferencing may amplify social insecurities. These communication anxieties are especially common when communications are not acknowledged (Feenburg, 1987).
- The absence of social context cues can make discussion somewhat more difficult. Nonverbal communication is not available to help interpret the message.
- Hardware and communications lines and equipment are not 100% reliable, which may cause a loss of work or delays in communications. Such problems tend to frustrate users and may reduce participation.

SUMMARY

Asynchronous communication is becoming more common than synchronous. Electronic mail is one of the most pandemic communication forms in the world. Information that used to be disseminated through live presentations, textbooks, or correspondence courses is now immediately available through bulletin board services. Asynchronous communication is changing the face of education. Asynchronous computer conferences have become one of the main features of most distance learning projects. In addition to disseminating information, designers agree that it is important to support communication among the students in the course. This is most often supported by asynchronous conferences. These conferences engage learners in evaluating information, discussing options, solving problems, and justifying their decisions, all of which require critical thinking. These electronic learning communities may consist of a few people in a focused conference or thousands of students corresponding through global conference networks. They are usually focused on a project or problem where learners co-construct meaning and collaboratively negotiate solutions. Those are meaningful outcomes for any student. Asynchronous conferences are increasingly becoming an essential part of educational processes at all levels.

References

Berge, Z. L., & Collins, M. (1993). Computer conferencing and online education. *Electronic Journal on Virtual Culture* [Online]. Available via FTP: byrd.mu.wvnet.edu.

Bull, G., Harris, J., & Drucker, D. (1992). Building an electronic culture: The Academic Village at Virginia. In M. D. Waggoner (Ed.), *Empowering networks: Computer conferencing in education.* Englewood Cliffs, NJ: Educational Technology Publications.

Cerbin, B. (1988, April). *The Nature and Development of Informal Reasoning Skills in College Students.* Paper presented at the National Institute on Issues in Teaching and Learning, Chicago, IL.

Cohen, M., & Riel, M. (1989). The effect of distant audiences on student writing. *American Educational Research Journal, 26,* 143–159.

Eastmond, D., & Ziegahn, L. (1994). Instructional design for the online classroom. In Z. L. Berge & M. Collins (Eds.), *Computer-mediated communication and the online classroom in distance education.* Cresskill, NJ: Hampton Press.

Edelson, D. C., Pea, R. D., & Gomez, L. (1996). Constructivism in the collaboratory. In B. G. Wilson (Ed.), *Constructivist learning environments: Case studies in instructional design.* Englewood Cliffs, NJ: Educational Technology Publications.

Feenburg, A. (1987). Computer conferencing and the humanities. *Instructional Science, 16,* 169–186.

Goodman, F. L. (1992). Instructional gaming through computer conferencing. In M. D. Waggoner (Ed.), *Empowering networks: Computer conferencing in education.* Englewood Cliffs, NJ: Educational Technology Publications.

Harasim, L. (1987). *Computer-mediated cooperation in education: Group learning networks.* Paper presented at the meeting of the Second Guelph Symposium on Computer Conferencing, University of Guelph, Ontario.

Harasim, L. M. (1990). Online education: An environment for collaboration and intellectual amplification. In L. M. Harasim (Ed.), *Online education: Perspectives on a new environment*. New York: Praeger.

Hiltz, S. R. (1986). The virtual classroom: Using computer-mediated communication for university teaching. *Journal of Communication, 36*(2), 95–104.

Howse, W. J. (1992, Spring). The Internet: Discoveries of a distance educator. *EDU Magazine*, p. 52.

Jonassen, D. H., & Carr, C. (in press). Mindtools: Affording multiple knowledge representations for learning. In S. Lajoie (Ed.), *Computers as cognitive tools, II: No more walls: Theory change, paradigm shifts, and their influence on the use of computers for instructional purposes*. Mahwah, NJ: Lawrence Erlbaum Associates.

Kwon, H. I. (1998). The effects of computer-mediated communication on the small-group problem-solving process. Unpublished doctoral dissertation, Pennsylvania State University.

Lea, M., & Spears, R. (1991). Computer-mediated communication, de-individuation and group decision making. *International Journal of Man-Machine Studies, 34*, 283–301.

Levin, J., Haesun, K., & Riel, M. (1990). Analyzing instructional interactions on electronic mail networks. In L. M. Harasim (Ed.), *Online education: Perspectives on a new environment*. New York: Praeger.

Mabrito, M. (1992). Computer-mediated communication and high apprehensive writers: Rethinking the collaborative process. *Bulletin of the Association for Business Communication, 55*(4), 26–29.

Margolies, R. (1991, January). The computer as social skills agent. *THE Journal*, pp. 70–71.

Merseth, K. K., Beals, D. E., & Cutler, A. B. (1992). *The beginning teacher computer network: Supporting new teachers electronically: An implementation guide for interested educators*. Cambridge, MA: Harvard University.

Palinscar, A. S., & Brown, A. L. (1984). Reciprocal teaching of comprehension fostering and monitoring activities. *Cognition and Instruction, 1*(2), 117–175.

Paulsen, M. F. (1994). An overview of CMC and the online classroom in distance education. In Z. L. Berge & M. Collins (Eds.), *Computer-mediated communication and the online classroom in distance education*. Cresskill, NJ: Hampton Press.

Pfaffenberger, B. (1986). Research networks, scientific communication, and the personal computer. *IEEE Transactions on Professional Communication, 29*(1), 30–33.

Phillips, G. M., & Santoro, G. M. (1989). Teaching group discussion via computer-mediated communication. *Communication Education, 38*, 151–161.

Riel, M. (1990). Cooperative learning across classrooms in electronic learning circles. *Instructional Science, 19*, 445–466.

Riel, M. (1993, April). *The writing connection: Global learning circles*. Paper presented at the annual meeting of the American Educational Research Association, Atlanta, GA.

Romiszowski, A. J., & de Haas, J. A. (1989). Computer-mediated communication for instruction: Using e-mail as a seminar. *Educational Technology, 29*(10), 7–14.

Romiszowski, A. J., & Jost, K. (1989, August). *Computer conferencing and the distant learner: Problems of structure and control*. Paper presented at the Conference on Distance Education, University of Wisconsin, Madison, WI.

Scott, D. M. (1993, January). *Teaching collaborative problem solving using computer-mediated communications*. Paper presented at the annual meeting of the Association for Educational Communications and Technology, New Orleans, LA.

Shum, S. B. (1997). Computer-supported collaborative argumentation resource site [WWW document]. URL http://kmi.open.ac.uk/~simonb/cscal.

Siegel, J., Dubrovsky, V., Kiesler, S., & McGuire, T. W. (1986). Group processes in computer-mediated communication. *Organizational Behavior and Human Decision Processes, 37,* 157–187.

Simón, C. (1992). Telematic support for in-service teacher training. In A. R. Kaye (Ed.), *Collaborative learning through computer conferencing.* Berlin: Springer-Verlag.

Voss, J. (1991). Learning to reason via instruction in argumentation. *Learning and Instruction, 1*(4), 337–350.

Winkelmans, T. (1988). *Educational computer conferencing: An application of analysis methodologies to a structured small group activity.* Unpublished master's thesis, University of Toronto, Canada.

PART SEVEN

Implementing Mindtools

art 7 describes the problems involved with implementing Mindtools in the classroom. These problems and concerns are discussed in the following chapters:

Chapter 14   Entailments of Mindtools
Chapter 15   Assessing Learning *with* Mindtools

Many technology-based innovations have failed because they were not properly implemented, and the intellectual and social challenges Mindtools present make them potential victims of a similar fate. The two chapters in Part 7 relate the responsibilities that you, the teacher, must accept if you choose to use Mindtools. These responsibilities are not insignificant. Mindtools represent a new approach to instruction and learning in which teachers must relinquish some of their intellectual authority and learners must assume more responsibility for making their own meaning. That will not be easy for today's learners, who may be used to simply repeating what they are told.

There is also the very difficult problem of assessing learners' higher order thinking and knowledge construction. Objective forms of assessment (e.g., multiple-choice test) are not acceptable. The Mindtools constructions themselves may be assessed, and because of their complexity, they must be evaluated using rubrics.

Entailments of Mindtools

THE ROLE OF MINDTOOLS IN SOCIETY

In recent years, national reports have documented a diminution among American students in the ability and willingness to think. Declining test scores are but symptoms of an intellectual disease in our society. Learning, thinking, and knowledge—and any efforts to develop them—are valued less and less. Learning is, at best, a necessary evil that is required in the relentless pursuit of material goods. What is needed in education at all levels is a revolution—not just a change in methodology, but a fundamental revolution in spirit. This revolution will be marked by learners who are energized by the personal growth that results from mastering something new rather than complaining about having to complete another assignment or grilling the teacher about the contents of the next test; by teachers who are invigorated by the intellectual challenges of their students and who model, coach, and facilitate thinking rather than telling students what is on the next test; and by educational systems that seek to prepare learners to adapt to changing environments by being lifelong learners, systems that revile mindless memorization of meaningless trivia. This is a tall order, and, although Mindtools alone will not cause or even catalyze such social change, they can be the tools of reform.

I do not presume that Mindtools are the only means for engaging students in meaningful learning. As I pointed out in Chapter 2, skilled teachers and purposeful learners have been doing that forever. If you believe that education is a process that should, at least some of the time, engage students in higher order thinking, and if you believe that computers can and should assist that process, then Mindtools can help. I hope there is no misinterpretation of the goals of using Mindtools. The goals are vigorous. They are challenging. They will work only if students and teachers agree that thinking hard is a meaningful goal unto itself.

CONSTRUCTIVE ROLES FOR LEARNERS

Why are learners often unable to think, to learn, to solve problems, and to reach their learning potential? Salomon and Globerson (1987) suggest three reasons. First, learners have not developed a repertoire of learning strategies for successfully accomplishing different kinds of learning tasks. Too often, they apply a "brute force" memorization strategy, and when that does not work they lack alternative strategies to employ. This is especially problematic with Mindtools, for which memorization strategies simply will not work.

Second, learners are poorly motivated. I believe that the most pandemic, yet most insidious, cause for underachievement in schools is lower expectations on the part of teachers, parents, and society. Salomon and Globerson (1987) also refer to factors such as learned helplessness, poor perceived self-efficacy, and improper attribution of success or failure. In the United States, people too frequently litigate personal responsibility rather than work to assume it. Students too often ask for help before investing any mental effort in solving problems. They have learned to be helpless, and they believe that it is not their fault.

Third, students tend to rely only on vague perceptions and global, quick-fix solutions to problems rather than thinking about and analyzing them—that is, engaging in effortful reasoning. When students are not motivated to perform, their initial strategy is to misapply their misconceptions rather than decompose the problem, analyze assumptions, elaborate on the information, and use other critical thinking skills.

Mindtools will work most successfully in a venue of educational reform where learners are perceived as constructors of ideas and defenders of those constructions.

Learners must approach learning mindfully, and they must realize and execute personal intentions to learn and think and to regulate those processes. Their productions must be taken seriously by educators, and their efforts must be rewarded by the educational system, their parents, and society in general. Mindtools can support both mindfulness and self-regulation, but they may not be able to cause them, although there are examples of that occurring. (Recall the students in Chapter 11 giving up their recesses and study halls to develop the multimedia program for the zoo.) Mindfulness and self-regulation must become a natural part of the learner's repertoire.

Mindful Learning

Mindfulness is the "volitional, metacognitively guided employment of non-automatic, usually effort demanding processes" (Salomon & Globerson, 1987, p. 625). Mindfulness is required for meaningful learning, learning that is applicable to similar situations and transferable to dissimilar situations. Mindful learning, according to Salomon and Globerson, is characterized by the following activities:

- suppressing initial responses and reflecting on aspects of problems
- gathering, examining, and personalizing information about problems
- generating and selecting alternative strategies
- making connections to existing knowledge and building new structures
- expending effort on learning
- concentrating
- reflecting on how a task was performed.

The goal of education should be to engage learners in mindful learning. This is not a level of activity that learners are inured to, but they certainly are capable of it. What is necessary is to provide them with a relevant purpose for thinking and the tools to guide the process. Salomon (1985) urges the use of computers not to drill "low-road" learning (drill and practice, leading to automatic responses) but rather to foster "high-road" learning (thinking-intensive, situation-dependent, mindful processing). High-road learning, he argues, depends on learners' mindfulness, which is dependent in part on the learning materials used. Mindfulness can be promoted by using the computer as a Mindtool, as an intellectual partner in the learning process (as described in Chapter 1). Ultimately, however, mindfulness is dependent on the students and their willingness and interest in learning.

Self-Regulated Learners

The goal of many educational reforms over the years has been the development of self-regulation skills in learners. Rather than functioning passively in classrooms, learners should be able to determine their goals for learning, plan for learning, prepare themselves to learn, engage in learning activities, monitor what and how they best learn, regulate the learning activities in light of that monitoring, and maintain motivation and a purpose for learning. While these activities seem to be intrinsically appropriate learning skills, they contrast sharply with most classroom routines, where teachers determine what the students will learn (or apply a mandated curriculum), seek the students' attention, deliver everything the students need to do or know, quiz them to be sure they are completing assignments, and assess whether they understand what they were told.

According to Simons (1993), self-regulated learners

- maintain an orientation to learning goals and activities
- plan learning activities to fulfill those goals
- select goals in light of personal ability, prior knowledge, and interest
- intrinsically motivate their own performance (self-motivation)
- access relevant prior knowledge to apply to new learning
- apply strategies for getting started
- attribute successes and failures to personal effort.

The key to self-regulation among learners is intentionality. Students must accept and even embrace the intention to learn and to perform. Those intentions are the purpose around which they can regulate their activity. Instruction needs to help learners first to articulate what those goals and intentions are and then to reflect on how well they have been achieved. This is the essence of self-regulation. Mindtools require learners to articulate such a purpose, so their primary goal, as knowledge representation tools, is to engage learners in reflecting on what they know.

Students normally do not approach learning mindfully, and few consistently exhibit self-regulation of that learning. Most have never been required to, so they do not know how. Most, if not all, of their learning careers have been directed by teachers, so making the transition to learner control and self-regulation will not be easy for them. In most cases, your efforts to help them become more mindful and self-regulated will be frustrated by their lack of ability, experience, and tenacity. You will need to ease the transition by providing guidance and encouragement. Persevere, for there are no more noble goals of education. And use all of the tools—including Mindtools—at your disposal to assist you in the process.

CHALLENGES TO TEACHERS

The most likely reason that learners are not mindful and self-regulated is because they have never been required to be. In most classrooms from kindergarten to graduate school, students are told what and when to learn and are tested to be sure that they have learned it. Too often, those tests examine only the ability to remember, rather than the ability to think. That is because writing and scoring assessments of higher order thinking is too hard. For teachers who believe that students should understand the world as they do, that they should remember rather than apply, and that they should conform to a rigid learning schedule, the use of Mindtools will be challenging. If you cannot accept at least some of the following premises, it is unlikely that you will be successful at attempts to integrate Mindtools in your classes. If you cannot, that is OK. Even the process of reflecting on your values vis-à-vis these assumptions should be enlightening. Effective learning and thinking require that we all be able to reflect on who we are and what we are able and willing to do.

Philosophy

Constructivists argue that we interpret our perceptions and experiences in terms of our past experiences, beliefs, and biases. So, to some degree, we all represent our experiences differently, because each individual's experiences and resulting perceptions are different. This does not mean, however, that each and every representation is equal. Experts are experts because their experiences have helped them to develop richer, better integrated, more useful representations of the world. What it does mean is that the meaning an individual constructs will depend on his or her intentions, needs, existing knowledge, and beliefs. The sense that any student makes from learning experiences will vary. To the student who is contemplating that evening's date, information about the War of 1812 will instigate very little meaning making.

Assuming that a constructivist philosophy represents a change (many teachers have practiced this philosophy for their entire careers), Mindtools will probably not require any change of beliefs. For teachers who are not as experienced with constructivist approaches, Mindtool use may require a huge change in educational philosophy (Healy, 1998). "For technologies to be used optimally, teachers must be comfortable with a constructivist or project-based, problem-solving approach to learning; they must be willing to tolerate students' progressing independently and at widely varying paces; they must trust students to sometimes know more than they do and to take on the role of expert teacher . . . and they must be flexible enough to change directions when technical glitches occur" (Foa, Schwab, & Johnson, 1996, p. 52).

This transition, if it occurs at all, will not occur immediately. Assuming a constructivist pedagogy will require considerable experience. Healy (1998) points out that even highly motivated teachers with access to state-of-the-art equipment take five or more years to make the transition.

Technology Skills

Effectively integrating Mindtools into the educational process requires that teachers be able to use the Mindtools. Computers, like other technologies, have too often been used in schools as electronic baby-sitters. Plug the kids into a film, video, or computer game and they at least present the illusion of engagement, and who knows, they may just learn something. Television allows learners to remain passive, uncommitted, mindless, and unregulated. That strategy will not work with Mindtools. You cannot "plug the kids into Mindtools" and expect them to work without your support and guidance, and you cannot model, coach, and scaffold learning unless you too understand them and their purpose. You should know how to use the tools well enough to facilitate their use by your students. This will show your commitment to the goals of Mindtools. If you communicate that you are not committed, then it is unlikely that your students will be either.

Teaching Skills

To effectively integrate Mindtools in the classroom, teachers may have to develop new teaching skills. Your role as the teacher must change from purveyor of knowledge to instigator, promoter, coach, helper, model, and guide of knowledge construction. Experience with implementing Mindtools has shown that this is difficult, that teachers are simply used to showing students how to do things and providing them with the answers they seek. We have often seen students' semantic nets, databases, and expert systems appear virtually identical, because the teacher (however well intentioned) directly taught the content and organization of the knowledge bases created by students. It will be difficult for you to observe the frustration experienced and expressed by your students as they try to think for themselves without intervening with the answer being sought.

Mindtools allow you to use perhaps the most powerful method of teaching. Rather than telling students what you know and hoping they will understand it as you do, you need to allow them to represent what they know and then "perturb" their understanding. Try to avoid telling students that the models that they construct are wrong (that is, they do not agree with yours). Rather, ask if their model has considered this, or represented that. Does the students' model accommodate another idea? Or what if something else happened? Viability of knowledge is assessed in terms of community standards. For example, to argue that human traits are in no way hereditary is not viable. The scientific community has too much evidence to support the claim. So if a students' model of human development ignored hereditary influences, you would merely need to ask students to explain their model in light of that evidence, that is, perturb their model. It is the model that you are questioning, not the student. While the students clearly have a significant intellectual investment in their models, perturbing their models is less offensive than perturbing or criticizing the students directly.

Authority

For Mindtools to be used most effectively, you must be willing to relinquish some of your authority as teacher, both your power-related authority and your intellectual authority. It is not necessary that you be an expert computer user before using any Mindtools. As Schoenfeld (1985) has shown, it is OK to admit that you do not know everything. When we admit to students that we do not know everything, then it is useful to model the process of searching through information sources to discover what we do not know. Relinquishing authority requires that you take some risks and admit that you do not know everything, but that you show that you do know how to go about discovering what you do not know and using that new knowledge to solve problems. Those are powerful lessons for students. We have had to do that on numerous occasions where we were barely a step ahead of the kids. They have no fear, and so their learning curve is flatter. They will push you.

There are many ways to perceive and understand most knowledge domains. It is not necessary that you or the textbook provide all of the ideas that students include in their Mindtools knowledge bases. You must become more willing to accept different perspectives and interpretations of the world and perhaps to allow students to challenge your perspective while supporting theirs. You are not the ultimate arbiter of meaning. You must be willing to permit students to express ideas in terms that are more meaningful to them, not necessarily as the textbook or the curriculum states them. The rewards will be obvious. When students have some ownership of ideas, they are more willing to generate and use them. The purpose of schools should be to educate, to "educe," which means to evoke, extract, or elicit something that is latent, that is, to draw out what learners know. That means that you cannot tell students what they should know; instead, your role should be to help them articulate what they know and come to know it better. Mindtools are computer tools for educing knowledge.

Administrative Support

Mindtools, like most innovations, will not work without administrative support. In most schools, the principal controls the intellectual tempo of the school. So, first and foremost, you need an administrative staff with a philosophy that begins with meaningful expectations for learning. Committed teachers are not enough if the administration is not committed to change and to student knowledge construction and critical thinking. The entire school culture has to believe that students can and will, given the opportunity, think meaningfully.

You will also need logistical support for using Mindtools, especially in terms of scheduling. Mindtools require engagement, and engagement cannot always reach fruition in 50-minute periods. Our experience has shown that flexible scheduling and interdisciplinary teaching arrangements greatly facilitate the use of Mindtools. Students need blocks of time to get involved and negotiate meaning among themselves. If your administration insists that your students move when the bells ring, then it will be more difficult to engage students and to use Mindtools.

Technology Support

To implement Mindtools, you need computers. Most schools have only one computer for every 20 students, so each student, on the average, is able to use it at best for only one twentieth of the time he or she is in school. I firmly believe that if computers are to become effective tools, then students must have consistent access to them. I am not arguing that there ought to be a computer on every desk. Since Mindtools are best used collaboratively, one computer for every three to four students might be ideal. What it does mean is that Mindtools are not best used in computer labs with one student per machine. I believe that computer labs are one of the major impediments to meaningful integration of technology in schools. In labs, computers become the object of instruction rather than tools for learning. Imagine teaching carpenters to build your house but allowing them to go to the carpentry lab where they can use saws and hammers for only one hour per week. The rest of the time they have to talk about building a house, listen to lectures, and take multiple-choice tests on home construction.

Parental Understanding and Support

Finally, using Mindtools may encounter resistance from parents. You may be required to sell the importance of these methods to parents and the community. While all parents espouse the importance of constructive, self-regulated, and critical thinking as important learning outcomes, most parents are really more interested in drawing numerical comparisons between their children and others than in understanding what children are learning. What they seek is accountability, but what they do not understand is that in order to be accountable, individuals need a personal stake or investment in determining the goals for which they are to be held accountable. Convincing parents of that will be an important challenge. Numerous outcome-based learning projects, in which students were truly accountable for learning, have failed because parents did not really want to know what their children were learning; they wanted normative comparisons (their kids, of course, deserve an A). We see this in schools at every socioeconomic level. Innovations in schools with the most highly educated parents in the country have failed, because the parents claimed that since they were obviously successful students, what was good enough for them was good enough for their children.

In my experience, the best way to win parental support is to show them their children's productions. At back-to-school nights, when parents can see the expert systems, hypermedia knowledge bases, and other intellectual artifacts produced by their children, they are usually amazed. Ultimately, we need to produce research that ties the use of Mindtools to increased scores on standardized tests.

SUMMARY

Mindtools pose a number of problems for schooling. Successfully implementing Mindtools assumes that the school staff and the society in which the school exists must respect and encourage critical thinking and personal knowledge construction as meaningful goals. It assumes that learners should spend their time in school mindfully engaged in thinking and learning (articulating what they know and reflecting on its personal and societal relevance) and that they should learn to regulate their own learning habits. Successfully implementing Mindtools also assumes that the role of teachers should change from purveyor to coach and that teachers must be skilled and committed to the goals of critical thinking and to Mindtools.

Finally, successfully implementing Mindtools in schools requires that the administration and the support system that it provides should also be committed to these goals and do everything they can to facilitate higher order thinking and meaning making among learners.

References

Foa, L., Schwab, R. L., & Johnson, M. (1996, May 1). Upgrading school technology. *Education Week*, 52.

Healy, J. (1998). *Failure to connect: How computers affect our children's minds—for better or worse*. New York: Simon & Schuster.

Salomon, G. (1985, April). *Information technologies: What you see is not (always) what you get*. Paper presented at the annual meeting of the American Educational Research Association, Chicago, IL. (ERIC Document Reproduction Service No. ED 265 872)

Salomon, G., & Globerson, T. (1987). Skill may not be enough: The role of mindfulness in learning and transfer. *International Journal of Educational Research, 11*(6), 623–637.

Schoenfeld, A. H. (1985). *Mathematical problem solving*. New York: Academic Press.

Simons, P. R. J. (1993). Constructive learning: The role of the learner. In T. M. Duffy, J. Lowyck, & D. H. Jonassen (Eds.), *Designing environments for constructive learning*. Heidelberg, Germany: Springer-Verlag.

Assessing Learning *with* Mindtools

ASSESSMENT AND LEARNING:
PROBLEMS POSED BY MINDTOOLS

What is taught and what is learned in most educational institutions is driven by what we assess. The tests, projects, and examinations we require of students determine what and how they study and learn. Though we may claim that our goals for learners include becoming critical, independent thinkers, if the only way we assess their thinking is through multiple-choice recall, we are communicating a clearer expectation of how we want them to think than all of the mission statements and educational objectives produced by school districts can ever convey. Most students are able to think critically enough to realize that we are not serious about the lofty goals included in the curriculum guides and that their primary responsibility is to memorize the material if that is the case.

Parents and educators decry the inability of students to solve problems independently and think on their feet. As the cartoon character Pogo once said, "We have met the enemy, and he is us." A primary reason why students cannot think independently is the overreliance of educators at all levels on a singular form of knowledge representation. We tend to use only one form of assessment in our courses. We may require students to complete multiple choice examinations, write essays, complete laboratory activities, whatever. Too often, we assign grades based on only one form of assessment. Representing what learners know in only a single way engages them in only one kind of cognitive skill. Single forms of assessment also betray the richness and complexity of any content domain. No content domain ever studied can or should be understood in only one way. Engaging students in instructional activities and assessments that employ only a single formalism for representing their knowledge necessarily constrains their understanding of whatever they are studying. Students in all levels of education have deficient understanding of content because they were required to represent what they know in only one way.

The implication is clear. If you want to use Mindtools to engage constructive, self-regulated, critical, creative, and complex thinking, then you are obligated to assess *those* kinds of constructive outcomes and not reproductive learning. If you integrate Mindtools into your instruction but then assess the learning outcomes with recall measures, your students will learn quickly that the Mindtools do not count and that, instead of thinking critically, they need to employ their well-rehearsed strategies for memorizing the content, because that's what counts. If you sow the seeds of critical thinking, then you should harvest critical thoughts and not reproductive learning.

Traditional assessment methods, especially those based on objective forms of examination, tend to

- decontextualize the learning being evaluated
- focus on reproductive learning outcomes
- focus on abstract rules and concepts that are not part of the real world
- remove prompts and supports that are part of meaningful situations in the real world
- make the evaluation process as stressful and artificial as possible.

Clearly, these attributes belie the assumptions and methods implied by the use of Mindtools. So, how do we evaluate the effects of learning with Mindtools? I have argued throughout this book that Mindtools engage personal meaning making, so how do we assess what meaning has been made?

The most obvious solution is to assess the products of student activities—the knowledge bases that students create. If students must engage in constructive, self-regulated, and critical thinking in order to use Mindtools, then the products they create ought to provide evidence of knowledge construction, self-regulation, and critical thinking. If you assess learning through the Mindtools products, then it is important that learners use a variety of Mindtools. You should not rely on one kind of Mindtool for assessing learning. For each content domain being studied, students should construct two or more knowledge bases, using a combination of databases, semantic networks, spreadsheets, expert systems, systems modeling, microworlds, information searches, hypermedia knowledge bases, and synchronous and asynchronous conferences.

If you use any other forms of assessment (essays, problems, examinations, etc.) in addition to Mindtools knowledge bases, they too should assess construction, self-regulation, and critical thinking. Again, if they do not, then students will easily decide that Mindtools don't count and will cease to invest serious effort in their construction.

The remainder of the chapter will focus briefly on some of the expected outcomes from using Mindtools—construction, collaboration, self-regulation, and critical, creative, and complex thinking. These are what you should be assessing in learners.

ASSESSING LEARNING WITH MINDTOOLS

Assessing Knowledge Construction

Throughout the book, I have claimed that Mindtools engage learners in knowledge construction. Because Mindtools engage learners in knowledge construction, it is important to assess the kinds and extent of knowledge construction by learners and not the regurgitation of ideas previously delivered to them. Genuine intellectual performance is inherently personalized, so the meanings students derive from knowledge construction experiences are inherently more personal and idiosyncratic. Common knowledge need not always be the goal of education. If learning is more like "contextual insight" and "good judgment" than it is like inert knowledge, we need to rethink our reliance on traditional assessment activities and methodology (Wiggins, 1993). Among the changes that are necessary are a redirection of assessment toward self-assessment by learners, and alternative forms of assessment that provide learners the opportunity to express what they know in the best way. So, have students self-assess their knowledge bases before they submit them. Then you can assess them. In each Mindtool chapter, I provided rubrics for assessing students' actions. Later in this chapter, I will provide some additional, generic rubrics for assessing student activities and products.

The rubrics listed in Figure 15.1 can be used to evaluate both the products of Mindtool activities and the processes in which students engage while using the Mindtools.

Assessing Self-Regulation

The purpose of assessment and evaluation with Mindtools is not to provide society with the information it needs to judge the individual, but rather to provide learners

Assessing Knowledge Construction

To what extent do students manipulate objects, make observations, and reason from those experiences?

Observation and Reflection

Students rarely think about or record the results of actions taken during activities.	Students often stop and think about the activities in which they are engaged.	Students share frequent observations about their activity with peers and interested adults.

Learner Interactions

Students manipulate none of the variables or controls in environment.	Students manipulate some variables and controls in environment.	Students manipulate all or nearly all variables/controls in environment

Originality of Interpretations

Knowledge bases include teachers' ideas or textbook material with no original interpretation.	Knowledge bases include some original ideas but are based on teacher/textbook interpretations.	Knowledge bases include original ideas that were conceived, organized, and represented by students.

Curiosity/Interest/Puzzlement

Students engage in learning activities only because they are required, rather than an intrinsic interest.	Learners' actitivites frequently motivated by a sincere curiosity about the topic of study.	Learners are consistently striving to resolve disparity between observed and what is known, operating on a sincere desire to know.

Constructing Mental Models & Making Meaning

Learners rarely create their own understandings of how things work.	Learners are often expected to make sense of new experiences and develop theories.	Learners routinely wrestle with new experiences, becoming experts at identifying and solving problems.

Figure 15.1
Rubrics for Evaluating Knowledge Construction in Students' Knowledge Bases

with feedback that will enable them to comprehend how much they have learned in order to better direct their learning. Another important assumption of this book has been that the use of Mindtools both requires and fosters self-regulation by learners. Self-regulated learners set their own goals, determine their own activities, and regulate those activities in terms of the goals they have set. To foster self-regulation, the most important kind of assessment is self-assessment, in which learners assess what they know (articulation) and how able they are to learn a particular skill or subject (reflection) in order to compare their base knowledge with what they need to acquire in order to meet their learning goals. These are essential components of self-regulation, which I have argued is an essential part of Mindtools use. To regulate their learning, learners must be able to self-assess their own knowledge growth.

Learners must also be aware of how they build their knowledge structures. Laveault (1986) argues for "adaptability" in the learner. He says that adaptability "accounts for four characteristics of adult intellectual evaluation: flexibility, stability, generalizability, and organizability of operations" (p. 2). These are essential characteristics of self-regulated learners and therefore should also be assessed when Mindtools are used to construct meaning. Assessment activities therefore should include self-assessment, which fosters articulation and reflection on the ideas the learners have constructed.

The rubrics shown in Figure 15.2 can be used to evaluate the level of self-regulation that students exercise while using the Mindtools.

Assessing Collaboration

Another important assumption of this book has been that Mindtools are most effectively used collaboratively. Students working together to negotiate their understanding will not only produce better knowledge bases with Mindtools but also learn more in the process. If your students use Mindtools collaboratively, then why should your students be evaluated independently? If the skills they are trying to acquire are best performed collaboratively, then removing collaboration during evaluation violates the most basic of assessment premises: that the conditions, performances, and criteria for the assessment ought to replicate those stated in the learning goals and employed during instruction. This is a compelling reason for assessing the knowledge bases that students produce, rather than relying on a separate examination.

The rubrics shown in Figure 15.3 can be used to evaluate the level of cooperation in which students engage while using the Mindtools.

Assessing Critical Thinking

The most important assumption of this book, as evidenced in the title, is that Mindtools engage students in critical thinking. Throughout the book, I have evaluated the critical, creative, and complex thinking skills engaged by each Mindtool. Because they are the *raisons d'etre* of Mindtools, it is important to assess whether or not any use of Mindtools actually engages them. In the figures that follow, rubrics are given that can be used to evaluate the level of critical, creative, and complex thinking engaged while using the Mindtools.

Critical thinking is difficult to assess. There is no universal agreement on what critical thinking means. There are a number of tests of critical thinking, such as the Watson-Glaser test and the Cornell Test of Critical Thinking, but they are not tied specifically to the outcomes of Mindtools, and there are questions about their validity and reliability. Norris (1989) contends that true critical thinking involves not only the ability to think critically but also the disposition to do so, and that it is

Assessing Self Regulation

To what extent do students articulate their goals and reflect on their accomplishments when using Mindtools? To what extent can learners explain their activity in terms of how the activities relate to the attainment of their goals?

Goal Directedness

$\longleftarrow$ ——————————————————————————————————— $\longrightarrow$

Learners are often pursuing activities that have little to do with the attainment of specified goals.	Learners are generally engaged in activities that contribute to the attainment of specified goals.

Setting Own Goals

$\longleftarrow$ ——————————————————————————————————— $\longrightarrow$

Learning goals are provided by educators.	Learners are sometimes involved in the establishment of learning goals	Learners are routinely responsible for developing and expressing learning goals.

Regulating Own Learning

$\longleftarrow$ ——————————————————————————————————— $\longrightarrow$

Learner's progress is monitored by others.	Learners are involved as partners in monitoring and reporting progress toward goals	Learners are responsible for monitoring and reporting progress toward goals

Learning How to Learn

$\longleftarrow$ ——————————————————————————————————— $\longrightarrow$

Little emphasis is placed on metacognition. There are few opportunities to discuss the learning process with peers or educators.	The culture of the learning environment promotes frequent discussion of the processes and strategies (both successful and unsuccessful) involved in learning.

Articulation of Goals as Focus of Activity

$\longleftarrow$ ——————————————————————————————————— $\longrightarrow$

Learners don't see the relationship between the activities in which they are engaged and specified learning goals.	Learners describe the activities in which they are engaged in terms that relate directly to the specified learning goals.

Use of Mindtools in Support of Learning Goals

$\longleftarrow$ ——————————————————————————————————— $\longrightarrow$

The use of Mindtools seems unrelated to the specified learning goals.	The use of Mindtools contributes to the attainment of specified learning goals.	The use of Mindtools makes a powerful contribution to the attainment of specified learning goals.

Figure 15.2
Rubrics for Evaluating Self-Regulated Thinking in Students' Knowledge Base Construction

---

Assessing Collaboration

To what extent do students collaborate to construct their knowledge bases? To what extent are learners developing skills related to social negotiation and learning to accept and share responsibility?

Interaction Among Learners

◄───►

Little of the learner's time is spent gainfully engaged with other students.	Learners are often immersed in activities in which collaboration with peers results in success.

Interaction with People Outside of School

◄───►

Students rarely seek information or opinions outside of school.	Students consistently seek information and opinions of others outside of school.

Social Negotiation

◄───►

Little evidence that learners work together to develop shared understanding of tasks or of solution strategies.	Learners are often observed in the process of coming to agreement on the nature of problems and on best courses of action.	Learners collaborate with ease. Negotiations become almost invisible, yet the ideas of all team members are valued.

Distribution of Roles and Responsibility

◄───►

Roles & responsibilities are shifted infrequently; more capable learners accept more responsibility than the less capable.	Roles and responsibilities are shifted often, and such changes are accepted by both the more and less capable.	Students make their own decisions concerning roles and responsibilities, freely giving and accepting assistance as necessary.

Figure 15.3
Rubrics for Evaluating Collaboration in Students' Knowledge Base Construction

unreasonable to attempt to measure judgment about when and how to think critically with a multiple-choice test. Furthermore, there is no evidence on what test takers actually consider when taking these kinds of tests. Are they actually thinking critically? These are generic measures of thinking ability that research has shown to be too insensitive to the kinds of thinking engaged by Mindtools (Wang & Jonassen, 1993). Why is that?

Critical thinking is context dependent. That is, thinking critically in different subjects (e.g., math, science, social studies) and in different real-world contexts engages different critical thinking skills or the same skills in different ways. Thinking critically to solve an engineering problem in a factory requires different thinking than solving a political problem at a city council meeting. Even transferring critical thinking within a subject domain is difficult to assess, because if transfer of learning fails to occur, you never know whether learners are unable to transfer critical thinking or simply lack subject-specific knowledge to be transferred (Norris, 1989). So, different measures of critical thinking would need to be developed for each context in which Mindtools are used. The only way to accommodate this problem is to assess the Mindtool product within the context of its use.

Critical thinking skills are stable and not easily altered. The development of critical thinking emerges over time and with lots of practice. You cannot expect to see significant changes in how someone thinks after constructing a single knowledge base. Any detectable changes in critical thinking would require the construction of several knowledge bases within a domain.

Despite these problems with assessing critical thinking, you are obligated to try, since the primary purpose of using Mindtools is to engage critical thinking. The rubrics shown in Figure 15.4 can be used to evaluate the critical thinking students use while using Mindtools to construct knowledge bases.

Do students evaluate information and ideas in their knowledge bases?

◄───►

Students use irrelevant, inaccurate unreliable information; do not judge quality of ideas or information

Students discriminate relevant/ irrelevant information; assess reliability and usefulness of information, identify criteria, and judge merit of information; recognize inaccuracies, untruths, propaganda

Do students analyze information and ideas in their knowledge bases?

◄───►

Students cannot distinguish elements or classes of information; do not recognize or evaluate assumptions; cannot identify main ideas or patterns of data.

Students examine and classify information normally; identify assumptions and positions; determine essential ideas and patterns in data.

Do students connect ideas and understand relationships in their knowledge bases?

◄───►

Students cannot distinguish kinds of information; cannot make inferences or determine causes and effects; cannot describe relationships among ideas.

Students compare/contrast similarities and differences, evaluate arguments and logic; infer from generalizations to instances; infer from instances to generalizations; identify causes and predict effects.

Figure 15.4
Rubrics for Evaluating Critical Thinking in Students' Knowledge Base Construction

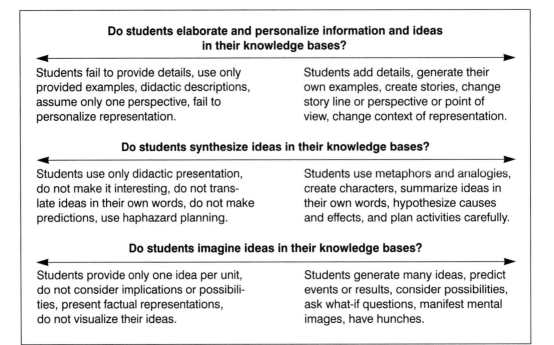

Figure 15.5
Rubrics for Evaluating Creative Thinking in Students' Knowledge Base Construction

The rubrics shown in Figures 15.5 and 15.6, respectively, can be used to evaluate the creative and complex thinking students use while using Mindtools to construct knowledge bases.

SUMMARY

The premise of this chapter is simple. If you provide learners with Mindtools, you are clearly encouraging the goal of thinking critically, so you are obligated to assess critical thinking and not something else. In this chapter, I have provided rubrics for assessing knowledge construction, self-regulation, collaboration, and critical, creative, and complex thinking skills in Mindtools activities and products. Assessing the critical thinking and higher order learning outcomes that Mindtools engage is difficult. It will require you to make different assumptions about assessment, to employ different methods of assessment, to relinquish some of your authority as a teacher by allowing students the opportunity to negotiate their goals and intentions and to self-assess, and to use multiple criteria when evaluating the outcomes of student learning. In doing so, you will allow your students to construct more flexible, mean-

Do students engage in problem solving while building knowledge bases?

◄──►

Students do not clarify problem, do not state assumptions, use only one information source, accept and use information without evaluation, use uninteresting treatment, accept any treatment.

Students visualize ideas, state assumptions, access different information sources, identify main ideas and summarize problem, assess information, determine most appropriate treatment, build consensus for solution.

Do students design coherent, meaningful products?

◄──►

Students produce without considering appearance, appeal, or effect of treatment; do not care how representation works; make no revisions to improve quality.

Students imagine their treatment, articulate its appearance and effect, assess its appeal and effect, revise product to maximize appeal and effect.

Do students systematically make meaningful decisions while building knowledge bases?

◄──►

Students cannot identify issues, do not consider alternative views, accept first option without review or evaluation.

Students articulate issues, consider alternative perspectives, evaluate the outcomes of each alternative, make choices, and evaluate and defend choices.

Figure 15.6
Rubrics for Evaluating Complex Thinking in Students' Knowledge Base Construction

ingful, stable, and transferable knowledge than if you dictate the goals and products of assessment. You will help them to become more insightful and self-reliant learners. That is sufficient for me.

References

Laveault, D. (1986, April). *The evaluation of adult intelligence: A new constructivism.* Paper presented at the meeting of American Educational Research Association, San Francisco.

Norris, S. P. (1989). Can we test validly for critical thinking? *Educational Researcher, 18*(9), 21–26.

Wang, S., & Jonassen, D. H. (1993, April). *Using computer-based concept mapping to foster critical thinking.* Paper presented at the annual meeting of the American Educational Research Association, Atlanta, GA.

Wiggins, G. (1993). Assessment: Authenticity, context, and validity. *Phi Delta Kappan, 75*(3), 200–214.

Index